Surviving Climate Change

Crisis Forum
Forum for the Study of Crisis in the 21st Century

The Crisis Forum is an independent initiative founded in 2002 by Mark Levene and David Cromwell, both based at the University of Southampton. Our premise is that humankind is in very serious trouble, and that at the root of the problem is an international economic and political system which, as both highly dysfunctional and dangerous to the planet, must yield to lateral, sustainable, compassionate, people-based solutions if we hope to survive as a species.

The Forum's aims are to bring together committed people from diverse college-based academic disciplines, as well as independent researchers, to analyse the nature of our twenty-first-century crisis in a genuinely holistic way; to put that knowledge to positive use by empowering people at grassroots level; and to develop this initiative as an independent research-based 'centre' through projects, publications and study programmes.

There are now a range of academics and activists across the UK and abroad who are associated with the Crisis Forum. As a network, it is open to anybody who shares our goals. For further information, please visit our website at http://www.crisis-forum.org.uk

Surviving Climate Change

The Struggle to Avert Global Catastrophe

Edited by
DAVID CROMWELL
and
MARK LEVENE

Pluto Press

LONDON • ANN ARBOR, MI

in association with

Crisis Forum

First published 2007 by Pluto Press
345 Archway Road, London N6 5AA
and 839 Greene Street, Ann Arbor, MI 48106

www.plutobooks.com

British Library Cataloguing in Publication Data
A catalogue record for this book is available from the British Library

Hardback
ISBN-13   978 0 7453 2568 2
ISBN-10   0 7453 2568 8

Paperback
ISBN-13   978 0 7453 2567 5
ISBN-10   0 7453 2567 X

Library of Congress Cataloging in Publication Data applied for

10   9   8   7   6   5   4   3   2   1

Designed and produced for Pluto Press by
Chase Publishing Services Ltd, Fortescue, Sidmouth, EX10 9QG, England
Typeset from disk by Stanford DTP Services, Northampton, England
Printed and bound in the European Union by
CPI Antony Rowe Ltd, Chippenham and Eastbourne, England

In memory of John Theobald,
our friend and fellow campaigner

Contents

Preface

Things are hotting up; and not just in terms of soaring temperatures. Politicians, opinion-formers, economists and business gurus all seem now to be jockeying for pole position in the climate change debate. It is almost as if, simply by demonstrating their supposed credentials and commitment, the 'answer', and with it salvation, will be found.

As this book goes to press, former US Vice President Al Gore arguably leads the pack; at least in terms of 'razzmatazz', with a 'star-studded' 24-hour-long music festival, dubbed 'Live Earth', on seven continents in July 2007: all geared to alerting us, as if we weren't already aware, to the impending climate crisis.

Not far behind is the departing UK Prime Minister, Tony Blair; a man, we are told, with a 'serious track record' on climate change. As his final leaving present he promised an international G8 summit which would involve not only major polluters like India and China, but even his friend, President George W. Bush. Not to be outdone, figures with a lesser international profile, such as Norway's Prime Minister, Jens Stoltenberg, are coming up strongly on the outside lane. Stoltenberg's assurance is that his country will be 'carbon neutral' by 2050, offering a powerful goad to other rich countries to follow his lead. Even the Pope is rumoured to be offering an encyclical on the matter.

Nor would it appear to be all just hot air. In the spring of 2007, much to the delight of Friends of the Earth, the British government unveiled its Climate Change Bill to commit the UK to the world's first detailed delivery mechanism for significant reductions in carbon dioxide emissions: a 60 per cent cut by 2050 from 1990 levels. Given that leading environmental campaigners believe this is one of the most important political landmarks of this generation – the beginnings of a transition towards a low-carbon economy, no less – surely we can rest assured that our leaders are not intent on destroying the world but are, instead, doing everything in their power to save it.

This book dares to question that assumption: and we do so by challenging the social, economic and political parameters within which diverse elite actors assume a basis for action (or inaction) on climate change. The essential inadequacy of the elite position rests on an unwillingness, indeed inability, to accept that anthropogenic climate change is an inevitable consequence of our globalising economic system. Only by rethinking the operating premises of *that* are we likely to have any chance of moving towards a safer and more sustainable future.

Mainstream institutions are, inevitably, waking up to the dangers ahead. Witness the entirely unprecedented UN Security Council debate in which climate change was posed, not only as a threat to international peace and security, but as 'a slow genocide'. By the same token, non-governmental organisations in the West have recently been much more vociferous in their own dire warnings. Christian Aid, for instance, recently spelt out the link between climate change and world poverty, warning that by 2050 as many as 1 billion people could be refugees because of water shortages and crop failures.

The Royal Society in the UK has gone even further, pointing to the danger that *Homo sapiens* will die out through nuclear weapons and/or climate change. That was the stark message from its president, Lord Rees, at a January 2007 conference of the Bulletin of Atomic Scientists, at which its famous 'Doomsday Clock' had its minute hand moved forward to five minutes to midnight.

Yet for all the anxiety, government and business efforts to stymie, let alone reverse, *accelerating* carbon emissions are at best unconvincing, and at worst entirely risible. Even the climate science experts in the shape of the Intergovernmental Panel on Climate Change (IPCC), postulating how a range of carbon-reducing technologies might help, have not been able to offer a greenhouse gas stabilisation target of anything less than a range of 445–534 parts per million by volume. This 'target' is already significantly beyond levels deemed in this book to be anywhere near safe. Indeed, at the top end of this range, the impacts would likely be utterly disastrous.

The IPCC's emphasis on smart technology, to be underpinned by serious financial backing, is, however, unsurprising. It is premised on the perpetuation of the current international political economy regardless of its dysfunctionality as exposed by climate change. The yawning chasm between what is needed and what is currently on offer is only further underscored by a recent European Union fiasco. This was when carbon permits doled out to serial polluters under the current Kyoto-sponsored carbon emissions market proved so generous that the market price collapsed, practically to the point of making the EU scheme meaningless.

Of course, a few would rather clutch at the straw that climate change is a load of baloney, anyway. They were given succour by the television broadcast of *The Great Global Warming Swindle* on Channel 4 in March 2007, a deceptive documentary that left many viewers befuddled and confused. Back in the real world, the scientific evidence that humanity is putting the planet under unprecedented stress is rapidly accumulating.

What this unequivocally points to, at this dread moment in the human saga, is the need for nothing less than a paradigm shift. In other words, the only logical response has to be one not of incremental but of revolutionary change; revolutionary, that is, without precipitating nations, societies, and communities worldwide into unmitigated and ultimately suicidal violence against each other. The book addresses the question: how is this to be done? Central to the answer is a framework which has been in existence since the early 1990s. Known as 'Contraction and Convergence', its case is argued eloquently in Chapter 1 by its original proponent, Aubrey Meyer.

With the Kyoto Protocol due to end in 2012 and, in any case, now defunct, an effective universal replacement is not just a matter of urgency but of the utmost gravity. Grassroots campaigners question why Contraction and Convergence is not yet squarely on the negotiating table. The next key round of climate talks beckons at Bali in December 2007.

The spotlight thus falls on political elites, administrative mandarins and scientific advisers. Here is *their* genuine opportunity, not just to act with political maturity but to take a giant leap on behalf of humanity. Can they break with all the vested interests, the inertial forces, the conventional wisdoms which are the historic lot of those in power, even while these have now lost all value? Through some collective Damascene vision might they at this late hour provide not only redemption for themselves, but for the rest of humanity too? One thing, though, is for sure: little time is left.

Mark Levene and David Cromwell
June 2007

Introduction: Survival Means Renewal

Mark Levene and David Cromwell

'Civilisations die from suicide, not by murder'[1]
Arnold Toynbee

INDICES OF A DYING PLANET

In the summer of 2005, *New Scientist* reported some of the latest findings on climate change. According to researchers who had been studying the permafrost of western Siberia, formed 11,000 years ago at the end of the last ice age, this, the world's largest frozen peat bog – as big as France and Germany combined – was not simply melting but could possibly unleash billions of tonnes of methane, a greenhouse gas 20 times as potent as carbon dioxide, into the atmosphere.[2] If this were to happen, the consequences for humanity and planet alike would be little short of apocalyptic.

Had the researchers uncovered one of the 'tipping points' repeatedly warned about by the climate science community? A point of no return: a threshold beyond which, whatever we try to do, it is going to be too late? Are we really, as historian Mike Davis – one of the most insightful commentators on the relationship between geophysical events and impacts on human society – has put it, 'living on the climate equivalent of a runaway train that is picking up speed'?[3]

If so, the speculation on what might happen could almost be endless. With both Arctic sea ice and the Greenland ice-sheet diminishing at accelerating rates,[4] the odds on the North Atlantic thermohaline circulation – the Gulf Stream being its most well-known component – weakening or even collapsing, would increase accordingly. And if that were to happen, the temperature of western Europe could plummet by five degrees Celsius or more, transforming its climate into that of Newfoundland, on the same latitude but minus the moderating effect of the Gulf Stream. Or will temperatures around the globe actually soar upwards by six or even twelve degrees, surpassing the torrid Cretaceous, even to that moment in the Permian period, 251 million years ago, 'when 90–95 per cent of all life on earth was wiped out and evolution virtually had to begin again'?[5]

1

Perhaps it is just as well that such questions cannot be answered by this book. Perhaps, indeed, we should leave the science to the Intergovernmental Panel on Climate Change (IPCC), the first stage of whose Fourth Assessment Report, published as this book neared completion in early 2007, confirmed that the world is not only radically hotting up but that the main cause is almost certainly anthropogenic – that is, human-caused emissions of greenhouse gases.[6] One might add that one hardly needs to be a climate expert to be aware that what is going on around us – both in terms of incremental shifts confusing, even suffocating, our normal seasons, or, more strikingly still, through repeated extreme heat, cold, storm and flood surges – are all signs that something is dreadfully amiss. What ordinary everyday observation cannot do is empirically test and explain causation or, having done so, chart likely, ongoing trajectories or outcomes. Without the science we would be none the wiser.

Whether this in itself means that the scientific analysis can be secure in its findings may be another matter. It may turn out, for instance, that the fourth IPCC report has insufficiently anticipated the combined effect of positive feedback processes of which a sudden jump in methane emissions is *only* one. A significant number of the report's own contributors take this argument a stage further through analysis of climate change impacts on the earth system as a whole, to suggest that we may be close to, if not past, that critical threshold beyond which human intervention cannot and will not be able to halt the 'runaway' scenario.[7]

Whatever the time-frames involved, and the degree to which the alarmist warnings turn out to be the most accurate, there is an almost universal scientific consensus that the necessary societal response must be one of very urgent and radical reductions in global carbon emissions. As John Holdren, President of the American Association for the Advancement of Science, has tersely put it: 'We have already passed the onset of dangerous climate change, the task now is the avoidance of catastrophic climate change.'[8] And it is that task which is the point of entry for this book. *Surviving Climate Change* is not about the science of global warming as such, though we certainly encourage our readers to become as well acquainted with it as they can.[9] Rather, its focus is on *human* consequences: international, national and local politics, the economic and social implications and, crucially, the cultural shift which will be necessary if humankind itself is to undertake at one and the same time a breakneck yet orderly shift towards a zero carbon economy, before the critical window closes shut on us for ever.

The reader might respond by asking why one should need such a book at all when the consequences of failure are so blatantly obvious. No longer mere background noise, media coverage on the dangers of climate change would appear to be so clamorous as to be practically deafening. In Britain, for instance, we may look back on 2006 as the year of the much-debated Stern Report, effectively the first occasion on which a British administration gave its official backing to a study predicting dire long-term consequences for the *economy* as a result of our increasing carbon emissions.[10] More likely, however, it will be popularly remembered for the personal plea by an individual regarded almost as a national institution, the natural history broadcaster, Sir David Attenborough, who, in the BBC television series *Climate Chaos*, warned viewers not only how dangerous the situation is but also just how far we are from averting catastrophe.[11] But if this is the case, and the seriousness of climate change really has become a dominant element in the contemporary *Zeitgeist*, why is there such a yawning gap between what we know of the looming crisis and what we are doing about it?

The answer, or answers, may be more than a little disturbing. Many historians have commented on the curious disconnect at the time of the Holocaust, between Western media reports on the extermination of European Jewry and how that knowledge was assimilated by politicians and populations alike. The evidence is not that people did not know what was happening; the newspaper coverage from 1942 onwards proves emphatically otherwise. Rather, what was involved was a failure to believe, to understand, or perhaps, simply to grasp the scale of the catastrophe.[12] Indeed, even after newsreel from the liberated camps was broadcast, it took a long time, several decades in fact, for a genuine appreciation of the tragedy to sink in.

Applied to the present, this might suggest that the failure thus far to tackle the climate crisis arises from an innate problem in our psychological make-up. Perhaps humans are simply not very good at dealing with stressful situations, or the prospects of an even more calamitous future – certainly not one whose roots lie in our own failings. Perhaps our present way of coping is to be locked in a state of denial. At least that way we can get on with our normal existences. After all, what exactly is the point of getting worked up about something we can do little or nothing to change?

But such an argument is deeply flawed. Yes, as increasingly atomised individuals, we are essentially helpless in the face of greater forces; which means, in turn, that an effective translation of *knowing* into *doing* is all but impossible. Yet, returning to the Holocaust, we know perfectly well that there were people in Britain, the United States and elsewhere, who strove tirelessly to tackle the ongoing nightmare. What ensured that nothing happened, at least not until quite late in the day, was the fact that these activists were marginalised by political establishments who were operating according to quite different criteria and interests.

Today, similarly, the blockages to effective action on climate change are determined not so much by the supposed psychic fragility of the human condition but much more by classic relationships of power in society. It may be a truism to remind ourselves that we are not all equal in the face of global warming, but it is necessary. Some of us on this planet bear a much heavier responsibility for global warming than others. And some of us – nearly all of whom are *not* those most culpable – are much more likely to be the first to suffer the consequences. If this distinction between the First and Third Worlds should be self-evident, it might also underscore that the climate change crisis cannot be placed in some splendid isolation distinct from other political, economic and social interactions, not least those which are bound up with realities of Western-led corporate globalisation or indeed concomitant drives towards a hegemonic world order.[13] If the climate crisis is *the* major symptom of what is wrong with our unsustainable dead-end system, it is still a symptom, nonetheless.

WHAT MOTIVATES THIS BOOK

It is with this in mind that we set out our two-part purpose. First, in order to understand the problem of human-made climate change and, thus, how we can break out of the present impasse, we have to grasp how those in hegemonic positions of economic and political leadership – or alternatively, cultural ascendancy – are thinking about the climate issue and responding to it (or not). We have in mind here, more exactly, policy makers, opinion formers, the rich, powerful or influential in corporate business, academic and scientific institutions, as well as in leading non-governmental organisations (NGOs). What is the nature of the climate debate – if it exists – at the level of such powerful actors; what actions have they taken (if at all), and what steps are they contemplating for the future?

Our focus is on the Western world: in particular the UK but also, to a significant extent, the United States, the globe's most powerful nation. We do not posit that only the First World is 'guilty' for the climate crisis, nor that the rich nations alone can solve it (indeed, perhaps they are the least likely to do so). The present pattern of global power, moreover, is undergoing rapid change, most dramatically through the inexorable economic rise of Asian nations; in particular, China and India, though a country such as Brazil, through the rapid development of its biofuel-based agro-industry may also prove to be very critical if this carries with it the complete destruction of the already radically damaged Amazon rainforest; otherwise one of the world's major carbon sinks.[14] Such trajectories will undoubtedly have a major impact on how fast carbon dioxide emissions rise beyond the current value of 383 parts per million by volume – already a huge increase over the pre-industrial level of around 280 ppmv.[15] Moreover, we should state that these realities underscore our endorsement of 'Contraction and Convergence' (C&C), the only serious framework presently available by which agreement on a global greenhouse gas emissions cap could be equitably achieved on a worldwide basis. C&C is presented in this book by its visionary exponent, Aubrey Meyer.

Any global framework, in turn, must translate into action at local, national, as well as multilateral levels. Given the background of the contributors to this volume, our attention focuses primarily on British state and society, that is both domestically, and in terms of its wider international relationships and commitments. Britain's contribution to overall global carbon emissions would, at first sight, appear to be no more than a small fraction of the total.[16] But even putting aside Britain's historical responsibility for the present crisis through its leading role in the industrial revolution, there is also contemporary practice to consider. The government's figures, for instance, do not include imported goods – for instance those from China – whose carbon emissions in production and transportation thereby are disregarded in the calculations. Nor, arguably more seriously, do they take account of the role UK business plays in global carbon emissions, a staggering 15 per cent of which, it has been estimated, derive from companies listed on the London stock exchange.[17] It may be that it has been several generations since Britain was *the* leading power on the world stage; nevertheless, in economic, political as well as scientific terms it remains highly influential, indeed currently fostering an international profile as the leading exponent of the need for a multilaterally agreed 'Climate Covenant'.[18]

Britain also has a significant dissenting tradition which may be of some importance. The country's projection onto the world stage, notably through military force, has always been opposed by vocal elements of its society. For example, the Campaign for Nuclear Disarmament (CND) has long demanded that Britain take a leading, even unilateral role in creating a world order based on social justice and peaceful resolution of conflicts, rather than on predatory self-interest and the amassing of weapons of mass destruction.[19] What British society does or does not do to tackle climate change – for instance, its willingness to back C&C at the international negotiating table – may well be a good indicator of broader political, economic and social trends towards survival, or otherwise.

The present prognosis is bleak. This motivates the second part of our purpose. If, as we argue, British elite thinking and planning, for all its apparent acknowledgement of climate change, is so bankrupt and at odds with the reality of the problem, what are the alternative visions and countercultural wisdoms which are going to deliver us from this tribulation?

To expect a set of neatly rounded answers to these questions is a tall order; one single volume certainly cannot provide them. What we offer is a series of commentaries on relevant aspects of our current systemic dysfunction as made manifest by the climate crisis. Our contributors also map out, however tentatively, possible personal and communal responses to it. Guided by their own empirical observations and intuitions in a variety of settings, all share an anticipation that this book might create a small breach in current hegemonic discourses, and thus help to open the floodgates to a lateral and alternative thinking coming genuinely from the grassroots.

Such a paradigmatic shift may seem a long way off, but over and beyond the small matter of urgency one might ask what is the alternative? The premise of the book narrows down to the argument that we cannot deflect a biosphere disaster except by radically rethinking the social, cultural, economic and political ground rules which govern our lives. Simply put, this implies a repudiation of current neo-liberal economics with its dependence on endless profit and 'growth': which actually equates to a *reduction* in the overall welfare of people and planet. In fact, though, more is at stake.

CHALLENGING CONVENTIONAL WISDOMS

The 'solutions' to climate change repeatedly proferred by Western leaders, think-tanks and board rooms – technical fixes, managerial reorganisations and diktats from on high – recall the workings and mindset of defunct communist regimes. Put aside political ideology, however, and the notion that technocratic, scientific and political elites have '*the* answers' by dint of their societal standing, practically ensures that the one thing rarely opened up to further examination is what drives *their* self-referential interests, values, hierarchies, mores, or – for that matter – epistemologies, in the first place. Even less discussed is the possibility that it might be exactly these imperatives which are acting as an inertial brake on meaningful action, or, worse still, lie at the very root of why we are in these dire straits.

Different contributors to this volume tackle this conundrum from various angles, unsurprisingly providing a range of views and approaches. It is perhaps unavoidable that there may be a certain tension between different sets of priorities from different writers, just as there will be in trying to set up grassroots initiatives that cut across various campaign 'constituencies'. For example, the two chapters here on the corporate sector – the first by Melanie Jarman, the second by David Ballard – take different, though not necessarily mutually exclusive, approaches. Jarman is more keenly focused on the obstructive tactics against international action on climate change pursued particularly by some leading US-based oil corporations. Ballard, by contrast, is more willing to give at least some elements, more specifically enlightened individuals, within major British and European major companies the benefit of the doubt. That one should be wary of treating elite groups as monolithic, or without the ability to break out from the value-laden compartments within which they operate, is clearly essential. And the very fact that, sometimes, it is those within those very boxes who most perceptively put their finger on the ghetto mentality, should also give us hope.

Some senior figures in academia, too, have been waving flags. For instance, Professor Mike Hulme, director of the UK's Tyndall Centre on Climate Change, following the December 2005 climate change summit in Montreal, has pleaded for a more holistic, cross-disciplinary and less obviously science-fixated approach to climate change research:

The recent negotiations reveal the full complexity, inequality and intractability of a troubled world, where different ideologies, cultures, faiths and economics battle for ascendancy and power. Climate change is now far more than a discovery of natural sciences and can no longer be defined, debated and defused through advances in scientific knowledge. It is, today, as much a cultural phenomenon as a physical reality. Nevertheless, debates about climate change still defer to the authority of the meteorologists and the earth system modellers who argue that this tipping point or that climate impact will provide the final piece of evidence to ensure a breakthrough in the negotiations.

Crucially, Hulme continues:

Climate science will never deliver the certainty about future change nor unambiguously define the probabilities of climate-related risks that will provide the world with the necessary tool-kit to decide what to do. We need a far richer array of intellectual traditions and methods to help analyse and understand the problem ... behavioural psychologists, sociologists, faith leaders, technology analysts, artists and political scientists, to name a few. And we ultimately must recognise that this is the most deeply geopolitical, not simply environmental, issue faced by humanity. Climate change will not be 'solved' by science.[20]

But if Hulme would seem to be travelling in the right direction, our key question is where are our elites more generally taking us?

THE 'NEW NORMAL', OR PREPARATION FOR SOMETHING MORE SINISTER?

The origins of this book lie in a workshop on the politics of climate change held in November 2004 at the University of Southampton. Organised by ourselves, as co-founders of an independent group known as the Crisis Forum,[21] the aim of the event was to do something almost unheard of in the academic world. We proposed to bring together 'thinkers' and 'doers': all too often two rather distinct categories. In particular, we wanted to foster exchanges between climate change academics and activists. Our intention was to promote a rethink of the climate change debate which we felt was increasingly being monopolised, diverted in unpalatable directions, or even suffocated, by government technocrats, business chiefs, professional 'contrarians', opinion formers within the mainstream media and sundry other 'experts'. At the time a particular concern of ours was that public figures from the Prime Minister downwards were expressing endless streams of noble sentiments, but with no real evidence of any shift towards a radical national action programme on climate change, which people could see was tangibly happening, let alone be actively involved in.

Our basic premise hasn't changed since then. But our sense of what is happening, in critical ways, has. Government, in particular, *is* thinking, and in critical ways *is* acting. It just happens that these actions not only are *not* geared towards tackling the problem at source, or empowering people to do something about it themselves, but rather to constructing emergency and contingency plans for the state's own hard-wired survival. This sounds conspiratorial. It should not, however, be taken quite so unproblematically. Individuals within elites, as we have already implied, like any other group of human beings, do not necessarily think and act alike. And as Dave Webb's contribution on *The Pentagon Report* amply demonstrates, even at the highest reaches of US power, a quite fraught struggle could be going on between those who want to make climate change central to government policy and those who would seek to thwart it.

What makes Webb's insights particularly illuminating, if sobering, is that nobody at this level of power appears to be thinking outside standard, received assumptions about society and economics, let alone the future of humanity. True, some military and intelligence strategists associated with the Pentagon may be ranged against a current ultra-reactionary and corporate-beholden Republican administration, but in itself, there is nothing intrinsically new here about an interdepartmental clash of interests. On the contrary, it is a classic restatement of what happens constantly and repeatedly behind closed doors in the corridors of power. And the crisis of climate change, even as thresholds for human survival are breached, is unlikely to change that.

Webb's key point about the thinking of even those more rational elements in the US elite who advocate change in the face of this crisis is that control remains the key issue; just as it always has been for ruling elites. What makes the present US military superstate different is that this means not just control over the domestic population, but over the entirety of global markets and resources too.[22] Steve Wright's following chapter reinforces the point by examining the technologies and strategies of control and surveillance currently under research and development, most particularly in the US. Such moves reflect *The Pentagon Report*'s relentlessly repeated motif: that of millions of environmental refugees swamping US borders. As Wright correctly notes, much of this R&D activity is not motivated by fear of climate change *per se* but by more immediate contingencies associated with the so-called 'war on terror'; reminiscent in itself of the way post-Second World War, corporate military industries were enormously enabled by a hugely hyped 'Cold War'.[23]

If – or rather *when* – the crisis of climate change really begins to bite, and existing societal and economic patterns break down, modern governments are thus likely to implement longstanding plans geared towards the preservation of their own survival regardless of the dangers to their publics. The risk of this happening is not new. In the era of the post-1945 threat of nuclear Armageddon, the British government had, at its fingertips, emergency powers designed exactly for such a contingency.[24] That in a future scenario of climate chaos, the suspension of civil liberties, or the draconian treatment of offenders would result, should not surprise.

Some readers might counter by arguing that this thoroughly dystopian forecast is an overstatement of the situation or is even wilfully 'off message' given that thinking on climate change should surely be concentrating on how we positively dig ourselves out of the hole we are in, not embedding ourselves further. But that in itself must raise, for anybody attempting to gauge the mindset of elite response, a fundamental but extraordinarily challenging question: 'How exactly do we understand the moment we are in?' A more benign reading, for instance, might seek to formulate it essentially in terms of democratic choice; one in which, not least as a result of the elevation of the charismatic David Cameron as leader of the Conservative party, it has become fashionable, even chic, to vaunt green credentials, enthuse about wind turbines, and cycle to work.[25] A healthy competition for the green vote between – at the time of writing – Labour Prime Minister, Tony Blair, on the one hand, Cameron on the other, and Menzies Campbell, for the Liberal Democrats in the middle, and, the 60 per cent cut in carbon emissions by 2050 to which the present administration has committed itself, seems almost plausible.[26] But even putting aside the discrepancy between what party political leaders claim and the tonnages of CO_2 emissions they squander on air travel, to say nothing of high-profile or prestige government-backed projects – Airbus, London Olympics (2012), a slew of proposed new airports or runways – which make of the green sound-bites fatuous nonsense, there is another reason why this more optimistic 'soft' forecast hits the buffers.

As James Humphreys, in his analysis of the British political framework suggests, the very nature of our electoral system, with its emphasis on swing voters and a relatively small number of marginal seats which could determine who does and does not become the next government, currently prevents any mainstream party doing anything which will take a climate change agenda radically forward through normative democratic processes. This is not necessarily because the majority of the public is unsympathetic to environmental exhortations – though the degree to which they have genuinely grasped the import of the issue is another matter – but rather because only a much smaller minority to date would be willing to pay much steeper environmental taxes, forgo oil-guzzling cars, air travel, or indeed, begin curtailing any of a heavily CO_2-dependent lifestyle options to which most have become accustomed in recent decades and which it would be necessary to reduce in order to achieve a nationally sustainable carbon regime. This, in turn, also suggests why in ceaseless internal government battles over the apportioning of resources and the pursuit of meaningful climate change policy, it is the environment ministry (Defra) which always loses out to the much mightier Department of Trade and Industry (DTI). Or why, at the very top of the government resource pyramid, no Chancellor of the Exchequer, of whatever political persuasion, will ever seriously tackle the climate crisis so long as the workings of the 'free' market remain supreme.[27]

From this perspective, what is interesting is the way negative pressures on elite action receive their vindication through a democratic mandate. But while this picture is worth painting it represents only part of the picture. Three points need to be made to supplement it. First, while it may be convenient to see government as irremediably short-termist in its aims, mostly looking ahead only as far as the next general election – if that – the country's administration is reliant on the bedrock of a civil service which has to plan according to much longer time-frames. Second, key civil service-based departments of state are recognising that our current situation is not sustainable and has to be transitional to something else. This assessment, significantly, is not purely about climate change but involves broader considerations associated with geopolitical instability as it may affect Britain in the near future, including the decline of global, and especially Middle Eastern, oil and gas reserves for projected energy needs.[28] Third, although contingency planning is normally off-limits to public purview, it is standard operating procedure for government, as advised by senior scientific, technocratic and intelligence staff.

Though we can assume that such planning *is* taking place outside public scrutiny, what public evidence is there to suggest that our present moment is characterised by these 'next-stage' preparations? Consider Blair's recent, apparently rapid 'conversion' to nuclear power, overturning his own administration's 2003 energy review in which the nuclear option was dismissed out of hand.[29] What is equally telling, however, is the way this regressive, not to say deeply unpopular, policy shift is being presented to the public as the primary route by which Britain can solve its climate change problems while at the same time meeting its 'transitional' energy requirements. Sir David King, the government's chief scientific officer, who has been outspoken on the threat from global warming, has been notably high-profile in providing the necessary expert imprimatur for this turnaround.[30] But also involved have been a bevy of public relations consultancies with significant government contracts to provide the ongoing hard sell.[31] Notwithstanding this PR exercise designed to appear as one of public 'consultation', what has actually taken place is on a par with the decision to upgrade Britain's nuclear weapons[32] – that is, to the exclusion of either parliament or *people*. Blair effectively announced the go-ahead for nuclear power at a Confederation of British Industry (CBI) dinner.[33] We can further expect implementation of actual nuclear plant through 'decisive government, eradicating avoidable delay and imaginative use of collaborative procedures'.[34] In other words, while dissent has been anticipated, not least through public inquiries that may impede the nuclear option, the government has already changed the legal ground rules to carry the day, regardless.

The point of considering the looming threat here is not to develop the case against nuclear power *per se* when this would require a book in itself. Its pertinence to our discussion rather lies in the degree to which it shows how government is gearing up to meet the future threat of climate change. As we have suggested, this is not so much to do with implementing policies to protect the public at large, but rather to preserving state 'security'. Thus, climate change feeds into and actually justifies what has increasingly become known as the 'new normal'. This piece of post-9/11 jargon has come to be associated with a political environment in which international society is perceived to be under a form of perpetual threat – regardless of its veracity or not – and to which the legitimate state response involves increased public surveillance and, where deemed necessary, abrogation of civil rights. The 'new normal' has also been applied to conditions in which uncertainty and instability also provide enhanced business opportunities.[35]

The risk of climate chaos thus offers governments a short to medium-term pretext – supplementing the convenient 'war on terror' doctrine – to monitor and control population movement both into and within the country, most obviously through the introduction of identity cards, while at the same embarking on a new programme of hi-tech solutions to the energy crisis whereby Britain might punch its way out of its perceived straitjacket. Sanity, of course, would seem to dictate otherwise, not least as Britain's territorial integrity literally begins ebbing away through ice cap melt leading to coastal and floodplain inundation, exacerbated by rising annual storm and flood sequences. But then, as we have tried to suggest, planning for the emergency state lies in defending core interests, even as they diminish. The real challenge, for the planners then – assuming as political leaders doubtless do, that whatever post-Kyoto deal they or their successors arrive at, it will not actually resolve the crisis – is how, *against* the grain of climate reality, as much of the 'business of usual' status quo can be kept intact, as we lurch from current transitional phase through to full-blown emergency.

CORPORATE OPPORTUNITIES, OR AN ENVIRONMENTAL WAR ECONOMY?

Just as science and technology has given us the evidence to measure the danger of climate change, so it can help us find safety from it. The potential for innovation, for scientific discovery and hence, of course, for business investment and growth, is enormous. With the right framework for action, the very act of solving it can unleash a new and benign commercial force to take the action forward, providing jobs, technology spin-offs and new business opportunities as well as protecting the world we live in.[36]

So proposed Blair in a much-publicised speech on climate change in September 2004. In so doing, he effectively laid out the contours of the British government's transitional phase response to climate change: acting in a more overtly centralised planning way as guarantor for nuclear power, carbon sequestration, or other more overtly green renewables projects, but with the real effort coming from a corporate sector which would be heavily incentivised to provide the necessary capital and wherewithal.

Much of the country's big business, not unsurprisingly, has been quick to repay the compliment. On 6 June 2006, the Aldersgate group, a coalition of businesses and environmental organisations, produced a report calling for market incentives to tackle climate change. This, they proposed, ought to be linked to an agenda of 'smart' regulation, eco-efficiency, and the encouragement of high growth environmental sectors, practically thereby parroting Blair's own platitudes. The very same day, senior executives of 14 British companies – including Vodafone, BAA, Unilever, Tesco, John Lewis, Scottish Power and Shell – wrote to the Prime Minister under the banner of the Corporate Leaders' Group on Climate Change, practically repeating the mantra.[37]

A couple of other things are noteworthy from this state–corporate meeting of minds. Jarman has astutely noted in her chapter how business elites share 'an almost religious belief that technology will get us there', which in turn would seem to justify their 'lining themselves up to jointly create the rules for the low-carbon society'.[38] The technological fix is a mantra, too, for that third arm of Britain's traditional power-money-knowledge nexus: a largely university-based scientific establishment. However, the Aldersgate group offers a more surprising partner still to the emerging government–business consensus, for the group also has at its core leading environmental NGOs. Even more remarkably, some of these NGOs' recent big-name campaigners have also given their endorsement to the oil-giant BP's latest PR ruse to 'neutralise' (sic) motorists' carbon emissions who pay into a BP charity which undertakes CO_2 reduction projects.[39]

With the likes of leading UK environmentalist, Sir Jonathan Porritt, on side to give a helping hand to this 'green' business flummery, one could be forgiven for assuming that climate change will hardly impact on the lives of ordinary people at all. Retail parks and giant supermarkets will still sell their wares, and the market-led requirements of hedonism and consumption will continue to be promoted. Moreover, as John Theobald and Marianne McKiggan demonstrate here in their searing dissection of the role of corporate media, climate change will continue to be portrayed as something where the victims are polar bears and coral reefs; or, when climate chaos strikes palpably at home in the form of the latest freak flood, worst storm or hottest summer, nothing actually to do with you or me.

An interesting facet of the contemporary 'peacetime' British political economy is the unwritten accord between government and the majority of people, in which the state provides the maximum latitude for citizens to live their lives, primarily in order to buy consumer products and services. In return, the people allow government to get on with serious and difficult matters of state. There is, of course, a critical bottom-line to this arrangement in the requirement that the government provide essential services, public health infrastructure and citizen security at home and abroad (so far as this is possible). Nor should we forget the expectation that a reasonable level of employment is achieved, founded on another mantra, shared by the majority of rulers and ruled alike, of 'market-led economic growth'.

The UK fuel protests in 2000 suggested the peacetime limits to this consensus. Here, the issue was of a perceived unjust rake-off on increasing fuel prices by the Treasury at the expense of the petrol pump consumer, leading to the government retreating rather rapidly in the face of popular disgruntlement. What, then, would it take for the tables to be turned? In the wake of Hurricanes Katrina and Rita in 2005, one had the unlikely image of President Bush gently requesting the most unrepentant nation of gas guzzlers in the world to go easy on fuel use while energy supplies remained disrupted.[40] In Britain, winter drought early in 2006 followed by a blistering summer led to hosepipe bans and even the possibility of potentially mandatory standpipe orders.[41] A series of scoping papers on the vulnerability of the electricity grid under extreme weather conditions, and of likely changes to NHS priorities as global warming-related epidemiological impacts kick in, reveals a heightened awareness of what future government 'duty of care' might actually entail.[42] As the bulk of the population wakes up to these new realities, can we assume that they will accept, or acquiesce in, whatever the government insists must be done? Might this include, perhaps, not just the embrace of nuclear power but much stricter limits on energy usage, reduction in foreign holidays and overseas travel? Will we even see a triage-like resource management in which key sectors of the economy have their fuel and water supplies ring-fenced, the rest of us learning to accept restriction and sacrifice?

We may be much closer than we might have imagined to what Andrew Simms, policy director of the New Economics Foundation, has called an Environmental War Economy (EWE),[43] or what Mayer Hillman, in this book's afterword and elsewhere, has posited as the absolute necessity of a national scheme of carbon rationing. The problem is that a readjusted government–people accord of this nature is unlikely to be founded on any such rational forward-thinking of the Hillman or Simms variety. On the contrary, the most likely circumstances for its occurrence are of an 'after the horse has bolted' kind, in line with Aubrey Meyer's 'C3 Impossible Risk' scenario of our first chapter and *after* a catastrophic sundering of the remaining planetary defences in response to unregulated capitalism's relentlessly upward trajectory towards the attainment of the unattainable.

There is absolutely nothing to suggest on current evidence that a post-Kyoto trading emissions scheme or any other proposed form of regulation, either market or government-led, will represent a limitation on this forecast. Consequently, energy projections are not set to fall, but to radically rise: in the case of oil, from 76 million barrels daily in 2003, to 112 million in 2020, much of it actually to feed electricity demand.[44] As another indicator of global trends, China will be producing 40 per cent of the world's total CO_2 emissions by 2050.[45]

Sweden is a welcome exception to the general rule, having announced a unilateral repudiation of oil dependency by 2020 without resort to nuclear reactors.[46] Policy makers in other industrialised countries surely know the consequences of not following the Swedish route, not least because of the looming crisis of peak oil. The point, however, is that other governments will *choose* not to follow Stockholm's path, effectively proving Jared Diamond's point about 'the sunk cost effect'; that is, a refusal to abandon a defunct policy (in this case, more exactly, a defunct corporate-led capitalist system) in which we have already heavily invested.[47] Indeed, when Tony Blair announced at the Clinton Global Initiative Conference in New York, in September 2005, that 'no country is going to cut its growth or consumption substantially in the light of a long-term environmental problem',[48] he was effectively endorsing not simply Diamond, but the Toynbee wisdom at the outset of this introduction.

The transition from an already fragile 'whistling in the wind' Aldersgate-cum-Blairite optimism to an entirely dystopian version of EWE is, of course, almost impossible to predict in detail. However, it is likely to contain the following macro-level components:

First and foremost, an abandonment of any genuine multilateral agreement on climate change, whether or not continuing lip-service is paid to it. Knowing full well they cannot change the parameters of what is endemically and systemically at fault, the leaders of the international system will operate on the basis of *sauve qui peut*, simply cutting adrift all the elements too problematic or costly to save. All poor countries, in particular those in sub-Saharan Africa, already recognised by key government reports as most at risk from climate change will come within these annihilatory parameters.[49] A dystopian EWE will signal the demise of the United Nations in any meaningful form as its inability to protect or succour humanity's most vulnerable becomes blindingly transparent.

Second, a hegemonic struggle for remaining energy resources, including pipeline infrastructure, will become even more intense than at present. This will embrace not just Iraq and Afghanistan, but the whole of Central Asia. There is also the potential here for armed conflict, especially between a US-led West and China, Russia or some broader Asian coalition.[50]

Third, insofar as there will remain a semblance of regional economic and political blocs such as the European Union, much cooperation will be geared towards controlling and patrolling the masses of environmental refugees.[51]

Fourth, as even such cooperation begins to fail, individual countries will gear themselves up for fighting their own resource wars, including over water. This possibility has been acknowledged by John Reid, then British Defence Secretary, in a Chatham House speech in February 2006. The use of nuclear weapons cannot be discounted from these encroaching conflicts.[52]

It should be obvious that the above description is but an extension of the paroxysm that large parts of the Third World already suffer regularly today. Dystopian EWE, on the domestic front, by comparison, will only kick in when all other 'business as usual' options have been exhausted. Once upon us, Britain will certainly be an ecologically aware society, but only because there is nowhere else to go. It will be heavily policed and extremely authoritarian. Strict conformity and rampant xenophobia against perceived outsiders is also a likely result. In short, far from being empowered, the people of Britain will be entrapped in this brave new world, to which the epithet 'eco-fascist' might well apply.

Is this 'Pentagon Report comes to Britain', the end-game? Possibly not. Again, though prediction in human affairs is notoriously risky, we should at least consider the possibility that the situation described above is but a medium-term station en route to some final denouement: the collapse of a global interconnected economy in the face of uncontrollable greenhouse warming and an international 'anarchy' in which residual states, or blocs, engage in all-out war for control of whatever fresh water, oil and other resources remain. Both Diamond and Toynbee have charted, in different ways, such complete civilisational or societal breakdowns in the past. But the contemporary *Oikoumene*, Toynbee's term for the habitat of humankind,[53] is so interdependent – and hence brittle – that the shock of nature's global Nemesis is not one from which we are likely to recover.

PRESCIENCE, COMPASSION AND RIGHT THINKING: A WAY OUT FROM DISASTER?

Our premise so far has been that normative elite thinking, wedded to a system that is inimical to the ongoing welfare of the biosphere, is structurally incapable of leading us to safety. An emphasis on corporate-led technological fixes as the way out is indicative not only of the hubris which helped get us into this disaster zone in the first place, but also of a mindset incapable of considering the problem holistically.

What about solutions arising from creative and independent activity inside academia? Alas, this is not likely either, according to Jonathan Ward's astute analysis here of the higher education system. Over and above their important contribution to 'pure' scientific research on climate change, there have been some welcome local initiatives which indicate how universities could become a beacon for a humane and wise principle and practice on climate change, and to which others in society might aspire and follow.[54] But these initiatives have been so minimal when set against the overwhelming tendency within academe, away from genuine interdisciplinarity and critical thinking, and towards corporatisation and marketable commodification, that any good effect is almost entirely nullified.

NGOs, such as environment or social justice groups, are perhaps another possible place to look for inspiration and possible answers. But, as George Marshall shows, there are deep-rooted problems here too. Marshall concedes that non-environmental campaigning groups are belatedly waking up to the reality that climate change is also a social justice and development issue. Yet even where some of the most influential and important of these groups, such as Oxfam and Christian Aid, have made common cause with clear-cut established environmental ones, including Friends of the Earth, Greenpeace and the World Wide Fund for Nature, the resulting umbrella body, Stop Climate Chaos,[55] has stopped well short of an unequivocal commitment to C&C, instead nailing its colours to the mast of the Kyoto protocol which James Lovelock, of *Gaia* fame, has described as 'a mere act of appeasement to polluters'.[56] Thus, although many

NGOs are now joining forces to ostensibly tackle climate change, their often self-referential thinking and policies typically fail to address the systemic roots of the crisis, any more than their corporate bedfellows in the Aldersgate group, or, for that matter, the senior bureaucratic echelons of the British state.

Something else is clearly needed. Writing before his death in 1976, and hence well before the scientific evidence on climate change became manifest, Toynbee – whose historical writing on human civilisation is now largely sidelined – in predicting the likely destruction of the biosphere through our 'suicidal, aggressive greed' saw the only possibility for salvation in the other side of the human condition: our innate spirituality.[57] Spirituality, in this sense, need not be restricted to organised religion but might equally encompass the deep reverence of an atheist for the planet, as well as a profound sense of the humanity we all share. For instance, anyone with any sense of moral compassion for our fellow humans would be appalled to learn that the average Briton burns up more fossil fuels in a day than a Tanzanian family uses in a year.[58] Or for that matter, that if everyone worldwide were to consume at current European rates, in terms of bio-capacity we would need 2.1 planet earths to sustain us, and that if we were all to follow the US example, the resources of nearly five earths.[59] As Gandhi succinctly put it, even in this overcrowded world there is 'enough for everybody's need but not for everybody's greed'.[60] Jim Scott has captured the essence of this simple aphorism in his contribution on enlightened self-interest.

Can a movement founded on spiritual environmentalism, linked to a conscious renunciation of Western consumerist gratification, thereby save us from destruction? In this very secular and materialist age, at least in the West, it is clear that any chance of a collective move in this direction would require a quite extraordinary sea-change in values. Perhaps, the churches, and other faith bodies, may have a very particular role to play in this regard, offering guidance, sound counsel, and that rather critical ingredient – hope – against a growing background of potential apocalypse.[61] One cannot deny how valuable a genuinely prophetic voice would be at this juncture in the human story. But that would still surely leave one critical item still missing; a recipe – a road-map – for what ordinary people might *do*.

The implication of much of this introduction has been that we are unlikely to be able to rely on mainstream politicians, business leaders, or even environmentalist gurus to help us achieve the 'change architecture' which Susan and David Ballard confirm as essential for combating climate change. They speak of the role of local 'champions': people in communities, schools and workplaces who are prepared to go against the grain of conventional wisdoms and organisational structures, and even face derision in the process. But the further implication here, despite the way the mass media promotes atomisation of individuals, is the degree to which collective action at the grassroots can provide the necessary substitute to conventional political power.

The good news is that there is already a plethora of local action groups, and coalitions of aware people, in Britain and elsewhere. Many have been considering, for example, how to develop decentralised sustainable energy projects in their own localities. Many others, particularly in the developing countries of the South, are challenging the very processes of corporate globalisation which represent the main economic and political obstacles to our human survival.[62]

Several of our contributors, notably Theobald and McKiggan, have suggested how a countercultural movement of this sort, 'a Movement for Survival' to use Scott's terminology, combining like-minded coalitions in the North and South, could begin subverting and replacing the very fabric of our redundant system. This recalls the mostly non-violent revolutions which helped topple a monolithic Soviet Eastern Europe in a few short weeks in 1989, albeit after decades of dissident activity and organising. The huge problem facing us now is that the post-1989 global market system is, for all its crises, more embedded, more monumental, more hubristic than ever. If revolution is the answer, it has to be not in any traditional Marxist sense but one founded on a fundamental realisation of our human place – indeed, to broaden to all other species – shared life, on this incredibly beautiful, yet fragile planet. The great paradox is that those within government, international bodies, corporate business and scientific establishment are not unaware of the problem. They simply are incapable of finding a way out from the shackles of this life-destroying system.

If reason and compassion, science and spirituality are, then, going to come together to generate fundamental action on climate change, this must involve a critical accretion of very disparate groups. These will include those who have repudiated the established society of which they are part, and those willing to support those critical pathfinders (in these pages particularly of the ilk of Aubrey Meyer and Mayer Hillman), who are not afraid to challenge conventional orthodoxy and who may even be able to show us the way, if only we would grasp it. This was the paradigm shift seen in India from the time around 1919 when Gandhi inaugurated *satyagraha*, a massive educational exercise in which people of all ages and from all walks of life devoted themselves to truth in order to dissolve British colonialism non-violently.

'Will mankind murder mother Earth or will he redeem her?'[63] asked Toynbee at the very end of his valedictory study. This actually translates, in terms of this book, into another question: will we learn to live with each other and each living thing on this planet through a path of healing, tolerance and basic loving kindness? Or will we perpetuate the inequality, injustice and violence – the symptoms, in other words of our relentless efforts to have mastery over everything – which have been our undoing for millennia, but which this time might augur some ultimate reckoning? All the evidence suggests that those in power will heed neither the prophets nor the critical pathfinders. The ball, thus, is very much in the people's court. If we are to survive as a species, and thus to renew, it can only be as actors, not passive victims awaiting our fate.

Finally, we need to understand and embrace what climate change really is: our last best chance to put our relationship with the planet on a sound footing. Throw that away – perhaps by imagining that through some final piece of technological conceit[64] we can trick our way out of catastrophe – and be assured: we will not escape the planet's Nemesis.

NOTES

1. Ironically, for all its much-quotedness, Toynbee appears not to have said exactly this in his book *Civilisation on Trial* (1948) but rather, referring to the demise of the Roman empire: 'It died not by murder, but by suicide.' www.myriobiblos.gr/texts/english/toynbee.html
2. Fred Pearce, 'Climate warning as Siberia melts', *New Scientist*, 13 August 2005.
3. Mike Davis, 'Melting Away', *The Nation*, 7 October 2005, http://www.thenation.com/doc/20051024/davis
4. Steve Connor, 'Climate change "irreversible" as Arctic sea ice fails to re-form', *Independent*, 14 March, 2006; Chen et al., 'Satellite Gravity Measurements Confirm Accelerated Melting of Greenland Ice Sheet', *Science*, 10 August 2006.
5. Duncan Law, supplementary notes to Ian Sample, 'Warming hits tipping point', *Guardian*, 11 August 2005.
6. IPCC Fourth Assessment Report, Working Group 1 report, summary for policymakers, published 2 February 2007, http://www.ipcc.ch/SPM2feb07.pdf.

7. David Wasdell interview in 'Climate Change, The Last Chance to Act?' www.tangentfilms.com/APGCC_C&C_FTSE.mp4. Thanks to director Mike Hutchinson for transcript. See also Richard Black, 'Global warming risk "much higher"', 23 May 2006; http://news.bbc.co.uk/1/hi/sci/tech/5006970.stm; Steve Connor, 'Review of the year: Global warming, Our worst fears are exceeded by reality', *Independent*, 29 December 2006.
8. Wasdell transcript, 'Climate Change, The Last Chance'.
9. Possibilities range through D. Wallace and J. Houghton, 'A guide to the facts and fictions about climate change', London: The Royal Society (2005) http://www.royalsoc.ac.uk/downloaddoc.asp?id=1630; H.J. Schellnhuber, ed., *Avoiding Dangerous Climate Change*, Cambridge: Cambridge University Press, 2006; Mark Lynas, *High Tide, Notes from a Warming World*, London: Flamingo, 2004; Elisabeth Kolbert, *Field Notes from a Catastrophe, Man, Nature and Climate Change*, New York: Bloomsbury, 2006.
10. Nicholas Stern, *Review: The Economics of Climate Change*, Cambridge: Cambridge University Press, 2006, or http://www.sternreview.org.uk, October 2006.
11. David Attenborough, 'Are We Changing Planet Earth?', *Climate Chaos*, BBC1, 24 May 2005.
12. See Tony Kushner, *The Holocaust and the Liberal Imagination, A Social and Cultural History*, Oxford and Cambridge, MA: Blackwell, 1994, esp. pp. 121–3.
13. See Franz Broswimmer, *Ecocide*, London: Pluto Press, 2002; Noam Chomsky, *Hegemony or Survival*, London: Hamish Henderson, 2003; also *Failed States*, Hamish Henderson, 2006; David Cromwell, *Private Planet: Corporate Plunder and the Fight Back*, Charlbury, Oxon: Jon Carpenter Publishing, 2001; John McMurtry, *Value Wars*, London: Pluto Press, 2002, for some of the books which broadly address these issues.
14. See http://www.biofuelwatch.org.uk/background5.php
15. Mayer Hillman, with Tina Fawcett, *How We Can Save the Planet*, London: Penguin Books, 2004, pp. 19–25.
16. See UK Defra/e-Digest/Environment Statistics, Global Atmosphere, http://www.defra.gov.uk/environment/ statistics/globatmos/gaemlimit.htm
17. Professor Doreen Massey, 'Geographical perspectives', *Today* Programme, BBC Radio 4, 1 January 2007, http://www.geography.org.uk/news/bbc-todayprogramme
18. Hillman, *How We Can Save the Planet*, p. 123.
19. See James Hinton, *Protests and Visions, Peace Politics in 20th Century Britain*, London: Hutchinson Radius, 1989.
20. Mike Hulme, 'We need a change of climate to survive,' *Times Higher Education Supplement*, 6 January 2006.
21. Forum for the Study of Crisis in the Twenty-first Century, http://www.crisis-forum.org.uk. Crisis Forum would like to acknowledge and thank the University of Southampton and Worldwide Universities Network (WUN), and more specifically, Southampton's vice-chancellor Professor Bill Wakeham and WUN's Dr David Pilsbury, for financial and moral support for the November 2004 workshop.
22. See Noam Chomsky, *Deterring Democracy*, London: Vintage, 1992.

23. Edward Herman and Noam Chomsky, *Manufacturing Consent*, New York: Pantheon Books, 1988; Alex Carey, *Taking the Risk out of Democracy*, De Kalb, IL: University of Illinois Press, 1994; Elizabeth Fones-Wolf, *Selling Free Enterprise*, De Kalb, IL: University of Illinois Press, 1994; for ways in which the corporate media, public relations industry and compliant academia have historically played crucial propaganda roles in pacifying the public for elite ends.

24. See Peter Laurie, *Beneath the City Streets, A Private Inquiry into Government Preparations for National Emergency*, London: Granada, revised edition, 1983.

25. Helene Mulholland, 'Cameron stresses Tories' green instincts', *Guardian*, 18 April 2006.

26. UK Defra/e-Digest.

27. See John Vidal, 'Miliband has youth on side but needs to earn green stripes', *Guardian*, 6 May 2006. The verdict is more recently confirmed with the Chancellor Gordon Brown's entirely tokenist increases in fuel duties on aviation and gas-guzzling cars. See Terry Macalister, 'Campaigners dismiss green measures as "feeble"', *Guardian*, 7 December 2006.

28. Paul Roberts, *The End of Oil, The Decline of the Petroleum Economy and the Rise of a New Energy Order*, London: Bloomsbury, 2004. See, however, James Howard Kunstler, *The Long Emergency, Surviving the Converging Catastrophes of the 21st Century*, London: Atlantic Books, 2005, for a much darker, but in our view, wholly more prescient view of a post-peak oil world.

29. Patrick Wintour and David Adam, 'Blair presses the nuclear button', *Guardian*, 17 May 2006.

30. Andy Rowell, 'Plugging the gap', *Guardian*, 3 May 2006, for more on the inside story. King, in fact, has been a long-time proponent of nuclear energy.

31. Ibid. Also see Andy Rowell, *Green Backlash*, London: Routledge, 2006, and http://www.nuclearspin.org/index.php

32. James Blitz, 'Brown in promise to replace Trident', *Financial Times*, 22 June 2006.

33. Wintour and Adam, 'Blair presses the nuclear button'.

34. Edward Fennell, 'Planning: it's a load of bananas', *Times*, 30 May 2006, quoting Tim Pugh, of Berwin Leighton Paisner. See also Terry Macalister, 'British Energy in profit and bullish on nuclear future', *Guardian*, 21 June 2006, on the likely routes by which government will seek to encourage industry supply contracts and promote future investment to nuclear.

35. 'Assessing the New Normal: Liberty and Security for the Post-September 11 United States', http://www action.humanrightsfirst.org/ct/n7111111B1Tx/ See also http://www.fastcompany.com/magazine/70/newnormal.html

36. PM speech on climate change, 14 September 2004. See http://www.number10.gov.uk/output/page6333.asp

37. Larry Elliott, 'Blue chips see the green light', *Guardian*, 12 June 2006; *Geographical*, the official magazine of the Royal Geographical Society, 'How green is your business', October 2006; http://geo.vnweb01.de/Features/Dossiers/How_green_is_your_business_-_October_2006.html

See also 'Aldersgate Group, Report', May 2006, http://www.ieep.org.uk/
publications/pdfs/press/Aldersgate%20press%20release.pdf

38. Jarman, 'First They Blocked', below, p. 123. Evidence for Jarman's case
has more recently been provided by the much publicised and vaunted
creation, in January 2007, of the CBI special task force on climate change',
ostensibly in direct response to the Stern review. 'The CBI and climate
change', 11 January 2007, http://www.cbi.org.uk

39. James Daley, 'BP targets green consumers with carbon-offset scheme for
drivers', *Independent*, 23 August 2006. The scheme's independent advisory
panel will be chaired by Sir Jonathan Porritt, and include Charles Secrett;
both are former Directors of Friends of the Earth.

40. James Wilson, 'Go easy on the gas, Bush tells America', *Guardian*, 28
September 2005.

41. John Higginson, 'Hosepipe ban to hit 8 million', *Metro*, 13 March
2006.

42. 'Energy firms plan how to cope as climate alters', *Reuters, UK*, 5 June
2006; 'What health services could do about climate change', *BMJ* (332),
10 June 2006.

43. Andrew Simms, *The Environmental War Economy, The Lessons of Ecological
Debt and Global Warming*, London: New Economics Foundation, 2001.

44. George Monbiot, 'Bottom of the barrel', *Guardian*, 2 December 2003;
also Paul Brown, 'Hotter world may freeze Britain', *Guardian*, 2 February
2006, for International Energy Agency rising fuel and electricity forecasts
over the next 25 years.

45. Jared Diamond, *Collapse, How Societies Choose to Fail or Survive*, London:
Penguin Books, 2006, p. 371.

46. John Vidal, 'Sweden plans to be world's first oil-free economy', *Guardian*,
8 February 2006.

47. Diamond, *Collapse*, p. 432.

48. Simon Retallack, 'Tony Blair and climate change; a change of heart?', 8
November 2005, http://www.opendemocracy.net/globalizationclimate_
change_debate/blair_3002.jsp 40.

49. See Stern Review on the Economics of Climate Change Discussion
Paper, 'What is the Economics of Climate Change?' 31 January 2006,
pp. 12–13, http://www.hmtreasury.gov.uk/independent_reviews/stern_
review_economics_climate_change/sternreview_index.cfm. Also Roger
Harrabin, 'Climate Change "harms world poor"', *BBC News*, 24 March
2004, http://www.news.bbc.co.uk/1/hi/sci/tech/14839834.stm

50. See Lutz Kleveman, *The New Great Game, Blood and Oil in Central Asia*,
London: Atlantic Books, 2003.

51. See Statewatch, reporting on civil liberties in the European Union, news
online updates, http://www.statewatch.org

52. 'Water wars – climate change may spark conflict', *Independent*, 28 February
2006. Also Michael Klare, 'The coming resource wars', 6 March 2006,
http://www.energybulletin.net/13605.html for valuable commentary
on Reid, including comparison with *The Pentagon Report*. The overview
here parallels in part, Chris Abbott, Paul Rogers and John Sloboda, *Global
Responses to Global Threats, Sustainable Security for the 21st Century*, Oxford:
Oxford Research Group, 2006. It is also significant that the dangerous

relationship between nuclear weapons and climate change has been drawn in the *Bulletin of Atomic Scientists'* recent decision to move the minute hand on their 'Doomsday Clock' to five minutes to midnight. See Steve Connor, 'Hawking: it is time to recognise the dangers of climate change', *Independent*, 18 January 2007.

53. Arnold Toynbee, *Mankind and Mother Earth, A Narrative History of the World*, New York and Oxford: Oxford University Press, 1976. *Oikoumene* comes, more specifically, from the Greek term for the 'civilised' world.
54. See, for example, Jess Goodman, 'Saving the midnight oil', *Guardian*, 14 June 2006; 'University launches first "carbon neutral" course', http://www.ncl.ac.uk/press.office/press.release/content.phtlml?ref=1146130414.
55. 'Stop Climate Chaos' website, http://www.stopclimatechaos.org/index.asp
56. Quoted in Robin McKie, 'Life on Earth, but for how much longer?', *Observer*, 12 February 2006.
57. Toynbee, *Mankind*, p. 596.
58. Johann Hari, 'Don't call it climate change – its chaos', *Independent*, 15 November 2005.
59. 'World economy giving less to poorest in spite of global poverty campaign says new research', 23 January 2006, http://www.neweconomics,org/gen/news.growthisntworking.aspx
60. Quoted in M.S. Dadage, 'Science and spirituality', http://www.mkgandhi.org/articles/sci.%20and%20sprituality.htm
61. See, for instance, http://operationnoah.org for the churches' network project on climate change.
62. See Appendix 2: Links.
63. Toynbee, *Mankind*, p. 596.
64. See for instance, David Adam, 'US answer to global warming: smoke and giant space mirrors', *Guardian*, 27 January 2007.

Part I

The Big Picture

1

The Case for Contraction and Convergence

Aubrey Meyer

I was born in the UK in 1947. I grew up in South Africa in the 'apartheid era' after the Second World War. 'Unity is Strength' was the motto of the then White Nationalist government of the country, yet 'Separate Development' was their decreed strategy. Even to a child, the segregation – or 'apartheid' – under this unity was a political oxymoron. This divided and asymmetric state made the Beloved Country weak for the lack of unity. This lesson now applies to our beloved but divided planet. Change is inevitable. May it be moderated for the better, even as we integrate cost and benefits of 'development' in the struggle to avoid the worst of global warming and climate change.

Early on my interest was focused by music. By the time I was 21, I was making my living playing and writing music in Europe. Still under this influence by the age of 40, I had become a parent and also very scared by the deeply asymmetric politics of global warming and climate change. There was nowhere to escape this. I became involved in efforts to correct these trends and 20 years on I am still.[1]

To musicians integration is everything. How music and musicians fit together, how we make the shared energy work to make music, is all about intelligent time measurement and design. Though creatively alive, music is very precise about counting. Timing and tuning to shared reference points are fundamental to the power of live music. It was not obvious to me when I was younger that principle precedes practice, and that this has both timeless stability and political relevance.

A current example of this is the East West Diwan Orchestra.[2] It was started in 1999 by the late Edward Said and Daniel Barenboim for children of Arab and Jewish families in the conflicts of the Middle East. The young players' attraction to music makes it possible for them to come together as equals from two sides of a conflict into the shared framework of music making. The Diwan Orchestra sets a global standard of peaceful cooperation, based on the musical principles of measuring and common reference points, and of working together despite differences, to produce something beautiful.

CONTRACTION AND CONVERGENCE LEADS PRACTICE WITH PRINCIPLE

The contemporary example of the East West Diwan Orchestra actually suggests a model for a global framework of reconciliation and ecological recovery in the years ahead. If, as a species, we are to avoid dangerous climate change and survive, we need to start counting from fundamentals with the core resonance of reconciliation. In practice this means keeping within the precautionary limits and using the pragmatic rationale of counting people's rights under these limits as equal.

This does not mean we are all equal. It means that to survive, we are all equally and collectively rationed by the limits that preserve us. The resonance of this in the text of the United Nations Framework Convention on Climate Change (UNFCCC) is 'common but differentiated responsibilities'.

Thus, the objective of the UNFCCC is to stabilise rising greenhouse gas concentration in the atmosphere at a value that is safe, based on principles of both precaution and *equity*. The UNFCCC necessarily adheres to contraction and convergence, first proposed by the London-based Global Commons Institute (GCI) in 1990 (see below). Contraction and Convergence is a policy framework that combines the precautionary principle and the principle of equity. The framework was explicitly approved by the UNFCCC Secretariat in 2003 with the statement that 'the objective of the UNFCCC inevitably requires Contraction and Convergence'.

We can restate the above key clauses of the UNFCCC as follows. Let us regard humanity, crudely, as being composed of two groups: high-energy users and low-energy users. The use of energy is directly related to carbon dioxide emissions (and that of other greenhouse gases, or GHGs). All of us share the common goal of atmospheric stabilisation, but some of us need to do more than others. Hence 'common but differentiated responsibilities'. Since the low carbon emitting nations can still increase their emissions before they reach the sustainable average, 'the share of global emissions originating in developing countries will grow to meet their social and development needs'. By implication, then, the high carbon emitting nations must contract fastest and greatest: 'the developed country Parties must

---

Key Clauses in the United Nations Framework Convention on Climate Change

Parties to the UNFCCC, 'acknowledge that change in the Earth's climate and its adverse effects are a common concern of humankind'. They are 'concerned that human activities have been substantially increasing the atmospheric concentrations of greenhouse gases, that these increases enhance the natural greenhouse effect, and that this will result on average in an additional warming of the Earth's surface and atmosphere and may adversely affect natural ecosystems and humankind'. (Preamble)

The Convention's objective – The Convention 'is to achieve ... stabilisation of greenhouse gas concentrations in the atmosphere at a level that would prevent dangerous anthropogenic interference with the climate system' (Article 2). In other words, greenhouse emissions have to contract.

The Principle of Global Equity – The Parties 'should protect the climate system for the benefit of present and future generations of humankind, on the basis of equity' (Article 3.1). They note that, 'the largest share of historical and current global emissions of greenhouse gases has originated in developed countries and that per capita emissions in developing countries are still relatively low' (Preamble). They therefore conclude 'that in accordance with their common but differentiated responsibilities and respective capabilities the developed country Parties must take the lead in combating climate change and the adverse effects thereof' (Article 3.1), while 'the share of global emissions originating in developing countries will grow to meet their social and development needs' (Article 3.3). In short, the Convention covers Convergence and a system of emissions allocation.

The Precautionary Principle – The Parties 'should take precautionary measures to anticipate, prevent or minimise the causes of climate change and mitigate its adverse effects. Where there are threats of serious or irreversible damage, lack of full scientific certainty should not be used as a reason for postponing such measures' (Article 3.3).

Achieving global efficiency – 'taking into account that policies and measures to deal with climate change should be cost-effective so as to ensure global benefits at lowest possible cost' (Article 3.3). In the past, cost-effective measures have been used to target pollutants, notably CFCs, in the form of trading via markets under a global maximum limit or 'cap'. More generally, the point to note here is that the idea of a framework based on precaution and equity had been established, with efficiency introduced in a subsidiary role purely to assist it.

---

take the lead in combating climate change'. Obviously the goal is sustainable emissions levels – so these two sides of the discussion inevitably lead to convergence. The lock opens and the water rushes out until both sides are level.

Many individuals, organisations and, indeed, nations have concurred that Contraction and Convergence (C&C) is the necessary policy framework that stems from the UNFCCC agreement, structured so that we are all in tune with each other, and in time to save the planet. What exactly then does C&C propose?

THE PRINCIPLE OF CONTRACTION AND CONVERGENCE

C&C is a global climate policy framework, formulated on the basis of equal rights, and has been proposed to the United Nations ever since 1990 by the GCI, as a means to achieving the UNFCCC climate change objectives.

C&C calculates a global carbon budget for what is deemed a 'safe' climate, e.g. limiting global temperature rise by 2° C. This enables greenhouse gas reduction scenarios to be calculated in the process of contraction. The global carbon budget can be shared by international negotiation, along a timeline with the final goal of achieving equal rights: this is the process of convergence. The commitment to a global treaty based on this negotiation can enable policies and measures to be organised at rates that avoid dangerous global climate change (see Figure 1).

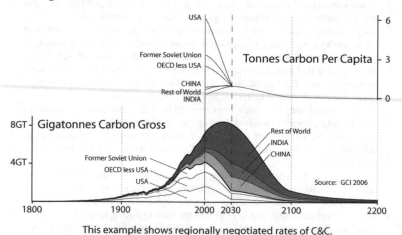

This example shows regionally negotiated rates of C&C.

Figure 1   Contraction and Convergence

Rates of contraction (Figure 2) and convergence (Figure 3) may be revised periodically as scientific understanding of the relationship between rising concentrations and their impacts on our world develops.

To get agreement to arrive at this juncture we need to concur with what Tony Blair has correctly called 'a rational science-based unity rather than more rounds of division'.[3] With the C&C definition closely based on the text of the UNFCCC which formalises into international law what must by definition be a numerate process,

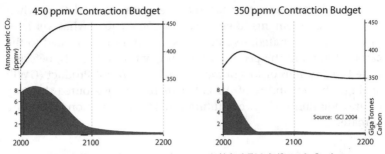

Annual Carbon Emissions contract over time to a sustainable level. This is the 'Contraction Event'.
The Choice of a 'safe' CO_2 stabilisation level determines the total tonnage of carbon to be burnt during the contraction event.
Two examples of CO_2 stabilisation levels are shown above, with their corresponding contraction budgets.

Figure 2   Negotiating Rates of Contraction

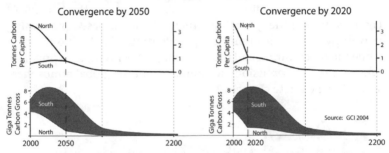

Per capita emissions entitlements converge on equality by a negotiated 'Convergence Date'.
Two examples of convergence are shown here, each within a 450 ppmv contraction budget.

Figure 3   Negotiating Rates of Convergence

The Contraction and Convergence framework proposes:

(a) A full-term contraction budget for global emissions consistent with stabilising atmospheric concentrations of GHGs at a concentration maximum deemed safe by the UNFCCC.
(b) The international sharing of this budget as a pre-distribution of entitlements that result from a negotiable rate of convergence to equal shares per person globally by an agreed date (for example, 2030).
These entitlements will be internationally tradable.

---

the issue thus unavoidably turns on the global measurement of GHG concentrations.

The C&C approach enables the UNFCCC process to be constitutionally numerate. It makes it possible to define a budget from a GHG concentration target and a convergence date by when per capita entitlements to emit have become equal, whatever rates of C&C are negotiated. Its calculus is first and foremost tied to the carbon limit and the people consuming within it; that is, before it is tied to any gain or loss of money or Gross World Product (GWP) arising. The tradability of the entitlements predistributed this way creates equilibrium between future carbon consumption and future climate.

'DOUBLE JEOPARDY' – ASYMMETRIC GROWTH AND CLIMATE DAMAGES

In stark contrast, the world at large is increasingly now haunted by the growth, divisions and conflicts of separate development. Money and power pursue each other and in this 'expansion and divergence' the 'disconnects' are discordant and dangerous. On the left side of Figure 5, we see the global asymmetry of dollar-based purchasing power: two-thirds of moneyless people routinely share 6 per cent while the other third spend the remaining 94 per cent, thus primarily causing the GHG emissions accumulating in the global atmosphere and driving climate changes.[4]

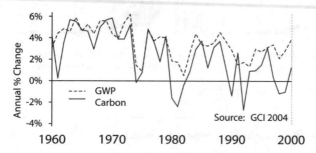

Figure 4   GWP, Carbon Lockstep

As Figure 4 shows, this money – or Gross World Product – is a close proxy for pollution, namely global carbon emissions. The growth of these emissions over the last 200 years of fossil fuel dependency has raised global temperature by one degree Celsius and triggered a rate of damages from an increasingly unstable climate that is twice the rate of growth in the economy (shown in Figure 5). The situation is critical. These trends are worsening and the poorest, particularly in small islands and Africa, are most vulnerable to the impacts of climate change.

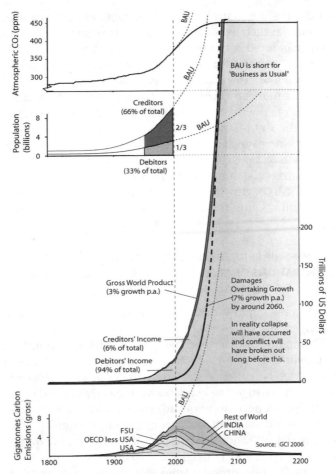

Figure 5   Asymmetric Growth and Climate Damages 'Double-Jeopardy'

A 3% per annum exponent in the path integral of growth is starkly asymmetric and unsustainable. Adhering to economic prognosis based on this is a measure of an increasingly dangerous economic 'growth illusion'.

When climate damages are added, it is already clear that the growth is *un*-economic. When damages are subtracted from this growth, it is clear the net growth is increasingly negative.

Asymmetric and damaging net-negative growth is a recipe for conflict. The bottom line is that there is no sustainable energy source that can realistically support this 'Expansion and Divergence'.

Contraction and Convergence can help cope with the limits to growth and structure and stabilise the transition to an equilibrium state based on:

(1) resource conservation,
(2) global rights,
(3) renewable energy and
(4) ecological recovery.

The injustice is acute. Many suffer great hunger or thirst. Many are forced to migrate as their lives are threatened. Many already die. This climate change induced mortality of innocent third parties is largely ignored; the poor and disadvantaged are discarded at the margins of the current system of expansion and divergence.

And while the monetary economy is compulsively force-focused on the 'benefits of growth', it is de-linked from the 'costs of climate damages'. As the right-hand side of Figure 5 indicates, climate-related damages increasing at a yearly rate of 7 per cent will overtake economic growth of 3 per cent per annum by the year 2060.

But, as the damage costs are subtracted from the benefit of economic growth, the benefits of growth are thus relentlessly deleted. For now, the accounts still disguise this as the necessarily cost-free discards of 'progress'.

THE RELATIONSHIP BETWEEN THE EMISSIONS AND ATMOSPHERIC CONCENTRATIONS OF GREENHOUSE GAS ON A GEOLOGICAL TIMESCALE OF 400,000 YEARS

Thanks to ice-core sampling, data for atmospheric concentration of CO_2 and temperature go back about half a million years before the present.[5] Throughout the ice-core record, up until the Industrial Revolution, temperature and greenhouse gas concentration moved up and down closely in step as shown in Figure 6. They oscillated because of natural change processes, between clearly defined upper and lower limits, but never went outside these boundaries. For CO_2, those limits were 180 and 280 parts per million by volume (ppmv); for methane (CH_4), 300 and 700 parts per billion by volume (ppbv); and for temperature, 5 and 15 degrees Celsius.

The leap in CO_2 concentration from 280 to 380 ppmv and CH_4 concentration from 700 to 1,700 ppbv in the last 200 years is faster and higher than anywhere in the geological record and has been accompanied by a one degree rise in global average temperature.

The rates of change in the human economy, since industrialisation began in the West around 1800, have had an impact on the atmosphere that is very different from the geological record. The ice-core records suggest very strongly that further global warming is to come.

Understanding this is fundamental to devising and being guided by a rational and strategic framework of GHG emissions for the purpose of restraining dangerous human-induced rates of climate change on the biosphere.

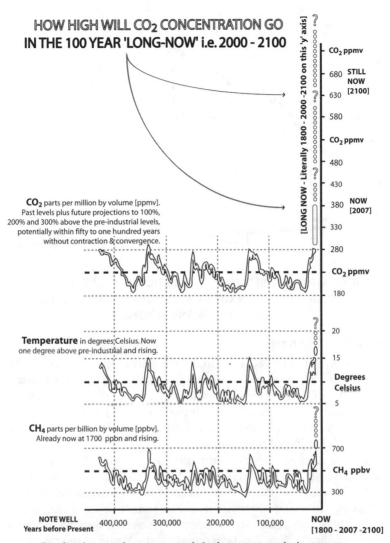

Figure 6   How high will CO_2 concentration go?

This chapter, and indeed this book, offers some insights into this, guided by the notion that to solve a problem you have to solve it faster than you create it. This is 'the battle of the rates' and we have to win it to survive.

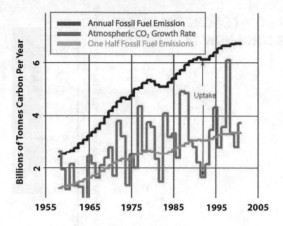

Figure 7   Atmospheric Growth Rate of CO_2

THE RELATIONSHIP BETWEEN THE EMISSIONS AND ATMOSPHERIC CONCENTRATIONS OF GREENHOUSE GAS EMISSIONS FROM 1800 TO NOW AND BEYOND

The battle of the rates

Over the last 200 years, human behaviour has disturbed the equilibrium of the natural carbon cycle and the balance of climate stability. CO_2 emissions from fossil fuel burning have raised atmospheric concentration by 40 per cent (see left half of curves plotted in Figure 9) until now, resulting in close to a one degree Celsius rise in global temperature.

Yet, in spite of the clear and present danger of increasingly dangerous rates of climate change beginning to take hold, uncertainty still surrounds the policy debate around how much to modify this behaviour in future. Over the next 200 years (see the right half of Figure 9), the uncertainties about what the overall systemic reaction to this 'policy' will be can be reduced to 'the battle of the rates'.

The questions are: what will the rate of atmospheric accumulation of greenhouse gas emissions from now on actually be, or how high will atmospheric greenhouse gas concentration be allowed to rise? In other words what does it really take to solve this problem faster than we are creating it?

To answer this it is necessary to look at the relationship between human source GHG emissions to the global atmosphere and the

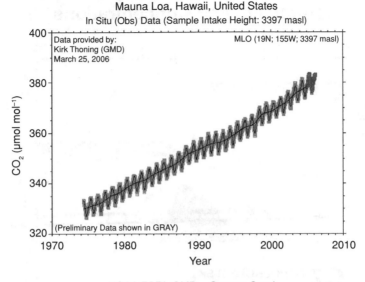

Mauna Loa, Hawaii, United States
In Situ (Obs) Data (Sample Intake Height: 3397 masl)

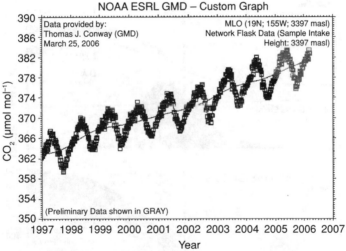

NOAA ESRL GMD – Custom Graph

Figure 8 CO_2 Measured at Mauna Loa Observatory

now varying extent to which these are increasingly retained there. The relationship between emissions and atmospheric concentration over this period has seen on average a constant fraction of each year's emissions remaining airborne. This so-called 'Constant Airborne Fraction' has until recently, been 50 per cent; i.e. 50 per cent of

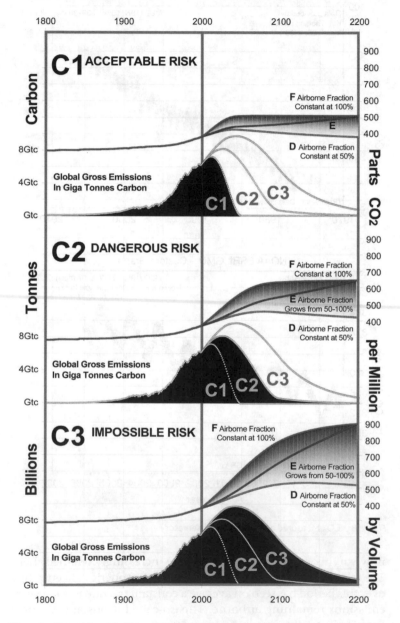

Contraction and Concentrations

Figure 9   Comparing risks from emissions budgets C1, C2, C3

Contraction and Convergence

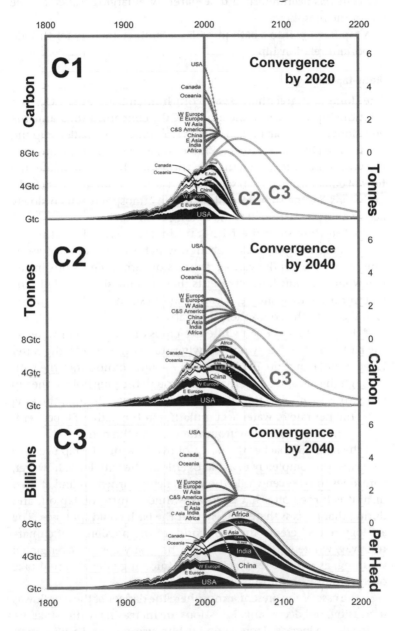

each year's emissions has been retained in the atmosphere, and 50 per cent has been returned to apparently enlarging 'sinks' for the gas in the biosphere.

A tap flowing into a bath provides a familiar analogy for this all-important relationship.

'Bath–tap' analogy

The dominant greenhouse gas from human sources is CO_2. The relationship between atmospheric CO_2 concentrations and the emissions of CO_2 from human sources is a 'stock-flow' relationship and can be thought of as a 'bath–tap' analogy. Just as the bath accumulates the flow of water to it from the tap, the atmosphere accumulates the flow of emissions to it from sources such as the burning of fossil fuels. Emissions are the short-term flow to the atmosphere which slowly accumulates a fraction of these as long-term stock.

On the flow side, the bath–tap analogy extends further by introducing the 'plug hole' through which water is drained away. The tap represents the various sources of carbon emissions in the real world; the plug hole represents their natural 'sinks'. Sinks in the real world are, for example, oceans and forests in which some of the 'extra' CO_2 in the atmosphere is 're-absorbed'.

If the plug hole is open while the tap is on, the level of water in the bath (the stock) may only slowly rise. In other words, the water level of the bath is the net balance of the rates of flow into the bath through the tap and out of the bath through the plug hole. If the tap water runs in at twice the rate that it drains away through the plug hole, the net rate of water accumulating in the bath is 50 per cent, or half the rate, of the flow from the tap into the bath.

If the bath approaches the point of overflowing, the tap needs to be turned off completely to avoid overflow. The bath level, however, continues to rise even while the tap is being turned off and at least until it is turned off. That is, it takes time to turn the tap off, and during that process there is a risk that the bath could spill over. The analogy refers here, in the real world, to the possibility of climate runaway, where we would no longer have any control over global warming, as positive feedbacks (self-reinforcing effects) would take over from human impacts.

In the case of the present atmosphere the danger of the overflow is increasing, not decreasing. Emissions are increasing, while sinks are failing due to increased forest combustion, warming and acidification of the oceans. Consequently the airborne fraction of emissions is increasing too.

In the analogy, the tap is opening wider, the pressure behind it is increasing, the plughole is blocking up, the rate at which the bath is filling is accelerating and there are more and more people in the bath wanting to fill it. The likelihood of the bath overflowing is itself rapidly growing.

PRESENT CO$_2$ 'PATH INTEGRALS' – EVIDENCE OF 'AGGRAVATED RATES OF ACCUMULATION' OF ATMOSPHERIC CO$_2$

Covering the last 200 years, good data exist for both CO$_2$ emissions from burning fossil fuel and atmospheric CO$_2$ accumulation, or concentrations in parts per million by volume (ppmv) and weight in gigatonnes (GTC). One part per million by volume of CO$_2$ in the global atmosphere equates to a weight in carbon of 2.13 billion tonnes (gigatonnes).

Observed data from the Mauna Loa Observatory (MLO) of the US government[6] shows that the 'Constant Airborne Fraction' (CAF) of emissions now appears to be changing.

On average the fraction of emissions from fossil fuel burning being retained in the atmosphere is growing, as is shown in Figure 7. The more recent trend in the raw data are shown in the two panels of Figure 8.

These data make it possible to determine the effect of having the higher – or 'aggravated' – rates of atmospheric CO$_2$ retention persist into the future. These are shown in the projections from the C&C model in the charts C1 (convergence by 2020), C2 (convergence by 2040) and C3 (convergence by 2040) that are in Figure 9. The rate of increase in atmospheric CO$_2$ until recently has been 1.5 ppmv per annum: the carbon weight of this annual increase is therefore approximately 3.3 GTC. This is around half the weight of annual emissions which is currently about 6.5 GTC.

The point of great concern here is that over the period 2003–05, the rate of atmospheric increase has jumped to nearer 3 ppmv per annum. This gives a loading of the atmosphere by weight that is roughly equal to, not half, but all the emissions from fossil fuel burning. This suggests that roughly the equivalent of 100 per cent of emissions were retained in the atmosphere in these years. This is 'aggravated accumulation'.

This was not foreseen in the carbon cycle modelling within the Intergovernmental Panel on Climate Change (IPCC) in the first three of its assessment reports between 1990 and 2001. These reports on the science of climate change, and the carbon contraction budgeting linked to different levels of GHG stabilisation in the atmosphere, did not as a result engage with the issue of 'aggravated accumulation'.

FUTURE CO_2 'PATH INTEGRALS'

The charts in Figure 9 project three scenarios for future rates of CO_2 stabilisation in the atmosphere. These 'path-integrals' are carbon consumption added up over time.

They project the contraction budgets for carbon emissions published by the IPCC in the 1995 Second and 2001 Third Assessments, for: (1) 350 parts per million by volume (ppmv), (2) 450 ppmv and (3) 550 ppmv. These IPCC reference curves are shown by path 'D' in each case against the emissions contraction budgets also quoted by IPCC.

In each of these three reference cases, the curves for atmospheric accumulation are projected using the C&C model to show the aggravated path integrals of rates of CO_2 accumulation in the atmosphere into the future at:

(a) 50 per cent CAF, as given with the original IPCC determined rates and integrals of emissions contraction budgets (path 'D' in the three examples shown);
(b) 100 per cent CAF, in other words the theoretical maximum rate of atmospheric retention of GHG emissions from human sources (path 'F' in the examples shown); and
(c) a rate of GHG retention in the atmosphere that gradually increases from 50 per cent to 100 per cent over the next two centuries (path 'E' in the three examples shown).

The scenarios shown are 'pairs' of emissions budgets and atmospheric concentrations that should have been stable at IPCC given values, but can rise faster along path 'E' (combined in first chart of Figure 9):

C1. An emissions budget for 350 ppmv as determined by IPCC, may well rise through 500 ppmv (here called 'acceptable risk').
C2. An emissions budget for 450 ppmv as determined by IPCC, may well rise through 650 ppmv (here called a 'dangerous risk').

C3. An emissions budget for 550 ppmv as determined by IPCC, may
     well rise through 900 ppmv (here called an 'impossible risk').

The justification for doing this relies on the data already returned
(and quoted above) showing that the aggravated rate of emissions
accumulation in the atmosphere is already occurring intermittently.
The purpose of doing this is to highlight the much greater extent
of risk with which we are already confronted as the likelihood of
aggravated rates of accumulation persisting into the future is real.
The point of concern is that conditions of runaway climate change
will take hold if preventive action is not urgently taken.

These 'aggravated rates of accumulation' are a fundamental
strategic consideration as we try and determine a stable future over
the next few decades since:

- governments are still caught in poor understanding and
  indecision about 'policy' to modify human fossil fuel
  consumption beyond 2012 when the Kyoto Protocol to the
  UNFCCC expires;
- politicians are operating under the increasingly challengeable
  assumption that there is still time to stop dangerous rates of
  climate change from taking hold.

Some commentators, notably scientist James Lovelock, already take
the position that it is all too late; in the 'bath–tap' analogy, the bath is
inevitably now going to overflow. The priority test to keep in mind for
policy to prevent this catastrophe is to compare path integrals for:

(a) the rate at which we cause the problem with our global emissions
     total where this rate is understood as the possible and likely rates
     of atmospheric accumulation and,
(b) these rates against the rates at which we are organising globally to
     stop triggering dangerous rates of climate change by contracting
     our global emissions total fast enough to avoid catastrophe.

We can reasonably measure the rate at which we presently still
continue to cause the problem much faster than we act to avoid
it by reference to the Kyoto Protocol. In its given time period of
2008–12, the Kyoto Protocol will theoretically and at best have
avoided emitting a few hundred million tonnes of CO_2 (measured

as carbon) into the atmosphere. During the same period we will have added several billion tonnes of carbon to the atmosphere from emissions: virtually business as usual. As soon as we factor aggravated accumulation into this it is clear that the end result will be that by 2012 we will be more, not less, deeply committed to the accelerating rate at which we are causing the problem than the response rates of C&C that are necessary to avoid it.

CAN WE SOLVE THE PROBLEM FASTER THAN WE ARE CAUSING IT?

As comparison of the three scenarios laid out here demonstrates, the risks of GHG concentrations rising faster and higher than has been suggested, and potentially completely beyond the ability of human decision taking to mitigate, are already clearly great and worsening. What is shown in the graphics of Figure 9 narrows and compares the ranges of uncertainty about concentrations to being between paths D (lowest) and F (highest) in each case.

This makes it possible to draw some very obvious conclusions about (1) the risks of acceleration in what we face and (2) what the accelerated rates of C&C are that it may take to avert these risks, in other words to solve the problem faster than we are causing it.

If the bath is not to overflow we need to be working more for scenario type C1, not giving in to C3 as is the case with Sir David King, the government's chief scientist.[7]

King, with an eye on the unresolved tension between the world's major GHG polluters – the US, India and China – has taken the view that the *realpolitik* driving this expansion of consumption now overshadowing the entire global community, is to aim for a cap of 550 ppmv CO_2 atmospheric concentrations. This, said King, was a 'reasonable' target. Anything less would be 'politically unreasonable'. Indeed, if King recommended a lower limit 'he would lose credibility with the government'.[8] But setting such a high limit means that the likelihood of preventing more than a two degree rise in global temperature is just 10–20 per cent. As *Guardian* columnist and green campaigner, George Monbiot, noted: 'Two degrees is the point beyond which most climate scientists predict catastrophe: several key ecosystems are likely to flip into runaway feedback; the biosphere becomes a net source of carbon; global food production is clobbered, and 2 billion people face the risk of drought. All very reasonable, I'm sure.'[9]

The truly alarming implication of King's stance is that his understanding of the contraction requirement to stay below this 550 ppmv maximum is based on IPCC carbon cycle modelling where the airborne fraction of emissions was assumed constant at around 50 per cent. When we allow for the aggravated rates of accumulation discussed above, King's 550 ppmv CO_2 prognosis is more probably headed to 1,000 ppmv and, hence, a runaway acceleration towards climate catastrophe. King, like many of the experts, appears either not to have understood the implications of aggravated accumulation in the C2 and especially the C3 scenarios. Or, perhaps for political reasons, he is ignoring this for now.

This is more than alarming. King has posed climate change as a greater threat than terrorism. But by saying, in effect, that the politically acceptable solution is to aim for 550 ppmv CO_2, his use of the word 'threat' is wholly misleading. It is certainly possible and almost inevitable that the aggravated rates of retention will increasingly become the norm if we persist with emissions control as envisaged in the Kyoto model. There is a point beyond which they certainly will become the norm, and on our present trajectory we are closing on it dangerously.

Avoiding this outcome means the underlying programme of global carbon emissions C&C must be agreed and internationally implemented at rates faster than those shown for 550 ppmv CO_2. The alternative is the slope of atmospheric concentration of CO_2 and other greenhouse gases, and temperature, running away out of control. To make the relevant comparison, contrast 'Acceptable Risk' C1,E with 'Impossible Risk' C3,D.

The contraction profile for C3 is three times the 'weight' (i.e. the total area under the curve) of C1, but the concentration trajectories cited are virtually the same.

WAR ON ERROR: TRANSCENDING FALSE DICHOTOMIES

The circumstances in which the next few decades of human development take place are inevitably going to be profoundly reflexive. The implications of failing to prevent dangerous rates of global climate change are almost too dreadful to contemplate. As argued by palaeontologist Michael Benton, mass extinction events such as the Permian 251 million years ago were almost certainly the result of rapid non-linear climate changes, triggered by sudden greenhouse gas loading of the atmosphere and temperature increases.[10] The difference is that then there were no human beings; now there are – us. Against this background, political integration of people on the left and on the right into a consensus-backed rationale for action is urgently required and already long overdue.

The economics of 'expansion and divergence' brings 'omnicide'

This globally 'separate development', just as in South Africa, is neither moral nor, since it has triggered a global security crisis, is it sustainable. Indeed a creeping madness inhabits this 'economic growth' and dealing with this is now fundamental to resolving our global dilemma. The very future of humanity as a whole is relentlessly deleted, when one-third of people are unwittingly attached to a false accounting which, in the words of Colin Challen, the Chairman of the all-party climate group of UK MPs, operates like the Third Reich as 'the economics of genocide'.[11] Uncorrected, this future increasingly warms to become how the rich finally commit suicide by continuing to rob the poor. As the historian Mark Levene puts it, this is the 'economics of omnicide' as all are inevitably vulnerable to the effects of climate changing out of control.[12]

In 1995 the IPCC Second Assessment Report was published. After bitter battles over the 'value of life' during its preparation, this intergovernmental 'consensus' report openly repudiated the global cost-benefit analysis of climate change carried out by economists who claimed to have demonstrated that it was cheaper or more cost-effective to adapt to climate change than to mitigate and prevent it. It was not the procedure *per se* that was condemned, it was the assumptions behind the valuation of the assets at risk. These said valuation was proportional to income, so the climate-caused death of a poor person was one-fifteenth the value of a dead rich person. When the climate mortality was summed globally, the net effect was to demonstrate that adaptation to climate change was the 'efficient' or cheaper option.[13]

It is this which demands a change in the accounting. Thus, we need a war on error, on the fixation with 'efficiency' and what former World Bank economist Herman Daly has called 'uneconomic growth'. It requires amnesty with the actuality of ecological limits and with each other as people. Success is possible if 'efficiency' is understood as at best a derivative of the principles of the UNFCCC, namely 'precaution' and 'equity'. Success is governed by the safe and stable limits that preserve us all and the global constitutional norm that values the right to life, regardless of income, as equal. This is a security proposition, more than any ethical construct. The alternative: to share the proceeds of unsustainable growth unequally, with conflict and failure the inevitable consequence.

SEQUENCING PRINCIPLE AND PRACTICE IN THE BATTLE OF THE RATES

The 'ultimate objective' of the UNFCCC (see box on p. 31) is to stabilise the rising atmospheric concentration of greenhouse gases at a level that prevents dangerous anthropogenic interference with the earth's climate system. The Convention declares 'qualitatively' that this must be done based on the principles of precaution and equity. Quantitative guidance, however, remains vague. It is expressed as aversion to danger by noting the per capita emissions differentials and 'differentiated responsibilities' of 'parties' for the historic contributions to the atmospheric build-up of GHGs. Subject to the limit that saves us, a quantitative methodology is required to reconcile the process to the limit. Without this there is the real danger of global failure swallowing local success.

It is said that principle without practice is useless, while practice without principle is dangerous. If ever the latter were true it is now and principle must precede and inform practice if we are to have any chance of avoiding dangerous rates of climate change. Specifically, this means that we have to solve the problem of climate change faster than we cause it. So consistency with a principled methodology for measuring the rate at which we cause the problem, against which we can demonstrate the faster rate at which we cause the solution, is a *sine qua non* for success.

The Convention uses the words 'ultimate objective'. As it stands, this does not sequence principle and practice. So some choose to limit the meaning of the word 'ultimate' to 'eventual', where the words mean merely the eventual future outcome of UNFCCC. Others recognise in 'ultimate' the sense of 'fundamental'. Here, the fundamental, perpetual and pervasive purpose of the Convention, before, during and throughout the process is recognised. It is in this sense that quantitatively principled methodology precedes process. Increasing momentum of human emissions on the atmosphere is already evident. Dangerous rates of climate change and its catastrophic damage effects will occur unless we stop this momentum by rapidly contracting these emissions. For this contraction to be globally effective and sufficient, it must be guided by an international C&C agreement with its practice quantitatively structured on that principle.

As the UN, through the vast majority of its members who were party to the Convention, are still legally committed to its achievement, the claim here, thus, is that the UNFCCC *is*, by definition, the 'United Nations Framework Convention for Contraction and Convergence' (UNFCC&C).

PRACTICE WITHOUT PRINCIPLE LEADS TO GLOBAL TRIAGE

The 'Berlin Mandate' was agreed at the first Conference of the Parties (COP-1) to the UNFCCC in Berlin April 1995, to establish a Protocol to the UNFCCC. Between 1995 and 1997, the 'ad hoc group on the Berlin Mandate' (AGBM) was chaired to this purpose by Raul Estrada Oyuela, a distinguished career diplomat from Argentina. In August 1997 the AGBM met for the seventh time, a few months before COP-3 in Kyoto, in December 1997 and the creation of what would become known as the 'Kyoto Protocol'.

During this meeting of the AGBM, Chairman Estrada appeared at a very large conference for the press and the NGOs to report on progress and take questions. Emission trading had come into play and everyone knew that the political argument had come to centre on one question above all others: 'How would the multilateral commitments on emissions control be defined and quantified?' A new word had resulted from the acronym of the point at issue, namely 'Quantified Emissions Limitation Reduction Options' or 'QELROS': or put more bluntly, who got how much and why.

By this stage, GCI had established two clear benchmarks in the debate. The first was C&C as the meta-concept for calculating QELROS in a scientific and constitutional manner. The second – considered notorious – was that the so-called Byrd-Hagel Resolution (BHR) of the US Senate, in July 1997,[14] amounted, in fact, to C&C.[15] The BHR was all or nothing. It embraced QELROS globally, as *quantified reductions* alongside *quantified limitations* of emissions for all of the developed and the developing countries all on the same account. GCI took the view that C&C was the only way to negotiate what the resolution called for, as anything devoid of a concentration target and more complicated than C&C would be rich in contested assumptions and recreate the arbitrary sub-global conditions that the US had been objecting to all along. In other words, the US rejects the notion that only part of the world, the developed nations (listed in Annex I of the Kyoto Protocol), should be made responsible for acting on climate change. Why, for instance, should the US have obligations to act but not China?

Indeed, whether the Senate had intended it or not, BHR was tentatively seen, by the US climate delegation *inter alia*, as C&C by definition. At a special series of meetings in Washington in July 1997, officials of the US government asked GCI to raise support for this understanding, particularly in India and in China. We did this on visits to those countries during July and when reporting back in August we also secured a collective statement to the UNFCCC from the Africa Group of Nations affirming the need for C&C. As the record shows, all this would feature clearly at the end of COP-3.

As he reported to the AGBM 7 press conference, Chairman Estrada was familiar with all these developments. His news, however, was desultory. The US continued objecting to the one-sided nature of the negotiations and the commitments on offer; the European governments and NGOs were effectively hostage to this BHR demand for a global solution. At the end of the session I publicly asked Estrada if the QELROS were seen as a function of an atmospheric greenhouse gas concentration target or whether it was the other way around, that the concentration value was simply seen as the result of whatever haggling had taken place in the QELROS negotiation. To much laughter from Greenpeace and its cohorts in the Climate Action Network, who had wrongly interpreted GCI's support for a global solution as support for the US position per se, he said, 'Aubrey in this process what happens in practice is what happens and you make up the principles afterwards to explain what happened in practice.' In other words, while Estrada afterwards apologised for the rebuff, what he was actually saying amounted to a case of 'make it up as you go along'.

A few years later Estrada published a paper in which he recalled the exchange thus:

In a meeting with NGOs during the Kyoto Protocol negotiations, Aubrey Meyer asked me which differentiation criteria were being used in the process. As negotiations were very flexible, I answered that at the end of negotiations I would explain those criteria, and that allowed me to get out of the situation among the laughs of the audience. When the negotiation ended and the Protocol was adopted, Aubrey Meyer asked me again which were the criteria, and since I didn't know the answer, I simply said that with QELROS agreed criteria were no longer relevant.[16]

Candid as he was, the blunt truth is that what Estrada had revealed was an example of aleatory – a term used in music for elements chosen at random – at the highest level of climate change politics, even more farcical than gesture politics. It is as if someone who waves their arms around believes that by doing so this makes them the equal of a great virtuoso violinist, say, of the ilk of Jascha Heifetz. The simile is harmless but what it illustrates is not. The UN climate negotiations are fundamentally flawed by the evolutionist folly that just plucking 'promising' numbers for QELROS out of a hat will do. The hope is that everyone will fail to notice the difference between the signal of what is required and the noise of what is actually happening. In the final hours of COP-3 the global allocation of tradable emission permits was debated. The US accepted in principle the C&C signal led by the Africa Group, India and China.[17] But while the UK remained silent, Estrada suspended the meeting saying that all the work done was in danger of being lost. The remnant noise became the Kyoto Protocol.[18]

Even 'evolutionists' could see by the end of 1997, however, that dangerous rates of climate change would not be averted by this aleatoric approach. Instead, it would collectively lead us to a kind of global triage – the sorting of the priority order of patients waiting for medical treatment – leaving us increasingly unfit to survive. Indeed, as matters are currently unfolding, such a process of triage has already begun.

A further insight into how this has been happening is provided through the person of James Cameron, an architect of Kyoto and emissions trading and a UK government adviser turned 'carbon trader'. In 1990 Cameron's 'Centre for International Environmental Law' (CIEL), in association with Greenpeace, encouraged the vulnerable Small Island States of the South Pacific and the Caribbean to form the Association of Small Island States (AOSIS). As the islands are mostly low-lying and very vulnerable to sea-level rise, the group took on the status of 'canary-in-the-mine', a *memento mori* for us all, if dangerous rates of climate change are not avoided.

By 1995, however, Greenpeace and CIEL had persuaded their clients that salvation lay in them presenting what became known as the 'AOSIS Protocol' to COP-1. Refuting the need for 'globality' defined by common sense and the US government, this stated that the developed countries should only tighten their emission reduction 'commitments', as in the UNFCCC, in exchange for no control of emissions by anyone else. At COP-2, in 1996, the US rejected this as 'unrealistic'. When the US presented their Byrd-Hagel Resolution a year later, Greenpeace attacked it as 'Byrd-brained'[19] whilst also arguing that global emissions must be reduced to zero by 2050 to avert a global climate disaster.[20] This was the same as the C1 scenario of 'Acceptable Risk' as defined above, a position GCI had argued since introducing C&C at COP-2 in 1996. As anyone could see that C&C was obviously required to achieve this, from that day to this it remains a mystery why Greenpeace and Mr Cameron have routinely denounced all calls for C&C. All the more peculiar, one might add, given that Greenpeace and others have described the paltry outcome of the COP-3 as 'a farce' and recognised that AOSIS have shifted from being an endangered species to being a certain discard in the emerging reality of triage. Moreover, since then Greenpeace has repositioned itself and the NGOs at the margins of the triage in a process now nearer the C3 scenario of 'Impossible Risk', and with Mr Cameron now operating as 'Carbon Capitalist' and trader par excellence at these lucrative margins. Indeed, Cameron has recently added Africa to the growing pile of discards that the C3 scenario inevitably causes and the economics of genocide inevitably requires:

The Africans are in a perilous position. They will not be rescued by 20 years of debate about C&C. Nor will they be rescued by the Carbon Market [or] beneficiaries of [it]. They're going to have to really look to the possibilities that do exist in altering their economies to cope with very high fossil fuel prices and Climate Change at the same time . . . some combination of looking at land use and land use change issues; of coping more effectively with the water resources which are there; of growing biocrops; of ensuring that renewable energy technology is made available at low cost.[21]

C&C IS 'QUANTUM' AND IT COUNTERS
DESPAIR WITH THE MOMENTUM OF HOPE

It is neither sane nor sanguine to defend the notion of unequal rights and simply discard vulnerable third parties. If we continue this, a growing global apartheid increasingly separates us from each other, sanity and the planet. If, and only if, we correct this 'in-time' and 'in-tune', can the really violent and potentially terminal 'corrections' of a changing global climate still be avoided.

The challenge is organising a C&C framework in preference to being further disorganised by structureless commerce of 'expansion and divergence', triage, conflict and chaos. It is simply not enough to rely just on more guesswork and patchwork and end up doing 'too little too late'.

Against this, counsels of despair are increasingly being voiced by eminent scientists such as James Lovelock, the creator of the *Gaia* theory.[22] He now suggests that it is already all too late. Although he has good reason to because of the 'aggravated rates' of GHG accumulation, this is nonetheless the 'victim's perception'. This must be weirdly amusing to the people who have said that there is no climate problem, only now to convert to saying that there *is* but there is no solution: it is all just too vast for the intelligence of humanity.

C&C says there still is time to define the goal-driven framework for solutions. However, for this to work, the international politics needs urgently to be freed from the stalemate by division that explains the failure of the Kyoto Protocol. For the last 15 years one half of the world has felt that it is being asked to do too much too soon in exchange for the other half of the world doing (or what is seen as doing) 'too little too late'. When the US oil industry took the position that 'there isn't a problem and you can't solve it without developing countries' (sic), this was simply the obverse of the juvenile 'green' organisations who took the position that 'there is a problem and you can solve it without developing countries'. The measurement challenges in this daft stalemate made effective negotiation of the UNFCCC impossible. The Kyoto Protocol was the result. Worse, the European Trading Scheme, seen as a gold standard by its 'free market' advocates, recently descended into bathos as European governments effectively took to bribing polluters to join it. Enron's fraud was mild by comparison but the pork-barrel basis of GHGs permits pre-allocation is the problem.

This hastens the danger of runaway climate change. To stop this requires measures that are congruent with the context of what is already an acute time-dependency. Survival for the human species is now a race against time. We have to solve this problem understanding that the 'we' involved is 'global', with all of us fitting into the available space-time that is left.[23] With a clear implication derived from 'do unto others', the context is almost biblical but it also raises fundamental questions of identity and culture as to:

- 'What' is being measured?
- 'How' are we measuring what is being measured?
- 'What' is the time-dependent unit of measurement?

- 'How' is value being assigned?
- 'Who' is doing the measurement?

As in love and quantum mechanics, the measurer and the measured are interactive; the observer's observation affects the observed. The strongest reason to deconstruct the inequality in the cost-benefit of expansion and divergence is simply that the economic science of inequality breeds climate failure. Kyoto's defenders unwittingly underwrite this. Though they reject the goalless model, or guesswork, of pure laissez-faire, they also reject the goal-focus of the C&C framework as somehow worse. Interestingly, it is for this reason that even transnational corporate leaders have taken to calling the Protocol an 'ineffective patchwork'. In the absence of a global GHG concentration target, they say they cannot address the drift into climate chaos.[24]

CONCLUSION: C&C DEFENDS ONLY TWO ASSUMPTIONS

The political equivalent of the quantum particle/wave dichotomy has Kyoto knowing where it is but not what its effect is or where it is going. C&C knows what its effect is and where it is going, because it defends only two core assumptions of numeracy (limits and equal rights), it is simple and simply says so. This science-based rationale gets increasing traction while Kyoto loses it to the goal-free poker-economics of 'multi-criteria trade-offs' and third party discards.

Consider again Einstein's vexed riddle as to whether God 'plays dice'. The game could not be played unless the dice existed. Principle simply precedes practice and so informs it. The dice are structured so and the game is programmed by the dice. Avoiding dangerous rates of climate change is the dice game we now play. Only in unity can we be determined not to lose. Contraction and convergence counters despair with the momentum of hope. Without such vision, much of humanity will simply perish.

FURTHER INFORMATION ON CONTRACTION AND CONVERGENCE

C&C definition statement and Bill:
http://www.gci.org.uk/briefings/C&C_Bill_Pledge.pdf
Zoom-able global past/future C&C 'map':
http://www.gci.org.uk/images/C&C_Bubbles.pdf
Animated C&C demonstration:

http://www.gci.org.uk/images/CC_Demo(pc).exe
C&C pledge statement:
http://www.gci.org.uk/kite/pledge-text.pdf
C&C support and background:
http://www.gci.org.uk/links/detail.pdf
C&C history:
http://www.gci.org.uk/Archive/Mega_Doc_1989_2004.pdf
C&C news service:
http://lists.topica.com/lists/GCN@igc.topica.com/read

NOTES

1. http://www.gci.org.uk/AubreyMeyer/CV_Aubrey_Meyer_1.pdf
2. http://en.wikipedia.org/wiki/West-Eastern_Divan
3. Tony Blair, 'Get real on climate change', *Observer*, 30 October 2005.
4. http://www.gci.org.uk/articles/Nairob3b.pdf
5. http://cdiac.ornl.gov/trends/co2/graphics/vostok.co2.gif; http://www.ncdc.noaa.gov/paleo/icecore/antarctica/vostok/vostok_data.html
6. http://www.mlo.noaa.gov/LiveData/FDataCCG.htm
7. David King, 'The nuclear option isn't political expediency but scientific necessity', *Guardian*, 16 December 2005.
8. George Monbiot, 'The chief scientific advisor has become a government spin doctor', *Guardian*, 25 October 2005.
9. Ibid.
10. Michael J. Benton, *When Life Nearly Died: The Greatest Mass Extinction of All Time*, Thames and Hudson, 2003.
11. Colin Challen, 'We must think the unthinkable and take voters with us', *Independent*, 28 March 2006.
12. Mark Levene, personal communication, 29 June 2006.
13. http://www.ipcc.ch/pub/sarsum3.htm#seven
14. http://www.nationalcenter.org/KyotoSenate.html
15. http://www.gci.org.uk/briefings/C&C&ByrdHagel.pdf
16. http://www.gci.org.uk/briefings/Paper7_EOyuela1.pdf
17. http://www.gci.org.uk/temp/COP3_Transcript.pdf
18. Aubrey Meyer, *Contraction and Convergence: The Global Solution to Climate Change*, Green Books, 2000.
19. http://thomas.loc.gov/cgi-bin/cpquery/T?&report=sr054&dbname=cp105&
20. http://archive.greenpeace.org/climate/arctic99/html/content/factsheets/carbonlogic2.html
21. http://www.gci.org.uk/speeches/Cameron_RSA_150506.pdf
22. http://observer.guardian.co.uk/shellenergy/story/0,,1793042,00.html
23. Challen, 'We must think the unthinkable'.
24. http://www.gci.org.uk/briefings/WEF_Statement.pdf

Part II

The State and its Apparatus

2
Thinking the Worst:
The Pentagon Report
Dave Webb

AN UNUSUAL WEATHER REPORT

'Now the Pentagon tells Bush: climate change will destroy us' – was the dramatic headline in the *Observer* newspaper on Sunday 22 February 2004. As if that wasn't enough to grab a reader's attention, the lead paragraph of the accompanying article by Mark Townsend and Paul Harris was printed in large bold letters, claiming that: 'The US President has denied the existence of global warming. But a secret report predicts a looming catastrophe – a world riven with water wars, famine and anarchy.'[1] This, together with sub-headings of 'Secret report warns of rioting and nuclear war', 'Britain will be "Siberian" in less than 20 years' and 'Threat to the world is greater than terrorism', guaranteed that the article would attract international attention and comment. And it did.

Entitled 'An Abrupt Climate Change Scenario and Its Implications for United States National Security', the report was written by Peter Schwartz and Doug Randall of the Global Business Network (GBN) a 'scenario and strategy consultancy', based in California. However, whether the report really was intended to be secret is another matter.[2] Dated October 2003, it appeared freely on the Internet and, early the following year, was picked up, first by David Stipp in *Fortune* magazine ('The Pentagon's weather nightmare')[3] and then other papers, including the *San Francisco Chronicle* ('Pentagon-sponsored climate report sparks hullabaloo in Europe'),[4] the *New York Times* ('The sky is falling! say Hollywood and, yes, the Pentagon')[5] as well as the British *Observer*.

By now known as *The Pentagon Report*, the newspapers' rendition of its substance was certainly correct. Schwartz and Randall depict global catastrophe due to sudden but extreme weather changes and the possible, consequent effects on US national security, over a relatively short time scale. These are summarised by Tables 1 and 2, as taken from the report.

Table 1   Conflict Scenario Due to Climate Change 2010–2020

Europe	Asia	United States
2012: Severe drought and cold push Scandinavian populations southward, push back from EU	2010: Border skirmishes and conflict in Bangladesh, India and China as mass migration occurs towards Burma	2010: Disagreements with Canada and Mexico over water increase tension
2015: Conflict within the EU over food and water supply leads to skirmishes and strained diplomatic relations	2012: Regional instability leads Japan to develop force projection capability	2012: Flood of refugees to southeast US and Mexico from Caribbean islands
2018: Russia joins EU, providing energy resources	2015: Strategic agreement between Japan and Russia for Siberia and Sakhalin energy resources	2015: European migration to US (mostly wealthy)
2020: Migration from northern countries such as Holland and Germany towards Spain and Italy	2018: China intervenes in Kazakhstan to protect pipelines regularly disrupted by rebels	2016: Conflict with European countries over fishing rights
		2018: Securing North America, US forms integrated security alliance with Canada and Mexico
		2020: Department of Defense manages borders and refugees from Caribbean and Europe

Table 2   Conflict Scenario Due to Climate Change 2020–2030

Europe	Asia	United States
2020: Increasing skirmishes over water and immigration	2020: Persistent conflict in South-East Asia; Burma, Laos, Vietnam, India, China	2020: Oil prices increase as security of supply is threatened by conflicts in Persian Gulf and Caspian
2022: Skirmish between France and Germany over commercial access to Rhine	2025: Internal conditions in China deteriorate dramatically leading to civil war and border wars	2025: Internal struggle in Saudi Arabia brings Chinese and US naval forces to Gulf in direct confrontation
2025: EU nears collapse		
2027: Increasing migration to Mediterranean countries such as Algeria, Morocco, Egypt and Israel	2030: Tension growing between China and Japan over Russian energy	
2030: Nearly 10 per cent of European population moves to a different country		

The report has violent storms destroying coastal barriers as early as 2007, with the possibility of people abandoning low-lying coastal cities such as The Hague, in the Netherlands. The creation of an inland sea in California disrupts the aqueduct system transporting fresh water from north to south; the melting of glaciers in the Himalayas causes large numbers of Tibetans to relocate. All of this is a scenario of what 'could' – not what 'will' – happen. Even so, the portrayal continues with rising sea-levels, by 2010 putting millions at risk of flooding, while fisheries are disrupted by water temperature changes. In Europe abrupt climate change results from disruption of the thermohaline circulation (THC),[6] the global ocean conveyor system that moves warm, saline tropical waters northward from the Gulf of Mexico across the Atlantic Ocean to form the Gulf Stream. With the melting of glaciers in Greenland and the subsequent flow of freshwater from them altering and then destroying the conveyor circulation, Europe's average annual temperature drops by more than three degrees Celsius by 2020. In particular, northern latitudes, including the UK – the principal beneficiary of the mild winters, as a result of the Gulf Stream – become colder, drier and more akin to Siberia.[7]

In the future depicted by Schwartz and Randall deaths from war, famine and weather-related disasters run into millions. There are riots and internal conflict in India, South Africa and Indonesia. Elsewhere, countries begin looking closely at their neighbours' resources as they lose their ability to feed and care for their own populations. Along the Nile, Danube and Amazon which serve a large number of states, the possibility of conflict over water resources increases. As the authors grimly put it, 'humans fight when they outstrip the carrying capacity of their natural environment. Every time there is a choice between starving and raiding, humans raid.'

With the world's major sources of grain subject to droughts and crop failures – even America's Midwest suffers severe disruption as strong winds, storms, droughts and hot spells create rapid soil loss and havoc for farmers – wealthy areas, including the USA and Europe become 'virtual fortresses' in order to prevent entry to millions of starving migrants. Immigrants from Scandinavia seeking warmer climes attempt to move further south. Southern Europe is beleaguered by refugees from hard-hit countries in Africa. China's huge population and food demand make it particularly vulnerable. Over 400 million people in subtropical regions are also at grave risk. Bangladesh becomes nearly uninhabitable because of a rising sea level, which also contaminates inland water supplies. As conflict between countries intensifies, the report envisages the inevitable proliferation of nuclear weapons. Israel, China, India and Pakistan all become poised to use their nuclear arsenals if they consider it necessary but other countries, too, including Japan, South Korea, Egypt and Germany, in addition to Iran and North Korea, also begin developing a nuclear capability.

GLOBAL WARNING OR PREDICTION?

Schwartz and Randall's report provoked concern, apprehension, denial and accusations of conspiracy. Some analysts and commentators believe that its purpose was to give a warning to the Bush administration as to what might happen if it rejected the idea of global warming and it turned out to be true. Others have suggested that it was to provide extra ammunition to those seeking to build up US military global dominance and control. For instance, the report proposes that 'because of the potentially dire consequences, the risk of abrupt climate change – although uncertain and quite possibly small – should be elevated beyond a scientific debate to a U.S. national security concern'.

This raises important questions about the scientific plausibility of the report's rapid/abrupt climate change scenario. The reference to Hollywood in the *New York Times* article on it was due to the imminent release of the disaster movie *The Day After Tomorrow*, which used exactly such extreme and abrupt climate change as a major pretext for its plot. Moving beyond reality to portray the effects of scientifically impossible and almost instantaneous changes in global weather – all in order for its special effects team to create an action-packed cinema experience – the movie has Manhattan covered in ice-sheet and western Europe virtually destroyed in a matter of days.[8]

Schwartz and Randall do not stray into this world of make-believe, arguing instead that 'the *actual* impacts [of climate change] would greatly vary depending on the nuances of the weather conditions, the adaptability of humanity, and decisions by policymakers'. Equally, they argue that the report is not a prediction but a worst-case scenario, the outcomes to which would depend upon what (if any) preventative measures were taken.

However, they also clearly state that any of the events they portray are potentially possible and some will definitely happen. This, then, is interesting, if only for the way the report would seem intentionally to consider the worst possible realistic scenario by way of a wake-up call for strategic planners in the Pentagon and in order to alert them to a range of events that are likely to challenge national security as a result of *inevitable* environmental and atmospheric climate change.

HOW RAPID IS ABRUPT?

It is now widely accepted, through scientific modelling or direct observation, that the human-induced global warming which will be experienced in coming decades is already locked in. Greenhouse gas levels can take a long time (perhaps centuries) to decay naturally and even if we were able to stop the emission of all greenhouse gases today further warming of around 0.5 degrees Celsius is still likely to occur. If we do nothing to limit emissions then surface temperatures are likely to rise by six degrees Celsius by 2100. Even with agreed global restrictions, an average global temperature increase of two degrees Celsius by this juncture is forecast.[9]

Of course, climate has changed considerably in the past, the term 'climate change' traditionally referring to a large shift that lasts for a significant period of time (perhaps hundreds or thousands of years). For instance, current understanding of long-term climate cycles is that for the past 800,000 years a series of ice ages, lasting for approximately 100,000 years each, have been interrupted by interglacial periods of approximately 10,000 years. These changes are thought to be due to cyclical variations in the earth's orbital parameters and evidence exists for changes in average temperatures, patterns of storms, floods or droughts over a wide area such as a country or continent over long periods of time – perhaps hundreds or thousands of years. Current forecasts indicate that we are nearing the end of our present interglacial period.

However, the writers of *The Pentagon Report* speculate about a rapid or abrupt climate shift, typically occurring in the space of a decade or so and with consequent acute adaptation difficulties for human and natural systems. Much of their evidence comes by way of North Atlantic ice-cores from the period of the Younger Dryas,[10] which occurred some 13,000 years ago, and lasted for around 1,300 years. During this time the North Atlantic polar front advanced south and some evidence suggests that the mean annual temperature in the UK dropped to around –5 degrees Celsius.[11] This period ended extremely abruptly around 11,500 years ago with much of the northern hemisphere affected by extraordinary cold, dry, windy conditions.

Possible triggers for such rapid climate change can be sudden, as with huge volcanic eruptions, or a more gradual build up of pressure which suddenly reaches a tipping point – such as when increasing the pressure on a switch will abruptly flip it 'on'. In the case of climate it could be slow pressure increases occurring through changes in oceanic circulation and/or the glaciers and ice-caps, which could act as the trigger. Or it could be modifications of atmospheric temperature, composition, humidity, cloudiness and wind; in land conditions, or possible external factors, such as changes or variations in the earth's orbital characteristics; in solar output, or even the impacts of large extraterrestrial bodies such as meteors. Whatever the cause, the possibility of such rapid climate change, and with it, indications that it may have occurred in the past, on a number of occasions, have been recognised for some time.[12]

Schwartz and Randall's possible future scenario however, is specifically based on the '8.2 kyr event' (so called because it occurred 8,200 years ago). This lasted for about 100 years and was probably caused by the catastrophic draining of prehistoric glacial lakes in Canada into the Hudson Bay. The sudden introduction of large quantities of fresh water is thought to have caused a dramatic change in the ocean currents that return water to the south in the North Atlantic conveyor belt. The subsequent cooling in the Northern Hemisphere, amongst other things, transformed previously established rain-based agriculture to irrigation-based agriculture.[13]

The key scientific question then, in terms of corroboration of *The Pentagon Report* scenario, is: how likely is it that such rapid climate change will occur again? Peter Challenor, and co-workers from the National Oceanography Centre, Southampton, for instance, have attempted to calculate the probability of a complete THC shut down, using global climate models. Their conclusion is that it constitutes 'a high impact/low probability event' but also point out that, though their models are normally used to deal with high not low probability conditions, their calculations – based on a variety of possible future CO_2 emission levels – suggest a much higher (perhaps ten times higher) than expected probability that the THC will collapse. Indeed, they put this at a 30–40 per cent likelihood, failing a radical reduction in global CO_2 emissions.[14]

SUPPRESSING THE FACTS?

If *The Pentagon Report* is interesting enough in terms of its controversial substance, arguably more interesting still has been its ultimate purpose – and, linked to that, the timing of its publication. US President George W. Bush has for some time now been closely associated with attempts to deny that human activity through increased industrialisation, pollution and over-consumption has anything to do with changing the climate. Moreover, while in the last six years most industrialised nations have managed to cut some greenhouse gas emissions, under Bush, America's emissions have increased by an average of 1 per cent per year. The BBC investigative programme

Panorama, for instance, quotes the President as saying: 'I told the world I thought the Kyoto deal was a lousy deal for America. It meant that we had to cut emissions below 1990 levels which would have meant I would have presided over massive lay offs and economic destruction.'[15]

As Melanie Jarman in a later chapter develops, behind these sorts of statements are oil companies; notably ExxonMobil, which has spent millions of dollars financing around 40 organisations working exclusively to repudiate the existence of global warming.[16] The company's CEO and Chairman, Lee Raymond, until his retirement in 2005, twice served as chairman of the Global Climate Coalition – set up exclusively to counter the Intergovernmental Panel on Climate Change (IPCC) – while also collaborating extensively with the anti-environmental Wise Use Movement,[17] as well as fringe groups such as Sovereignty International. He is said to believe that global warming is a plot to enslave the world under a United Nations-led 'world government'. An article in the *Guardian* in June 2005 also revealed how documents obtained by Greenpeace, under the US freedom of information act, link Bush's repudiation of Kyoto to lobbying from ExxonMobil, among others.[18]

In the US, suppression of the basic facts about global warming, however, has gone even further than that. About the same time as the *Observer* article appeared on *The Pentagon Report*, the Union of Concerned Scientists (UCS) (an influential and non-partisan group of established US scientists including 20 Nobel laureates) issued a 38-page report accusing the Bush administration of deliberately distorting scientific fact to serve its policy agenda. The UCS report detailed how Washington 'systematically' twisted government scientific studies, suppressed others, stacked panels with political and unqualified appointees and often refused to seek independent expertise on many issues.[19] Similarly, in June 2006, a BBC *Panorama* investigation specifically revealed how US scientific reports on global warming were systematically changed or suppressed for political reasons. For instance, Bob Corell, author of an 'Arctic Assessment Report' which disclosed that Arctic ice was melting at an unprecedented rate, claimed in the programme that the publication of the report was deliberately delayed because of the US presidential election in 2004.[20]

James E. Hansen, a climate modelling scientist at NASA's Goddard Institute for Space Studies, is another who has publicly warned about the long-term threat of global warming since 1988. Although invited to brief Vice President Cheney and other US cabinet members on climate change in 2001, he fell out of favour three years later when he backed Senator John Kerry in the presidential election. Hansen has claimed that government scientists were being stopped from speaking out about climate change, citing as an example how, following a lecture he gave in December 2005 – calling for prompt reductions in greenhouse gas emissions – NASA attempted to censor his publications and warned him of 'dire consequences' if he continued to speak out.[21] A few weeks later, Hansen suggested publicly that scientists at the National Oceanic and Atmospheric Administration (NOAA) were also experiencing censorship. As a case in point he has stated that a March 2004 draft report on the widespread bleaching of coral due to sea temperature rises, inferring the impact of global warming, was doctored to remove these references in its final July 2005 version.[22]

The knock-on effects of US government denial have also extended across the Atlantic. For instance, in January 2004, Sir David King, chief science adviser to the then British Prime Minister, Tony Blair, in an article in *Science* (an international weekly journal published by the American Association for the Advancement of Science: AAAS),[23] severely criticised the Bush administration for its failure to take climate change seriously as well as its refusal to sign the Kyoto Protocol. Yet while in the article King unequivocally asserted that 'in my view, climate change is the most severe problem we are facing today, more serious than the threat of terrorism', Blair, during a Parliamentary committee meeting, on 3 February, actually tried to counteract King by saying that although terrorism and global warming are both of 'critical urgency, I think you can get into a rather cerebral debate about which is more important than the other'. More pointedly, a 10 February memo was sent by Ivan Rogers, the Prime Minister's principal private secretary, advising Sir David to 'decline [interview requests from] the UK or US national media' during a forthcoming visit to Seattle to deliver a lecture at the annual AAAS meeting.

This rather transparent attempt to stifle the government's top scientific adviser was uncovered when Sir David's personal press secretary, Lucy Brunt-Jenner, inadvertently left a computer disk in the AAAS press room where it was picked up by Michael Martin, a freelance journalist.[24] The disk included scripted answers from Rogers, suggesting how King might answer a list of 136 questions that might be put by reporters. For example, if he were asked to say whether terrorism or climate change was the greater threat, he was supposed to say that 'Both are serious and immediate problems for the world today.' However, when asked on the BBC radio morning news programme *Today* how he had come to the conclusion that global warming was more serious than terrorism, Sir David replied that this was 'based on the number of fatalities that have already occurred' – implying that global warming had already killed more people than terrorism.

Not surprisingly, the incident produced a slew of articles and public statements including a sensationalist report in the *Independent*, and criticism from the Liberal Democrat's environment spokesperson, Norman Baker MP, accusing the Prime Minister of 'muzzling' his chief scientific adviser.[25] However, what was becoming manifest for the Bush administration, is that its primary British ally, not least through the person of Blair, was finding it literally impossible to maintain any sustained congruence with the official US position on climate change.

Thus, some months later, in a speech made on 14 September 2004, Tony Blair stated:

What is now plain is that the emission of greenhouse gases, associated with industrialisation and strong economic growth from a world population that has increased six-fold in 200 years, is causing global warming at a rate that began as significant, has become alarming and is simply unsustainable in the long-term. And by long-term I do not mean centuries ahead. I mean within the lifetime of my children certainly; and possibly within my own. And by unsustainable, I do not mean a phenomenon causing problems of adjustment. I mean a challenge so far-reaching in its impact and irreversible in its destructive power, that it alters radically human existence.[26]

This is not to suggest that Her Majesty's Government has abandoned 'business as usual' as its response to the crisis. On the contrary, as firmly heralded in his 14 September speech, Blair's administration promoted 'science and technology' as the road to protection from the dangers of climate change and not least through the revival of nuclear power to 'protect high living standards' and reduce the need for possibly unpopular 'lifestyle changes'.[27] On this score, both the Prime Minister and his chief scientific adviser would appear to be at one.[28]

But if this has become the official British view, *The Pentagon Report* suggests an alternative US one, which actually recognises that scientific models alone are inadequate in predicting the social impacts of climate change while at the same time proposing that the administration, and more particularly the US Department of Defense, should be planning 'no-regret (military) strategies' for worst-case, global warming-induced eventualities.

There is a more benign interpretation, of course: that the information the *Report* offers provides grounds for the US to support global environmental treaties such as the Kyoto Protocol. Or, indeed, for the implementation of policies that will slow down the rate of climate change to give the US time to adapt and prepare for the likely environmental and social upheaval. But a more dystopian reading would be that Schwartz and Randall are setting the ground rules for the US to start building a virtual wall around its national boundaries: restricting the movement of people into the country, developing technologies of political control, and preparing for increased threats from nuclear war.

IF THE WORST COMES TO THE WORST

If the *Report*, thus, appears to present difficulties for a US administration which has gone out of its way, through denials and reassurances, suppression of the facts, and an alternative spin for popular consumption to suffocate a public debate on climate change – all designed, of course, to counter economic instability, the loss of popular support, and equally importantly, backers and friends, not least in the oil industry – there is no doubt that it is in line with other facets of emerging US administration planning. In the next chapter, Steve Wright describes how many governments, with that of the US at the forefront, are investigating – and implementing – military strategies and technologies for dealing with the expected public disorder following large scale and extended environmental and social disasters previously considered very low risk and, in particular, the attempted mass movement of populations across borders. In fact, some of the methods being considered for surveillance, public order and 'fortress'-style control along borders would also be very useful in urban war fighting situations – as recently experienced in Iraq or in the US's continuing 'war on terror'. This sort of thinking and practice is very indicative of a situation in which human rights, international law and democratic processes are peremptorily sacrificed so that governments can continue to exercise complete control. There is certainly nothing in the conclusions of *The Pentagon Report* which would demur from these implications.

A STORM OF CONTROVERSY

Paradoxically, then, the Pentagon found itself, on the *Report*'s release, with a press furore on its hands which had much less to do with the military scenarios it set out and much more to do with the fact that environmentalists and the media were able to use it to demonstrate that President Bush was out of touch with his own experts. Some critics challenged it actually on the grounds that it was purely speculative and that no recognised climate experts were involved in formulating its possible scenarios. Others made much of the authors' insistence that the *Report* was a 'not implausible' reinforcing of their own calls for climate change to become a prime US national security concern. A Pentagon spokesman, Lt. Commander Dan Hetladge, could only declare that the press and media outcry amounted to 'a tempest in a teacup'.[29]

So, who was behind the *Report* and what was their purpose?

IN THE BEGINNING ... THE MARSHALL PLAN

The Pentagon paid $100,000 for the *Report* which was commissioned by 83-year-old US Defense Department futurist planner Andrew Marshall – often referred to by Pentagon insiders as 'Yoda'. It was he who sent the report to *Fortune* magazine and he has also been quoted as saying that: 'The Schwartz and Randall study reflects the limits of scientific models and information when it comes to predicting the effects of abrupt global warming. Although there is significant scientific evidence on this issue, much of what this study predicts is still speculation.'[30]

Marshall has a long history of working in US national security. He joined the RAND Corporation in 1949 as an analyst and in 1972 was hired by Henry Kissinger to work in the National Security Council. The following year Richard Nixon appointed him as the first director of the newly formed Office of Net Assessment (ONA) and he has been reappointed to that role by every President since.

ONA is not widely known to the general public but has been very influential in forming US military and political strategies. It was formed to look ten or twenty years into the future to determine possible future threats to US security. Its evaluation, for instance, of the Soviet threat and its analysis of Soviet military investment were used by Secretary of Defense James R. Schlesinger to reverse the US decline in military spending in the 1970s. During the Reagan years, Marshall helped to write a secret report calling for the US to develop the ability to fight and win a nuclear war with the Soviets. He has also been an enthusiastic supporter of Missile Defence and Star Wars programmes, arguing that the US could soon face the threat of ballistic missile attack from North Korea. In the 1990s Marshall began to speak about a 'revolution in military affairs' (RMA) driven by advances in information technology and a recognition that battle management and planning systems need to be integrated across the whole spectrum of war fighting capability (the 'Full Spectrum Dominance' of land, sea, air and space).[31]

The influence that Marshall holds in his position became clear when, in 1997, an attempt to downgrade ONA by incoming Defense Secretary William S. Cohen was rebuffed by Marshall's supporters in Congress, the aerospace industry and the press. Not least of Marshall's defenders was his former aide, James G. Roche (who, at that time was Corporate Vice President and President of Electronic Sensors & Systems at the major defence contractors Northrop Grumman – later he became Secretary of the Air Force). Other followers and supporters of Marshall include Vice President Dick Cheney,[32] former Defense Secretary Donald Rumsfeld,[33] and former Deputy Secretary Paul Wolfowitz who helped found the Project for a New American Century (PNAC),[34] a Washington-based think-tank created in 1997 which believes in, and works towards, the establishment of a global American empire.[35] Its White Paper produced in September 2000, and entitled 'Rebuilding America's Defenses: Strategy, Forces and Resources for a New Century', describes 'four essential missions' for the US military:

- Homeland Defence – to counteract possible threats to the homeland from lesser states
- Large Wars – to fight and win multiple, simultaneous large-scale wars
- Constabulary Duties – to shape the security environment in critical regions
- Transform US Armed Forces – to exploit the advanced technologies developed as a 'revolution in military affairs'.[36]

At the time of writing there are indications that PNAC is 'heading toward closing down' with the feeling of 'goal accomplished'.[37] None of this particularly explains why Marshall commissioned Schwartz and Randall, rather than, for instance, a group of climatologists to produce the *Report*. As a futurologist, however, Marshall was probably more interested in the challenge of unexpected future scenarios than potentially inconclusive scientific models or predictions. What, then, of his commissioned authors?

Peter Schwartz is Chairman of GBN a consultancy based in Emeryville, California. He has a Bachelor's degree in aeronautical engineering and astronautics, was director of the Strategic Environment Center at SRI International in Menlo Park, Silicon Valley, before becoming head of planning for Royal Dutch/Shell Group in London, from 1982 to 1986, where he continued the work of Pierre Wack, using scenario planning to introduce change in individual and institutional behaviour.

Scenario planning was used in the 1940s, by Herman Kahn at the RAND Corporation, to explore possible situations leading to and resulting from nuclear war. Schwartz uses the same technique of creating possible future scenarios to help organisations 'think the unthinkable'.[38] During his time with Shell, Schwartz led the team that correctly speculated the collapse of oil prices and of the Soviet Union. His method is to develop a 'thinking tool' by investigating the possible response of an organisation to a major but unexpected shock. He also claims he prophesied the 9/11 tragedy:

We wrote for the Rudman Commission [Hart-Rudman Commission into US national security in the twenty-first century] that the forces of Bin Laden and al-Qaeda would fly a Jumbo jet into the World Trade Center and major buildings in Washington. We weren't the first or the only ones who said that ... You just had to read what Bin Laden said and look at history and his behaviour. He went after the World Trade Center before, and he comes back for his targets if he doesn't get them. You couldn't know that it would be on 11 September but you knew it was coming.[39]

In fact Schwartz hasn't always got it right. In 1997 he offered the possibility of 25 years of global prosperity, freedom and a better environment generated by an economic boom that would double the world's economy twice in that period. This scenario optimistically envisioned five great waves of technology – personal computers, telecommunications, biotechnology, nanotechnology and alternative energy – that would produce sustained growth without destroying the environment.[40] Unfortunately, this has not happened, but perhaps the article was an attempt to influence as much as to predict. As he says, 'without an expansive vision of the future, people tend to get short-sighted and mean-spirited, looking out only for themselves.

A positive scenario can inspire us through what will inevitably be traumatic times ahead.'[41]

In 1987 Schwartz co-founded GBN[42] which is now part of the Monitor Consulting Group and has clients that include the US Defense Advanced Research Projects Agency (DARPA) and the CIA. He has worked as a script consultant for Hollywood films such as *War Games*, *Deep Impact* and *Minority Report*, which portrays a world where crimes are predicted and prevented before they actually occur – perhaps the ultimate in futurist thinking.

Doug Randall is co-leader of the GBN consulting practice and a former senior researcher at the Wharton School in Pennsylvania, where he studied tools and techniques for managing uncertainty. He is quoted as putting the question:

Do advanced technologies and globalisation make this sort of [abrupt climate] change less impactful, because we can adapt more quickly, or do they make it worse, because our systems are more brittle and we're more reliant on one another? That's a key question ... It's certainly plausible to imagine the impacts being worse ... leading to a sharp decrease in the carrying capacity of the planet, and that would lead to even more conflicts over food, water and other resources; more instability.[43]

POLICING THE FUTURE EFFECTS OF CLIMATE CHANGE

As Randall further admits, it is not clear where gradual climate change will hit the hardest or how abruptly climate change might unfold. To effectively plan will require more information. However, it is equally unlikely that we will have created a sustainable global society before the negative effects of climate change (abrupt or gradual) fully take effect. In many respects the effects of climate change are merely an epiphenomenon. They will certainly hit hardest those who are less prepared and less able to cope – hence emphasising issues of global inequality and lifestyle protection.

The experiences of Hurricanes Rita and Katrina have already demonstrated how lack of civil preparation can quickly lead to a widespread breakdown in public order and so to rapid policing or military responses. The way Morocco flew out and then dumped plane loads of African migrants to Senegal, who had tried to storm razor-wire fences to get into the Spanish enclaves across the border, is a further indicator of things to come.[44] Meanwhile, a US programme costing $500 million over five years, ostensibly to counter terrorism in the Sahara region, seems to defy evidence of terrorist threat but has been linked to US moves to build a presence in the region where there are potentially large oil reserves.[45] Perhaps this is another example of futurist strategy planning, with the US ensuring access to oil, or establishing a military presence in Africa where refugees from abrupt climate change may number many millions – or possibly both. Certainly, current US political ideology is underpinned by an aggressive military programme of global dominance – perhaps best illustrated by the US Space Command's 2020 Vision document:

The ultimate goal of our military force is to accomplish the objectives directed by the National Command Authorities. For the joint force of the future, this goal will be achieved through full spectrum dominance – the ability of US forces, operating unilaterally or in combination with multinational and interagency partners, to defeat any adversary and control any situation across the full range of military operations.[46]

With the US currently developing its hi-tech superiority in space – satellites, telecommunications, weapons, and the like – to sustain the current status quo, it is hardly surprising that the military have another angle on climate change: the possibility of controlling the weather, and even using it as a weapon.

MILITARY WEATHER MODIFICATION

Throughout history the weather has played an important part in planning and fighting wars and so is of particular interest to the military. Nearly 2,500 years ago the Chinese general Sun Tzu proclaimed: 'Know yourself, know your enemy; your victory will never be endangered. Know the ground, know the weather; your victory will then be total.'[47]

More recent times have produced all manner of occasions when the weather has been crucial to the success of troop deployments, attack or defence, especially where commanders have been forewarned of the meteorological forecast. Indeed, it is mainly due to the military interest in accurate predictions of cloud cover, wind direction and strength for reconnaissance and surveillance, or possible sea conditions, that so much research into weather modelling and forecasting has been funded by governments around the world.

However in the 1990s the US Air Force developed another interest in the weather by introducing the concept of weather exploitation: 'the deliberate use of knowledge about friendly and enemy operating capabilities under given natural environmental conditions to set the terms of battle, resulting in optimal performance of the friendly force and reduced effectiveness of the enemy force'.[48] One step beyond that would be the military developing the ability to change the weather to suit them – or even use it as a weapon. Far-fetched? Perhaps, but in the 1970s, former national security adviser Zbigniew Brzezinski wrote: 'Technology will make available, to the leaders of major nations, techniques for conducting secret warfare, of which only a bare minimum of the security forces need be appraised ... Techniques of weather modification could be employed to produce prolonged periods of drought or storm.'[49]

Twenty years later, in 1996, a 'futurist' research paper from the US Air Force described how:

US aerospace forces can 'own the weather' by capitalising on emerging technologies and focusing development of those technologies to war-fighting applications. Such a capability offers the war fighter tools to shape the battlespace in ways never before possible. It provides opportunities to impact operations across the full spectrum of conflict and is pertinent to all possible futures.[50]

The paper cites a 1957 advisory committee on weather control which explicitly recognised the military potential for weather modification, suggesting that it could become a more important weapon than the atom bomb. Weather modification might be controversial, the paper admits, so not totally acceptable to all segments of society. However, against that:

The tremendous military capabilities that could result from this field are ignored at our own peril. From enhancing friendly operations or disrupting those of the enemy via small-scale tailoring of natural weather patterns to complete dominance of global communications and counterspace control, weather-modification offers the war fighter a wide-range of possible options to defeat or coerce an adversary.[51]

In fact, while on the one hand all manner of technical wizardry – robot planes, unmanned aerial vehicles (UAVs) for cloud generation, seeding and dispersal, plus microwave generators to cause localised atmospheric disturbances – are all envisaged, the one thing the research paper does not mention is that there are legal restrictions on tampering with the weather. The Convention on the Prohibition of Military or Any Other Hostile Use of Environmental Modification Technique (ENMOD) was adopted by a UN General Assembly resolution, in

1977, the signatories pledging to refrain from any military or other hostile use of weather modification which could result in widespread, long-lasting or severe effects.[52] In spite of this, research into weather modification has continued amid accusations that commercial and non-profit enterprises are being used as fronts for military experimentation. One openly military experimental operation, however, is of marked pertinence to our broader consideration.

STRUNG ALONG BY HAARP?

The High Frequency Active Auroral Research Program (HAARP), an assembly of 180 radio aerials situated near Fairbanks, Alaska, is jointly managed by the US Air Force and US Navy. The antennae can project 3.6 Megawatts of radio energy into the ionosphere and heat many square kilometres of it by several degrees. HAARP can certainly influence the naturally occurring electrical current systems that exist in the upper ionosphere, one defence application of its work being to generate and modulate such currents to turn it into a giant transmitter for Very Low Frequency (3–30 kHz) and/or Ultra Low Frequency electromagnetic (radio) waves (0.003–3 Hz).[53]

These may certainly have various applications for enhancing 'communications and surveillance systems' as the HAARP website describes.[54] But not only conspiracy theorists are convinced that it is also being developed as a secret weather-modification weapon. A number of concerns and accusations by the NO HAARP movement are documented in *Angels Don't Play This Haarp*,[55] while world-renowned public health expert and author of *No Immediate Danger: Prognosis for Radioactive Earth* (1985), Rosalie Bertell, in November 2000, was reported as saying: 'US military scientists ... are working on weather systems as a potential weapon. The methods include the enhancing of storms and the diverting of vapour rivers in the earth's atmosphere to produce targeted droughts or floods.'[56]

Michel Chossudovsky, an economics professor at the University of Ottawa, who has studied official military documents about HAARP, has recently gone further to propose that 'It is time people began focusing on these weapons instead of concentrating solely on global warming ... Both are a serious threat.'[57] Significantly, in February 1998, The European Parliament's Committee on Foreign Affairs, Security and Defence Policy held public hearings on the HAARP programme and submitted a 'Motion for Resolution' to the European Parliament that: 'Considers HAARP ... by virtue of its far-reaching impact on the environment to be a global concern and calls for its legal, ecological and ethical implications to be examined by an international independent body'.[58] The Committee also noted the repeated refusal of the US to give evidence on HAARP to its hearings. Its efforts to further examine 'the environmental impacts of military activities' through a 'Green Paper' were sidelined on the dubious technicality that the European Commission lacks the required jurisdiction to delve into 'the links between environment and defence'.

None of this has prevented the US Senate from receiving a bill in March 2005 to establish a Weather Modification Operations and Research Board in the Department of Commerce whose purpose would be to:

implement a comprehensive and co-ordinated national weather modification policy ... with respect to ... improved forecast and decision-making technologies ... and ... assessments and evaluations of the efficacy of weather modification, both purposeful (including cloud-seeding operations) and inadvertent (including downwind ... and anthropogenic effects).[59]

Approved by the Senate Commerce Committee in May 2006, with a proposed appropriation to the Board of $10 million every year from then until 2014, it was subsequently introduced to the House of Representatives as HR 2995, on 20 June 2006. Its proposer, Senator Hutchinson, was quoted as saying: 'Hurricanes Rita and Katrina and the recent tornados and violent storms in the Midwest took many lives and destroyed both property and the environment ... By developing sustained research we can provide answers to the issues of predictability and reliability of weather modification research.'[60]

Conspiracy theories abound on the US military and weather control. Some extremists believe that it is their experimentation that is, or will be, the cause of abrupt climate change.

CONCLUSION

The newspapers and media made the most of the apocalyptic scenario described in *The Pentagon Report* in 2004. Uncontrollable weather conditions brought on by abrupt and unexpected climate change causing famine, pestilence, war and death (all four biblical Horsemen of the Apocalypse unleashed at once), leaked secret reports, disagreements between the government and the military – each of these is a good story on its own and here they all were in one headline-grabbing article.

However, rather than being mysteriously leaked, it was Andrew Marshall, the *Report*'s commissioner, who sent it to *Fortune* magazine. It was therefore unclassified (at least in the version that has now been openly published). Why did Marshall do that? Was he concerned about its findings and thought the public should know about them? Perhaps this is unlikely for someone heading a secretive government department. Or did he, or someone else, want to influence and/or initiate public debate on climate change and national security ?

Certainly, in involving GBN – in other words, scenario-planner specialists, rather than a whole range of other experts on climate change – to write it, Marshall does seem to have chosen his ground rather deliberately. Was he directly challenging the President's line on global warming – and at the beginning of a presidential election year – indicating that he wanted senior figures in the business world as well as policy makers to take note of the ongoing administration's attempts to ignore, alter or distort the views and findings of the IPCC, the National Academy of Science and the vast majority of the scientific community on climate change? Did he set out, indeed, to commission an extreme scenario in an attempt to demonstrate that climate change is the most severe problem that we face today – greater even than terrorism?

Clearly, the US Department of Defense has to be ready for – or at least consider – any eventuality. However, this chapter has attempted to demonstrate that the implications for national and global security as suggested in the *Report* are not necessarily at odds with the US military's current way of thinking. The portrayal of the future as presented by the *Report* could be used to help drive the strategy of Full Spectrum Dominance and the adoption of technologies and methodologies arising out of the 'revolution in military affairs'. Although beset by many critics, the US government sees its role as a heavily armed, technologically superior police force acting across the globe. It behaves accordingly.

The military interest in weather and its possible modification can also benefit from the *Report* – which could be used to argue that an understating of weather conditions in advance will give the US the advantage over those lacking that ability and without the requisite techniques. The *Report* may even support the view that the possibility of combating climate change with high-tech military weaponry is worth considering. Some of this is science-fiction, some political reality – but that seems to be the way that the most powerful nation on earth thinks and plans at the moment. Perhaps that's even scarier than the consequences of rapid climate change itself.

NOTES

The author would like to thank Dr Steve Wright from the Praxis Centre for many useful and interesting discussions and suggestions; Dr Lesley Jeffries of the University of Huddersfield for very useful comments on early drafts, and Leeds Metropolitan University for assistance with this work.

1. Mark Townsend and Paul Harris, 'Now the Pentagon tells Bush: climate change will destroy us', *Observer*, 22 February 2004.
2. The report can be obtained from the *Global Business Network* website at http://www.gbn.com/ArticleDisplayServlet.srv?aid=26231
3. David Stipp, 'The Pentagon's weather nightmare: The climate could change radically, and fast', *Fortune* magazine, 9 February 2004.
4. Keay Davidson, 'Pentagon-sponsored climate report sparks hullabaloo in Europe', *San Francisco Chronicle*, 25 February 2004.
5. Andrew C. Revkin, 'The Sky is Falling! Say Hollywood and, Yes, the Pentagon', *New York Times*, 29 February 2004.
6. *Thermohaline* – from the Greek words for heat, *'thermos'*, and salt, *'halos'*.
7. In fact, the ocean conveyor system could be slowing down already – see H. Bryden et al., 'Slowing of the Atlantic Meridional Circulation at 25°N', *Nature* 438, 1 December 2005, pp. 655–7. The IPCC also states: 'beyond 2100, the thermohaline circulation could completely, and possibly irreversibly, shut-down in either hemisphere' if global warming is 'large enough and applied long enough'. IPCC, *Climate Change 2001: The Scientific Basis*, Cambridge: Cambridge University Press, 2001, 'Summary for Policy Makers', p. 16.
8. *The Day After Tomorrow*, Dir. Roland Emmerich; see http://www.the-dayaftertomorrow.com
9. IPCC, *Climate Change 2001*, 'Technical Summary of Working Group I', p. 26.
10. The name comes from the pollen of a tundra wildflower – *dryas octopetala* – that was unexpectedly discovered in a core sample taken from a lake bed in Denmark.
11. T.C. Atkinson et al., 'Seasonal temperatures in Britain during the past 22,000 years, reconstructed using beetle remains', *Nature* 325, 1987, pp. 587–92.
12. See, for example, W.H. Calvin, 'The great climate flip-flop', *Atlantic Monthly*, 281(1), 1998, pp. 47–64. Further discussion at http://williamcalvin.com/1990s/1998AtlanticClimate.htm
13. E. Linden, *The Winds of Change: Climate, Weather and the Destruction of Civilisations*, New York: Simon and Schuster, 2006. Linden uses the 8.2 kyr event, two less well-defined climate changes around 5,200 and 4,200 years ago, a possible volcanic event in 536 AD, the Mayan collapse around 800 AD, and the Norse colony collapse in Greenland to make the

case that societies are vulnerable to abrupt shifts in rainfall, temperature and so on.

14. P.G. Challenor, R.K.S. Hankin and R. Marsh, 'Towards the probability of rapid climate change', in H.J. Schellnhuber et al., eds, *Avoiding Dangerous Climate Change*, Cambridge: Cambridge University Press, 2006, chapter 7.
15. 'Bush's Climate of Fear', *Panorama*, BBC1, 4 June 2006.
16. Andrew Gumbel, 'An immovable obstacle to action on climate change', *Independent*, 1 June 2006.
17. An anti-environmentalist organisation founded in the late 1980s dealing mostly with timber and mining issues – more information at http://www.sourcewatch.org
18. John Vidal, 'Revealed: how oil giant influenced Bush', *Guardian*, 8 June 2005.
19. Seth Borenstein, 'Bush administration Accused of Suppressing, Distorting Science', *Knight Rider*, 19 February 2004. For the UCS report, 'Scientific integrity in policymaking – an investigation into the Bush Administration's misuse of science', see http://www.ucsusa.org/scientific_integrity/interference/specific-examples-of-the-abuse-of-science.html
20. 'Bush's Climate of Fear'.
21. Andrew C. Revkin, 'Climate expert says NASA tried to silence him', *New York Times*, 29 January, 2006.
22. Juliet Ailperin, 'Scientists say they're being gagged by Bush – White House monitors their media contacts',*Washington Post*, 16 April 2006.
23. D.A King, 'Climate change science: adapt, mitigate or ignore?', *Science*, 303 (5655) 2004, pp. 176–7, available at http://www.ost.gov.uk/policy/issues/
24. M. Martin, M., 'Cooler Heads on Climate Change', *ScienceNOW*, 217, 17 February 2004, also on http://www.weeklyscientist.com/ws/PM_Memo/ScienceNOW%20Martin%202004%20(217)%202.htm
25. Steve Connor and Andrew Grice, 'Scientist "gagged" by No. 10 after warning of global warming threat', *Independent*, 8 March 2006.
26. Speech available at http://www.number10.gov.uk/output/Page6333.asp
27. Marie Wolf, 'Blair demands nuclear power to protect high living standards', *Independent*, 9 May 2005.
28. David King, 'The nuclear option isn't political expediency but scientific necessity', *Guardian*, 16 December, 2005.
29. Davidson, 'Pentagon-sponsored climate report sparks hullabaloo'.
30. Ibid.
31. B. Berkowitz, *War in the Information Age*, The Hoover Digest – Research and Opinion on Public Policy, no. 2, Spring, 2002, The Hoover Institution, Stanford University, available online at http://www.hooverdigest.org/022/berkowitz.html; E. Halpin, P. Trevorrow, D. Webb and S. Wright, eds, *Cyberwar, Netwar and the Revolution in Military Affairs*, Basingstoke: Palgrave Macmillan, 2006.
32. Dick Cheney, a former CEO of Haliburton, has links with the Carlyle Group (a global investment firm that has considerable investments in defence and high-tech, space, security-linked information technology,

nanotechnologies and telecommunications, and whose members include a slew of former US, British and assorted other state leaders plus some bin Laden family members for good measure. See 'Meet the Carlyle Group', http://www.hereinreality.com/carlyle.html

33. In 2004 Donald Rumsfeld sold shares he held 'in at least five companies after they were identified as doing business with the Pentagon, according to his latest financial disclosure form'. See Jim Wolf, 'Rumsfeld sold stakes in Pentagon contractors', *Boston Globe*, 22 September 2004, available online at http://nucnews.net/nucnews/2004nn/0409nn/040922nn.htm#400

34. Former Deputy Secretary of Defense, currently President of the World Bank, though perhaps best known as a leading proponent of the Iraq War in 2003 and in the development of the 'Bush Doctrine' (the National Security Strategy of the US, issued in September 2002 in response to the 9/11 attacks – a policy that moves away from deterrence to first strike or preventive war).

35. See http://www.newamericancentury.org

36. Available from http://www.newamericancentury.org/RebuildingAmericasDefenses.pdf

37. Jim Lobe, '"New American Century" project ends with a whimper', *Inter Press Service*, 13 June 2006. See http://www.commondreams.org/headlines06/0613–05.htm

38. See P. Schwartz, *The Art of the Long View: Planning for the Future in an Uncertain World*, New York: Currency, 1996.

39. As quoted in an article in the Business news section of the *South African Sunday Times*, 26 January 2003.

40. P. Schwartz and P. Leyden, 'The Long Boom: A History of the Future, 1980–2020', *Wired,* Issue 5.07, July 1997, available online at http://www.wired.com/wired/5.07/longboom.html.

41. Ibid.

42. GBN (see http://www.gbn.com/) was co-founded with Jay Ogilvy (former director of SRI research in the 'Values and Lifestyles' Program), Stewart Brand (founder of the *Whole Earth Catalog* and the Well computer network), Napier Collyns (Shell planning group) and Lawrence Wilkinson (president of Colossal Pictures).

43. Interview with Alex Steffen on *World Changing Interviews*, http://www.worldchanging.com/archives/000760.html

44. BBC News, 'Morocco flies out dumped migrants', 10 October 2005. See http://news.bbc.co.uk/2/hi/africa/4326670.stm

45. Jason Motlagh, 'US opens new war front in North Africa', *Asian Times*, 14 June 2006.

46. United States Space Command, *Vision for 2020*, Peterson Air Force Base, 2nd Printing, August 1997, http://www.fas.org/spp/military/docops/usspac/visbook.pdf

47. Sun Tzu, *The Art of War*, 500 BC, Chapter 1, Laying Plans, X. Terrain, #31 – as translated from the Chinese by Lionel Giles, 1910. See online reference http://www.chinapage.com/sunzi-e.html

48. J.M. Lanicci, 'Integrating weather exploitation into airpower and space power doctrine', *Airpower Journal*, Summer 1998, pp. 52–63.

49. Z. Brzezinski, *Between Two Ages: America's Role in the Technetronic Era*, New York: Viking Press, 1976.
50. T.J. Huse et al., 'Weather as a force multiplier: owning the weather in 2025', Air Force 2025 Final Report, August 1996, http://csat.au.af.mil/2025/volume3/vol3ch15.pdf
51. Ibid.
52. Full text available at: http://www.sussex.ac.uk/Units/spru/hsp/ENMOD.pdf
53. D. Hambling, *Weapons Grade – Revealing the Links Between Modern Warfare and Our High-Tech World*, London: Constable, 2005, pp. 303–4.
54. See http://www.haarp.alaska.edu
55. N. Begich and J. Manning, *Angels Don't Play this Haarp: Advances in Tesla Technology*, Earthpulse Press, 1997; see also *The Military Pandora's Box* at: http://www.haarp.net; Jim Phelps, *Star Wars, Space Shields, UV, and the Weather:* http://www.gargoylemechanique.com/chama/chemtrails_overview.html
56. Quoted in Michel Chossudovsky, 'Washington's new world order weapons can trigger climate change', 26 November 2000, http://www.mindfully.org/Air/Climate-Change-Weapons.htm. See also Rosalie Bertell, Background of the HAARP Program, 5 November 1996, http://www.globalpolicy.org/socecon/envronmt/weapons.htm Also, Bernard Eastland, 'Systems considerations of weather modification experiments using high power electromagnetic radiation', *Proceedings of Workshop on Space Exploration and Resources Exploitation*, Explospace, 20–22 October 1998, Calgary, Sardinia, Italy.
57. 'Weather War? – new evidence', *Daily Express*, 8 October 2005, see http://www.infowars.com/articles/science_technology/weather_modification/weather_war.html. Other Chossudovsky articles on HAARP including 'The ultimate weapon of mass destruction: owning the weather for military use', 27 September 2004, are available from the *Centre for Research on Globalization* website: www.globalresearch.ca
58. European Parliament, Committee on Foreign Affairs, Security and Defense Policy, Brussels, doc. no. A4–0005/99, 14 January 1999.
59. Senate Bill 517 introduced by Senator Kay Bailey Hutchinson, 3 March 2005, 109th Congress, 1st Session, see http://www.theorator.com/bills109/s517.html
60. 'Committee approves bill establishing weather modification program', *KWTX.com*, 13 June 2006, http://www.kwtx.com/home/headlines/1985602.html

3
Preparing for Mass Refugee Flows: The Corporate Military Sector

Steve Wright

Whilst political, scientific and the specialised environmental communities argue intensely about the realities of climate change, practical steps to obviate the colossal anticipated impact on human settlements are few. The official version now seems to be settling towards an increased reliance on nuclear power generation: an option discredited on economic grounds not to mention the ludicrous folly of relying on processes accelerating the creation of fissile material in a time of growing political upheaval.

Meanwhile, military think-tanks, especially in the United States, are planning sophisticated new area and perimeter denial technologies and deployment rationales and strategies under the catch-all diktat of preparing for the asymmetrical 'war against terror'. These developments have come about because of a coalition of coincidences rather than a pre-planned response to climate change. Nevertheless, with current estimates of up to 100 million people being forced to migrate because of environmental disasters,[1] and in an international society where state boundaries provide firm reminders of geographic, political and ethnic exclusion, we should not suffer any illusions about the willingness of future politicians to deploy such zone exclusion technologies to seal off the human migrations associated with climate change.

The Pentagon, in particular, is beginning to see the issue in security terms. Thus, while many governments are now working on a hi-tech range of advanced paralysing technologies to immobilise people at borders, legitimised on the grounds that they are less-lethal flexible responses to the changing nature of modern warfare, in the US, considerable sums of money have been released for cutting-edge concepts and prototypes in this field.

A short survey like this can merely scratch the surface of current area-denial research and development. For many readers, even what is covered here will read like science-fiction. Few critical researchers undertake work in this area of mass human rights violation. While torture rehabilitation centres work at the coal face,[2] the Praxis Centre, at Leeds Metropolitan University, of which this author is a member, works with human rights, peace and development NGOs to share our concerns about the human rights impacts when such technology is in place. Therefore, where possible, named company websites are provided to enable others to follow up on future developments. This chapter also builds on previous work, undertaken in critical part with Professor Brian Martin, where we have questioned whether or not researchers can or should remain neutral in this debate, or instead use the political ju-jitsu framework advocated by ourselves to find ways of overcoming some of the operational mechanisms of this border control technology to make their policy rationale 'backfire'.[3]

With the Hurricane Katrina disaster in New Orleans, in August 2005, we saw the after-effects of an over-emphasis on protecting state infrastructure, rather than prioritising the real-time, or immediate needs of ordinary citizens. A telling phrase which has emerged is that 'homeland security runs through my back yard': a reminder in itself that the juggernaut of state security concerns should not override the basic needs of common humanity in a 'time of terror'. Thus, a key challenge for conflict researchers is to share information about more humane alternatives – implementing security as if people mattered.

With this in view, our technological discussion is three-fold. Firstly, an examination of some of the emerging algorithmic systems which, counter to the premise that a potential target in some sense makes a choice whether to breach a boundary or not, are geared towards actively seeking targets. Secondly, emergent systems based on neural networks, combining both surveillance and identity recognition processes to punish certain groups of people, whilst leaving others untouched. Finally, some thoughts on what kind of semi-intelligent active border patrol technology lies on the horizon, including armed unmanned aerial vehicles and robot gangs.

SHIFTING CLIMATE CHANGE PARADIGMS AND CONFLICTS

The 2003 Schwartz and Randall report for the Pentagon, previously analysed in this book by Dave Webb, has predicted that climate change conflict will soon not only become more important than the current 'war against terror' but with an estimated 100 million people on the move as a consequence, could see rich areas such as

Europe and the US becoming virtual fortresses against this people-tide. Their scenarios paint a frightening picture of massive numbers of migrants arriving at Southern European shores from a devastated Africa; mega-droughts affecting the world's major bread baskets and with particularly disproportionate effects on countries such as Bangladesh, predicted to become virtually uninhabitable because of rising sea levels. China, too, will be especially vulnerable because of its huge population but also, as elsewhere in the world, because many of its key population centres are in cities by seaboards and thus threatened by flooding.

Moreover, with weather damage around the world in 2005 rated by the UN Environment Programme (UNEP), at $200 billion, as the costliest ever – not least as the result of the highest number of hurricanes and tropical storms since records began more than 150 years ago[4] – *The Pentagon Report* is no longer being dismissed as simply alarmist. The then British Defence Secretary, Dr John Reid, in a Chatham House speech in February 2006, not only warned that British Armed Forces would have to be prepared to cope with conflicts over shrinking resources over the next 30 years but, in particular, expressed his fears of a violent collision between a growing world population and increasingly scarce and contaminated water resources as global warming causes ice fields to melt and arable land to become desert.[5] It is significant that soon after making this statement, Dr Reid went on to parrot the current US line that the Geneva conventions should be redrawn.[6]

Of course, when Western leaders make such statements they rarely refer to the advanced weapons technologies supplied by the more affluent nations which lead to the direct displacement of civilians. Nor that affluence itself might be creating conditions for climate change, not least through resource wars required to sustain unsustainable lifestyles. Nevertheless, climate change has increasingly been seen in security terms even in the EU, where member states are constitutionally prevented from strategically integrating their military forces. A report to the European Parliament in 1999 thus observed that an 'estimated 25 million people are refugees from drought, soil erosion and other environmental problems, which may be compared with 22 million "traditional" refugees'.[7] Analysts, such as John Vogler, have commented that whilst the EU has resisted labelling refugees as a security threat, it has warned that refugee flows are putting 'direct pressure on EU immigration and justice policies'.[8] While enhanced intermediate controls in Europe will begin with automated biometric visitor processing,[9] for countries which border Africa, like Spain, the issue has taken on an altogether more visceral turn, not least in 2005 when migrants were forced to cross a Saharan army minefield after having failed to breach barbed-wire fences protecting the Melila enclave.[10]

THE EMERGENT PHILOSOPHY OF TUNEABLE LETHALITY

How could military forces possibly deal with hundreds of thousands of refugees swarming over borders? With the ending of the Cold War, notions such as Military Operations Other Than War (MOOTW) could provide part of an emerging answer. Some of this thinking has focused on evolving a second generation of incapacitating technology, hi-tech, lucrative and capable of industrialising repression.

Post-9/11, US homeland security initiatives have rapidly encouraged new blue-skies thinking from corporates, who see state security supplies as potentially one of the most rapid and profitable areas of growth in future defence markets. It has previously been argued that the impacts of some of the crowd control weapons in this burgeoning market are 'tantamount to torture' and that we are witnessing the beginnings of a new policy, using the macro-induction of pain to control both mass movement and large protests.[11] The technologies discussed below include lethal electroshock fences; automated sentry guns; taser mines which shoot out darts carrying 50,000 volts; optical and acoustic technologies; directed energy systems that project lightning at crowds or heat them up to unbearable temperatures; bio-chemical weapons which target specific human receptor sites to induce fear and terror; and energy projectiles which create a disabling shock wave by turning the water which surrounds our body as a by-product of metabolism, into plasma.

The technologies being developed link in with emergent military doctrines such as 'layered defence', which imagines it will be possible to produce a rheostat-like controlled violence from maiming at one end of the spectrum, to full scale 'tuneable lethality' at the other. The problem, when it comes to using new technology for these alleged purposes (such as directed energy weapons which have effects which can be increased in severity), is, as Dominique Loye of the International Committee of the Red Cross (ICRC) points out, that in the context of hostile operations, the temptation for security forces will always be to use the maximum setting.[12] Otherwise how can they predict which maimed or dazed target still has the wherewithal to fire back? Even with the best intentions, experts at specialist security and border control conferences, tend to corroborate these state rather than human security perspectives. It is easy within this context to reframe the refugee issue from a matter of humanitarian assistance into one for a new techno-politics of exclusion.

CURRENT IMMOBILISING BORDER SECURITY TECHNOLOGIES

There are essentially two classes of immobilising technologies, namely: (i) current off-the-shelf technologies which are already on the market and (ii) future variants at stages of research and development yet to exist in a commercial format. Some are passive or victim activated; others are active or victim seeking. Existing non-lethal border control technologies include the familiar razor-wire barriers and electrified fences (though some of these are now twin switched to provide a lethal option). Commercial off-the-shelf variants also include fences with semi-intelligent integral sensor technology, which detect an intrusion, report the proximity of people or vehicles and automatically alert a central control or security guard.

More lethal variants are essentially the outlawed anti-personnel landmines (APL) which continue to infest border zones including Cambodia and Thailand, North and South Korea and the borders of India, Pakistan and Kashmir. This technology itself is changing, as companies attempt to circumvent the Ottawa anti-personnel landmine treaty of 1997. Whilst 154 states have signed up to the treaty, 40 others, including Russia, China and the USA, have not.[13] Potential markets thus remain.

New systems include the allegedly less-lethal claymore mine which is filled with rubber balls (manufactured by Alliant Tech Systems Inc. of Edina, Minnesota, in conjunction with Textron Systems of Wilmington, Massachusetts), and currently fitted to vehicles in Iraq as a modular crowd control munition; the taser mines (discussed below), area-denial systems based on laser dazzlers and semi-intelligent mine networks such as the Matrix and the Spider. These last two can be switched on or off via a master unit increasing the uncertainty around whether an area is safe or not. The US has engaged in a substantial research programme to develop alternative mines. These include the Hornet Wide-Area Munition Product Improvement Program (WAM PIP) – a so-called self-destructing mine system and a non-self-destructing alternative system, or NSD-A which has software which enables a man in the loop to switch a minefield on or off.[14]

Such programmes will include both lethal and allegedly 'non-lethal' variants.[15] However, there are differing perspectives on the safety of these non-lethal versions. At a Japanese anti-landmine conference I asked a high-ranking US military officer and his diplomatic counterpart about their reliability. The diplomat was willing to take his family through a switched off or self-destructing minefield: the soldier said he valued his comrades too much.

Other lethal systems rely on victim-seeking small arms. Examples include the US-based Autaga Arms, which is a camera-mounted gun with some basic intelligence. The gun can be set on automatic or the camera used merely to set a safe distance between the weapon and firer. Another US Company, Precision Remotes, produces a similar system which has both a 'man-in-the-loop' or an automatic capacity. A truly robotic sentry gun is slowly emerging and even garage inventors can see big-bucks opportunity in this field of security.[16]

BORDER CONTROL SYSTEMS ON THE HORIZON

Brian Martin and I[17] have identified at least eight new mechanisms for such immobilising technologies including (i) taser anti-personnel mines; (ii) immobilising nets; (iii) stickums and slickums; (iv) high-powered microwaves; (v) acoustic devices/vortex rings; (vi) ionising and pulsed energy lasers; (vii) chemical calmatives, incapacitants, convulsants, bio-regulators and malodorants; and (viii) robotic self-deciding vehicles. These technologies are roughly consistent with those being announced in recent Joint Non-Lethal Weapons Program newsletters.[18]

Examining selected variants of weapons already considered for a future border control function, we find a range of companies pitching actual technologies or fielding the following prototypes:

Taser anti-personnel mines: A taser is an electroshock weapon. It delivers a high voltage, typically 50,000 volts, to the target, resulting in excruciating pain and a shutdown of major muscle groups, causing physical collapse. A typical weapon used in policing fires two darts at the target, with trailing wires. Once an electrical connection is made, the voltage is turned on, disabling the target even through clothing, with an extremely painful electrical shock. When a group of volunteers experienced the effect of a taser, only one was willing to accept exposure for the full five seconds before the voltage was automatically cut off, and not a single one volunteered for a second shock. The idea of the taser landmine is to arm a landmine not with an explosive but with a taser. A person triggering the mine would be hit by multiple taser darts and immobilised. The taser gives regular shocks over an extended period, up to an hour. A field of taser landmines could serve as a form of non-lethal border protection. An area would be mined; a few guards would be available to arrest or release victims of the mines.

The turning point in this technology came when two US companies, Primex (which became General Dynamics) and Tasertron (which became Taser Technologies), teamed up to successfully bid to the US Joint Non-Lethal Weapons Directorate (JNLWD) for a Technology Insertion program (TIP).[19]

High-powered microwaves: These devices enable a pencil beam of microwave radiation to be focused on a human body at some distance. The result is near instant pain that can only be alleviated by moving out of the beam's path.

At the time of writing this device is a mobile platform but it is not difficult to imagine such technologies being deployed at borders in roving beam fashion. It has obvious countermeasures including either physical destruction of the device via some form of disruption, including rocks, or mirroring the beam back to source. The danger of such resistance is that it is likely to provoke the deployment of more lethal technology. A more defensive technology might be to set up a water curtain spray (if water is readily available), because this would dissipate the directed energy into the water as heat. For individuals, aluminum foil blankets and mirror sunglasses afford some protection and could be used on vehicles too. A high-tech form of countermeasure might be the use of 'microwave bridges' to redirect the radiation back to source. However, whilst such techno-ju-jitsu devices are appealing in principle, without the ability to properly field test them the upper hand is likely to remain with government-funded countermeasure programmes.

Acoustic devices/vortex rings: These can cause disorientation by producing very loud noises. Infrasound can be created using two ultrasound beams. Pyrotechnically generated sound rings can create either knock-down effects at a distance or carry other incapacitating agents.[20] However, critics have brought attention to the potentiality of permanent damage to the ear from some acoustic weapons. Vortex-ring technology is still at the prototype stage but blunt trauma injuries are likely to be similar to those associated with water cannon.

Ionising and pulsed energy lasers: Laser light in the UV spectrum can ionise the air sufficiently for it to conduct high-voltage electricity, thus making possible directed energy weapons. Their hazards are essentially those associated with electroshocking a diverse population including susceptibility to stress-induced heart attacks, pacemaker failure, acidosis and the induction of post-traumatic stress. Advertising brochures for these devices, produced by US company Ionatron, explicitly identify their products for 'partial denial systems' and 'effective perimeter security devices on stationary objects'.[21]

A new variant has recently been reported from the JNLWD, namely the pulsed energy projectile that is scheduled to hit the streets this decade. It started life as the 'Pulsed Impulsive Kill Laser' but has been retuned to create a shock wave by vaporising the first thing it hits.[22] Its technical specifications have been well guarded but some superfluous injury and traumatic shock induction seem likely.

Calmatives, incapacitants, convulsants, bio-regulators and malodorants: There are a wide range of chemicals that create a paralysing effect which can be delivered to targets by existing weapons systems designed for delivering chemical or malodorous agents. Bio-regulators would be targeted at interfering with body functions that maintain steady body temperature, heart rate, breathing and other stabilising body functions. However, one person's tranquilisation is another's lethal dose and in field circumstances it would be impossible to guarantee a uniform effect. Further advances in molecular biology are being directed at specific receptor sites in the human brain that can induce fear and anxiety. These breakthroughs could create capacities that no government has ever been shown to use responsibly. The developments pose a huge challenge to NGOs wishing to avoid an arms race in the life sciences. Yet the strongest objection to their future development remains the fact that they are illegal in most plausible scenarios of future use.[23]

Robotic self-deciding vehicles: These are intelligent mobile devices armed with either lethal or sub-lethal weapons and capable of operating as border patrol agents. What was once science-fiction is now a reality. Robots bearing incapacitating technologies are now marketed as programmable sentinels of organised violence that will work without respite. The potential hazards are those associated with weapons operating without the finer points of discrimination or being deliberately deployed in an abusive configuration especially when on automatic mode and hunting in packs.

Isaac Asimov's science-fiction was predicated on rules that no robot should ever be programmed to harm a human being. That design criterion remains fictional: these devices have the potential to be a form of ruthless border patrol that could make rottweilers passé. Unlike rottweilers, such 'self-deciding vehicles' will not be able to be lured off with a juicy piece of steak. However, all such devices must be mobile and their patrol route governed by terrain. Like fictional Daleks, old robots could not go up stairs or negotiate steep hills or holes, so setting up suitable obstacles would enable robot-free bridges to be temporarily secured. For new robots, such as the Foster-Miller armed military robots, stairs are not a problem. The fact that one of their manufacturers, Foster-Miller, is owned by semi-British company Qinetiq might, however, yield some form of political pressure point.

HARMLESS WEAPONS?

Many of the technologies being touted for future border control duties have been promoted on the basis of their alleged non-lethality. Harmlessness, however, is a much more difficult state to achieve in any weapon. It depends on a complex interaction of a number of factors including (i) an adequate technical evaluation of the characteristics of the weapons, such as muzzle velocity, accuracy, impacts on human health (both short, medium and long term); (ii) non-lethality based on absolute adherence to rules of engagement re: distance to target, avoidance of vulnerable spots, etc; (iii) sufficiently good weapons design to avoid abuse; (iv) adequate quality control specifications to ensure that the weapon actually delivers technical effects as specified; (v) evidence that if a weapon is capable of delivering sub-lethal effects that these do not permanently debilitate, maim or yield long-term disablement, disease or mental impairment; (vi) a security force responsible for deploying the technology which is democratically accountable and does not have a track record of torture, grave human rights abuses and extra-judicial killings.

These criteria will determine how harmful a particular weapon system actually is. We should also be mindful of the processes of technological mission and decision creep. What starts out as a relatively mundane system can gradually undergo a series of cumulative transitions into something much more sinister, which would have been rejected at the outset if it had originally appeared in that format. Using the example above, given the high level of pain caused by even a few seconds of taser shocks, the consequences of many minutes of exposure are truly horrific and would likely result in post-traumatic stress disorder, if not worse.

Microwave weapons pose all the hazards associated with microwave radiation, with the eyes being particularly vulnerable to a cooking effect. The pain induced is meant to make the dose self-limiting but much higher exposure would become likely if lethal force or barriers blocked off escape routes. The official line is that the microwave devices are safe, though little official technical data have been released. A November 2004 conference at Bradford University on non-lethal weapons questioned the assumption of safety.[24] A participant observed that the natural response to intense eye pain is to shut the eyes – hence making targets effectively blind so that they could no longer navigate a safe way out. Another expert said as far as he knew there was no automatic cut-off on the device which would close it down once a human reached a disabling temperature. Such blind targets would microwave cook en masse. An effective challenge to the apologists for such weapons is to advocate transparency and legal accountability. We will need to establish ways to control or oppose such innovations or face the prospect of successive generations of refugees and activists being the guinea pigs for each successive newcomer to the growing arsenal of unconventional disabling weapons.

Indeed, the International Red Cross has severe reservations about the use of rheostatic weapons, such as the Vehicle Mounted Area Denial System (VMAD) which heats people up to an unbearable 140° F. The device is meant to be self-limiting since victims are expected to move away from the pain beam – but would fleeing refugees do so if they were being chased by armed hit squads? Who would treat them to avoid post-traumatic stress?

David Hambling's features in *New Scientist* have questioned the future role, function and ethics of weapons such as wireless tasers which can project lightning at crowds by spraying them with a conductive plasma.[25] Hambling found other variants including the Xtreme Alternative Defense System's Close Quarters Shock rifle which projects ionised gas[26] and a star wars variant made by Mission Research Corporation (MRC) which uses lasers to create Pulsed Energy Projectiles (PEP) to ionise a target's clothing and sweat.[27] Already hints of strategy have emerged in Department of Defense (DoD) contracts wishing to use VMAD and the PEP together: VMAD for general pain induction to target crowds and PEP to 'ablate' serious ring leaders.[28]

Human testing is proceeding and over 900 volunteers have been microwaved so far, with over 2,370 shots fired in 2004 alone.[29] Steps have already been announced by the US Air Force Research Laboratory to take some of this mass pain technology airborne.[30]

LEGAL CONTROLS – NECESSARY BUT INSUFFICIENT

Much of this technology transcends existing notions and contexts of weapons which violate international norms, existing conventions or international human rights legislation, but some does not.[31] ICRC was one of the first NGOs to recognise that various emergent so-called 'non-lethal' weapons would violate the Geneva conventions. It was particularly worried about these new weapons breaching established principles such as the clauses against weapons that (i) cause superfluous injury or unnecessary suffering; (ii) breach the principle of distinction between civilians and combatants; (iii) and in the case of the so-called Martens Clause which states that even when neither treaty nor customary law clearly applies, civilians and combatants remain under the protection and authority of the principles of international law derived from established custom, the principles of humanity and the dictates of public conscience.[32]

Other conventions also apply to the development and deployment of this class of technology including the Ottawa Anti-Personnel Landmine Treaty of 1997, the prohibition on 'booby traps' contained in Protocol II to the Convention on Restrictions on the Use of Certain Conventional Weapons, of May 1996; the 1993 Chemical Weapons Conventions; the Biological and Toxins Convention of 1972; and the 1980 UN Inhumane Weapons Convention.[33]

Of course, a much more detailed examination of the issues is required if existing International Humanitarian Law (IHL) is not to be eroded by the short-sighted demands of an emergent war-fighting doctrine from a tiny minority of states. ICRC, for instance, has recently published an update on what constitutes a prohibited weapon.[34] Unfortunately, the prospects do not look good if we examine these debates in the context of recent efforts to control the proliferation of even the most medieval of military supplies: instruments of torture. Europe is justifiably proud of its democratic traditions. It might be thought that we have legal frameworks sufficiently robust to resist any border technologies capable of facilitating human rights abuse. It would be comforting to think so. It still seems astonishing that even in the Western liberal democracies, states have failed to prevent corporate bodies supplying torture technologies, by either sale, licensed production or via brokerage. And even when a decision is made in principle to outlaw equipment of abuse, official foot-dragging still enables business as usual. Why did the EU, for example, take from January 2003 until the summer of 2005 to agree measures controlling technologies which facilitate execution, torture and human rights abuse?

Strong lobbying by NGOs pressured the Council of Ministers to belatedly approve diluted new export controls. Death-penalty equipment and technologies which can be solely used for torture will be banned. Perhaps it was fear of centralised Brussels controls? Earlier drafts giving the Commission ultimate oversight were stripped out – policing of these regulations and whether some are banned or simply 'controlled' will now be at member states' discretion.[35]

Why does this matter? The answer is a 'no brainer'. If we can't control the supply lines of the crudest, medieval technologies used to violate human rights, or for that matter, more 'advanced' electro-shock 'therapies', then the prospects of domestic populations facing algorithmic, advanced, mass human pain-inducing or rendering systems at borders, or on our streets in circumstances of MOUTW, are far from implausible. Moreover, the British comedian and human rights investigator, Mark Thomas, has revealed just how significant the wider implications are when he showed that even children in this country could set up an 'After School Arms Club' and successfully broker prohibited weapons to embargoed states.[36]

Mirroring this concern at the international level, the UN Special Rapporteur on Torture, Theo van Boeven, before resigning in 2005, proposed that new 'non-lethal weapons', including devices which employ high-decibel sounds and microwaves, were being marketed internationally and whose use in practice had revealed a substantial risk of abuse or unwarranted injury. 'A number of countries', the Rapporteur noted, were developing this 'equipment for the purpose of crowd control ... these new technologies have the potential to be used for torture and ill treatment, including collective punishment if abused'. He went on to suggest that the 'effects of these products should have been subject to rigorous inquiries by medical, scientific and law enforcement experts who are fully independent of the manufacturers, traders and law enforcement agencies promoting them, and whose proceedings and conclusions are transparent and subject to peer review in public scientific literature'.[37]

This proposal is far from current practice. Indeed delegates at the Non-Lethal Defence IV conference (March 2005)[38] were advised by a representative from the Office of the US Assistant Secretary of

Defense for Public Affairs, to really go after their critics, not inform them.[39] This has certainly been the case with Taser, whose stock took a tumble after Amnesty International said their weapon was involved in over 70 fatalities in North America.[40] In March 2006 Taser sued two forensic scientists who raised safety concerns. According to the *Guardian*, both men facing legal action say they've been putting forward legitimate technical arguments but 'the company is using the courts to extinguish dissent'.[41] This is a worrying case since, if successful, it introduces a precedent which could help silence future critics of the more complex technologies discussed here.

Despite the rhetoric, there is a super-sensitivity about informed challenges to the ethics of such systems. One key proponent of advanced paralysing technologies at a recent conference could not help himself reacting angrily to an editorial in the *New Scientist* concerning new pain weapons and torture.[42] Thumping the podium with a rolled-up copy of the journal, he fatuously suggested that you can use it to hurt people or use it as a torture instrument with the addition of Vaseline. 'Maybe what we should do is ban *New Scientist?*'[43]

ALGORITHMIC BORDER CONTROLS

Older colonial torture technologies depended on technique to produce bespoke torture on a one-to-one or several-to-one human basis. Advanced pain-inducing technologies are capable of paralysing one-to-many and potentially industrialising torture by undermining the right to maim-free protest using semi-automated networks.

In this context algorithmic systems mean a combination of electronic nervous system, some computation capability and accompanying pain-delivery mechanisms. Thus, algorithmic systems are semi-intelligent, and have some autonomous decision-making facilities. A good contemporary lethal example of such a system is the so-called self-healing minefield. This minefield uses neural network technology to monitor any breaches and thus its own vulnerability, if there is a gap from a previous intrusion. Each mine has a piston-style foot. The mines communicate with each other and can physically jump to fill any breach.[44] The innovation is again being supported by the Defense Advanced Research Projects Agency (DARPA) via commercial contracts with several US military companies including Alliant Tech Systems, Sandia National Laboratories, SAIC, Foster-Miller, ITT Industries and Quantum Magnetics Inc.

The Metal Storm systems outlined below lend themselves to such quasi-intelligent functions but rapid developments in both unmanned aerial vehicles and robot soldiers are where we should focus most attention. The JNLWD have already heralded unmanned vehicles as a suitable platform for deploying incapacitating weapons. We are already seeing in Iraq an increasing use of drones and robots and we can anticipate warbots replacing soldiers for riskier missions.[45] Foster-Miller, based in Massachusetts, has already fielded the Talon robot which mounts a M240 or M249 machine gun, and a less-lethal alternative, or both. This unit is remote-controlled, not automated, but experts think the potential is there if thermal target detection and automated navigation systems are added. The SWORDS version already has sniper functions.[46] Such warbots can be used to avoid 'friendly fire' fiascos, but in operations targeted at civilians, who will take a robot to a tribunal if it has violated human rights or been involved in episodes of extra-judicial execution?

ON EARTH AS IN HEAVEN

After 9/11, big dollar budgets became available for this weaponry; for instance, $3.2 million was awarded to MRC in 2004 and some of the contracts are specifying both lethal and non-lethal applications. The work has become institutionalised and time-lined with rapid innovation. At the 2005 Force Protection Equipment Demonstration (FPED) V exhibition inside Quantico (HQ of the the US Marine Corps and JNLWD), victim-activated taser landmines were on show, which shoot darts carrying 50,000 volts to paralyse targets for up to an hour. Metal Storm was there too, grant funded by DARPA after a successful test of its mortar system, in March 2005.

Both of these companies have explored the possibility of remote activation either from satellite observation or by using an automatic process of remote detection and response. Metal Storm, for example, has managed to create virtual mine fields which are held in a database in an earth-orbiting satellite. Anyone actually crossing the ground is detected by space-orbiting cameras which then trigger an attack. The company is highly innovative and has done away with mechanical firing systems for its weapons which can deliver ammunition almost like pixels. Rates per minute of between 500,000 and 1,000,000 are being reported in the press. The company recently has been given a contract by DARPA to look at sub-lethal systems. Yet since pixallation of an area can be triggered by cameras on satellites containing a virtual mine field with no actual ordnance in the ground, such technologies are landmine-treaty proofed.

CONCLUSION

Alas, we are already beyond the prototype stages for some of these victim-activated systems; some implemented by non-human algorithms to create human-rights-free area-denial zones, others invisible weapons designed to achieve group paralysis, produce compliance through pain or deny entire zones through mass immobilisation. The lessons of the Moscow Theatre Siege where the ill-prepared use of a fentanly derivative killed at least 118 hostages have not been learned. The Russian authorities have already weaponised and subsequently used similar calmatives,[47] while at the Third Non-Lethal Weapons Symposium in Germany, in May 2005, Czech medics from the Prague-based Institute for Clinical and Experimental Medicine advocated using their skills as anaesthetists to build new 'calmative' weapons.[48]

It would be reassuring but futile to believe that the Pugwash mission of an ethical code for scientists can now prevent such scientific irresponsibility.[49] Nor will the recent Royal Society's welcome call for global cooperation to prevent misuse of science through codes of conduct be sufficient.[50] Ideally, scientists should be subject to professional sanction and prosecution if they knowingly create tools of punishment which can violate international standards of human rights. Currently they are given fat contracts. A major concern is the current US propensity to outsource their uglier research and rendering programmes to places where even expressing notions of account-ability would make critics ripe for similar processing.

Where does this leave us ? It would be comforting to believe that conflicts arising out of rapid climate change might be technically fixed. It would be even more comforting to think that the resolution of such issues can be separated from the US 'war on terror' and that it is a passing phase. The challenge to us is that all these processes are essentially linked into what one might sum up as an unsustainable programme of future growth. We know that such programmes will become increasingly militarised and that little political will currently exists to thwart this juggernaut and its consequences.

If this is to be a David and Goliath struggle, then our best hope is to collectively attempt to slow down the introduction of some of the scarier technology using existing democratic protections and controls to question the legitimacy of such systems. However, this should be undertaken in the knowledge that merely using official channels is unlikely to be sufficient. What should concerned social and environmental scientists do? There is a clear need for new alliances between so-called research activists to use their organised knowledge to make new control measures politically backfire. Should we also contemplate work towards providing counter-technologies to enable people to swarm over the techno-limits installed at borders?

It is a subject addressed by myself and Brian Martin in terms of non-violence theory.[51] It is a perspective which focuses on the idea of processes by which an attack on non-violent refugees can backfire against the attackers. Several standard operating procedures have been identified to facilitate this political ju-jitsu, loosely designated as the five R's:

Reveal: expose the injustice, challenge cover-up.
Redeem: validate the target, challenge devaluation.
Reframe: emphasise the injustice, counter reinterpretation.
Redirect: mobilise support, be wary of official channels.
Resist: stand up to intimidation and bribery.

Of course there are various techniques that repression technologists and apologists will use to inhibit this political ju-jitsu. Yet without a new way of thinking on these matters, most countermeasures to border control technologies will be ad hoc and amateur. In a time of rapid climate change more of us will be on the move than we can currently imagine. Here we simply ask, in the future, must we become more concerned about creating the means to breach borders rather than secure them?

NOTES

The author would like to thank his colleagues at the Praxis Centre (Professor David Webb and Dr Edward Halpin) and the Threshold Group for their help and encouragement in developing the concepts presented in this chapter. Much of the conceptualisation of resisting inhumane and repressive technologies and the potential for political ju-jitsu or backfire derives from my collaboration with Professor Brian Martin of Wollongong University, Australia, who continues to be a great source of inspiration. The author would also like to thank the Joseph Rowntree Charitable Trust and the Social Science Research Council, for financial support to develop the background research for this piece.

1. P. Schwartz and D. Randall, 'An abrupt climate change scenario and its implications for United States national security', October 2003.
2. Torture rehabilitation centres throughout the world include, in Europe, the Medical Foundation for the Care of Torture Victims: http://www.torturecare.org.uk/articles/weblinks/c161/ and the International Rehabilitation Council for Torture Victims in Denmark: http://www.irct.org/
3. For previous studies see S. Wright, Scientific & Technological Office of Assessment Panel of the European Parliament (STOA) Report, 'An Appraisal of the Technology of Political Control, European Parliament', PE166 499, January 1998, http://www.statewatch.org/news/ 2005/may/steve-wright-stoa-rep.pdf/; Landmine Action, 'Alternative anti-personnel mines – the next generations', London, 2001: http://www.landmine.de/fix/English_report.pdf; Amnesty International, 'The Pain Merchants: security equipment and its use in torture and other ill treatment', Amnesty International Secretariat, AI Index ACT 40/008/2003, London: http://web.amnesty.org/library/Index/ENGACT400082003; B. Martin and S.Wright, 'Countershock: mobilising resistance to electroshock weapons', *Medicine, Conflict and Survival*, 19(3), 2003, pp. 205–22. For a comprehensive list of Brian Martin's analyses of the backfire process see: http://www.uow.edu.au/arts/sts/bmartin/pubs/backfire.html Excellent examples are included in B. Martin, *Justice Ignited: The Dynamics of Backfire*, Lanham, MD: Rowman & Littlefield, 2006.
4. *Independent* Online, 7 December 2005: http://news.independent.co.uk/environment/article331621.ece
5. http://www.terradaily.com/reports/British_Defense_Secretary_Warns_Of_Looming_Water_Wars.html
6. Richard Norton-Taylor, 'International laws hinder UK troops – Reid', *Guardian*, 4 April 2006.
7. European Parliament Committee on Foreign Affairs, Security & Defence Policy, 'Report on the Environment, Security and Foreign Policy', (Rapporteur: Mrs. Maj. Britt Theorin), 14 January 1999, A4–0005/99.
8. J. Vogler, 'The European Union and the "Securitisation of the Environment"', in E.A. Page and M. Redclift, eds, *Human Security and the Environment – International Comparisons*, Cheltenham: Edward Elgar, 2002.
9. See Statewatch, 'EU: border control for the 21st century: automated passenger processing', 16(1), 2006, pp. 1–2.
10. 'Migrants made to cross Sahara army minefield', *Observer*, 23 October 2005. For the broader implications see also Omega Foundation, 'Crowd Control Technologies: Crowd Control Technology Options For the European Union', STOA, European Parliament, 2000: http://www.europarl.eu.int/stoa/publications/studies/19991401a_en.pdf
11. S. Wright, 'Future sub-lethal, paralysing and incapacitating technologies: their coming role in the mass production of torture', London, 2002. See http://www.statewatch.org/news/2002/nov/torture.pdf; Amnesty International, 'The pain merchants'.
12. For a discussion see D. Loye, 'Non-lethal capabilities and international humanitarian law', in Proceedings of the Second European Symposium on

Non-Lethal Weapons, Ettlingen, Germany, 13–14 May 2003, Fraunhofer Institut Chemische Technologie, 3(1–8), 2003.

13. For an update of Ottawa Treaty signatories see the landmine Monitor website: http://www.icbl.org/lm/

14. http://www4.nationalacademies.org/news.nsf/isbn/0309073499? OpenDocument

15. Ibid.

16. Two US college kids for example have set up a company, USMechatronics, to market a human-seeking gun based on a college project. See http://www.technovelgy.com/ct/Science-Fiction-News-Comments.asp?NewsNum=502

17. B. Martin and S. Wright, 'Looming struggles over technology for border control: organisational transformation and social change', Special issue on Designing Governance: http://www.imresearch.org/RIPs/2005/RIP2005-3.pdf

18. See for instance, Safeguarding Peace–Safeguarding Lives (2005), 2nd Quarter, which highlights that the Active-Denial system is on track; that hand-emplaced NL munitions (taser mines) were successfully demonstrated; that their Technology Investment Program (TIP) had identified two efforts focusing on laser-induced plasma applications; and that the Crowd Control Exploration Programme had identified High Intensity Directional Acoustics (HIDA), Tactical Unmanned Ground vehicles (TUGV) and the Multi-Tube Launched munition Portable Active-Denial System (PADS) as priorities.

19. TIP initiatives focus first on evaluating the technology before creating a munition. See D. Murphy, 'Taser Anti-Personnel Munition', 2002: http://www.dtic.mil/ndia/2002mines/murphy.pdf

20. L. Deiming et. al., 'Infrapulse generator: an effective non-lethal weapon', Paper presented at conference on 'Non-lethal weapons: new options facing the future', Ettligen, Germany: Fraunhofer, Institut Chemische Technologie, 25–26 September 2001.

21. Ionatron Directed Energy technologies brochure 2006, which admits that 'the specifics of the technology remain classified': http://www.ionatron.com

22. H. Moore, 'Laser Technology Update: Pulsed Impulsive Kill Laser (PIKL)', paper presented to NDIA 2000, Joint Services Small Arms Symposium, 29 August 2000: http://www.dtic.mil/ndia/smallarms/Moore.pdf

23. For a more detailed discussion see M. Dando, 'Future incapacitating chemical agents: the impact of genomics', in N. Lewer, The Future of Non-Lethal Weapons: Technologies, Operations, Ethics and Law, London: Frank Cass, 2002, pp. 167–81: http://www.mindfully.org/Technology/2003/Electric-Shock-Weapons21may03.htmmay 03

24. Bradford Peace Studies Non-Lethal Weapons reports: http://www.brad.ac.uk/acad/nlw/

25. D. Hambling, 'Star Wars hits the streets', New Scientist (176), 12 October 2002, pp. 42–45; updated in 'Stun weapons to target crowds', New Scientist (182), 19 June 2004, p. 24.

26. http://www.newscientistlist.com/article.ns?id=dn6014

27. http://www.newscientist.com/article.ns?id=mg17623645.300

28. Office of Naval Research (2004), Sensory Consequences of electromagnetic pulses emitted by laser induced plasmas (Contract No M67854-04-C-5074): http://www.thememoryhole.org/milweapons/navy-ufl.pep_contract.pdf

29. http://www.defensetech.org/archives/cat_lesslethal.html

30. Air Force Research Laboratory, 'Non-lethal technology going airborne', AFRL Press Release, 4: http://www.de.afrl.af.mil/News/2004/04-46.html

31. D.P. Fiddler, 'Non-lethal weapons and international law', *Medicine, Conflict and Survival*, 17(3), 2001, pp. 194–206, for an excellent detailed discussion of these points.

32. Robin M. Coupland, International Committee of the Red Cross, 'The SIrUS Project: Towards a determination of which weapons cause "superfluous injury or unnecessary suffering"', ICRC pamphlet, 10 November 1997.

33. V. Wallace, 'Non-lethal weapons: R^2IPE Arms Control Measures', in Lewer, *Future of Non-Lethal Weapons*, pp. 141–66, for discussion.

34. See ICRC, 'A guide to the legal review of new weapons, means and methods of warfare: measures to implement Article 36 of additional protocol 1 of 1977', Geneva: ICRC, 2006. The guide largely focuses on a legal review of new weapons, means and methods of warfare, particularly with reference to implementation of Article 36. A useful example of how the Article might clarify the challenge relates to taser mines. As these do not have explosives they are not covered by the Ottawa Treaty. They would, however, be covered by Article 36's provisions against booby traps.

35. House of Commons European Scrutiny Committee, 'Trade in products used for capital punishment, torture, etc', 11th Report, 2004–2005, Document Considered by Committee, 15 March 2005, Para 11.5.

36. M. Thomas, *As Used On the Famous Nelson Mandela*, London: Ebury Press, 2006; broadcast Channel 4, 3 April 2006. The young people were able to successfully set up brokerage deals involving weapons and torture equipment even though the stated destinations were ostensibly embargoed.

37. UN Economic and Social Council, Commission on Human Rights, Civil and Political Rights, Including the Questions of Torture and Detention – Torture and Other Cruel, Inhuman or Degrading Treatment, 'Report of the Special Rapporteur on the Question of Torture', Theo van Boeven, Sixty First Session, Item 11a,E/CN.4/2005/62, 15 December 2004.

38. http://www.dtic.mil/ndia/2005nonlethdef/2005nonlethdef.html

39. http://www.bradford.ac.uk/acad/nlw/research_reports/docs/BNLWRPResearchReportNo7_May05.pdf

40. Amnesty International, 'United States of America: excessive and lethal force? Amnesty International's concerns about deaths and ill treatment involving police use of Tasers', AI Index, AMR51/139/2004.

41. J. Randerson, 'Stun gun makers sue experts over safety criticisms', *Guardian*, 9 March 2006.

42. http://www.newscientist.com/channel/mech-tech/mg18524894.500

43. Information from Col. John Alexander, at the Third Non-Lethal Weapons Symposium, Ettlingen, May 2005.

44. http://www.darpa.mil/ato/programs/SHM/proginfo.html

45. http://www.physorg.com/news62940690.html
46. http://web.mit.edu/ssp/seminars/wed_archives_05spring/machak-platt.htm
47. In Nalchik over 100 victims were reported to have been taken to local clinics following a similar military operation to free hostages. *The Caucasus Knot/News*, 15 October 2005: http:/kavkaz-uzel.ru/printnews/news/id
48. J. Schreiberova, J. Fusek and H. Kralove, 'Pharmacological non-lethal weapons', paper presented to the Third Non-Lethal Weapons Symposium, Ettligen.
49. See for example: http://onlineethics.org/codes/
50. Royal Society Press Release, 'Global Cooperation needed to prevent Misuse of Science', 9 June 2005.
51. Martin and Wright, 'Looming struggles'.

4

Climate Change and the Political Process: Consequences for Government Action in Britain

James Humphreys

'a challenge so far-reaching in its impact and irreversible in its destructive power, that it alters radically human existence'

Tony Blair[1]

The reality of climate change is now acknowledged, it would seem, by leaders around the world. The affluent states of the West who are the most serious polluters; the developing countries who will suffer the most from the effects of climate change; the leadership in China, who have the power to avert a catastrophic increase in emissions over the next few decades; even President George W. Bush, long resistant to the idea that human activity was the root cause; all have spoken of the need for the international community to act.

This ought to be a cause of celebration for those who have stood helpless as those with the power have debated the best approach, traded off the benefits of action against the costs, argued over whose job it is to solve the problem; and, in the case of the United States and a few allies such as Australia, rejected the evidence and undermined the science. Naturally, this inaction has bred frustration, bafflement and anger. President Bush in particular is alternately mocked as too stupid to understand climate change, or too self-interested or venal to do anything about it. The links between Bush and the oil industry – the deep involvement in the business of key aides and of his own family, plus massive campaign donations from oil interests – are used to explain his hostility even to the idea that the rise in CO_2 concentrations may be the result of human action. Even those who fall short of accusing him of having been bought by Big Oil would say that his failure to challenge US dependence on the automobile, air conditioning, coal-fired power generation or air travel is a sign of political cowardice and a dereliction of duty. As Commander in

Chief, the President's ultimate role is the safety and security of the nation: if climate change will, as predicted, kill many Americans, then his responsibility is clear.

Some of the same anger is aimed at other leaders in the West, albeit tempered by their comparative lack of power. Whether it is John Howard's unholy alliance with the US against the Kyoto agreement, or Jacques Chirac's smug reliance on France's already low CO_2 output (courtesy of investment in nuclear power), or Tony Blair's failure to use his 'special relationship' to persuade Bush to join Kyoto, no one escapes criticism that is often couched in crude and accusatory terms.

This frustration and anger have been justified. The science of climate change is relatively straightforward, even if the exact ways in which rising concentrations of greenhouse gases will interact with the earth's weather, ecology and geology are not fully understood. The underlying processes were first posited in the 1930s, and the rise in CO_2 levels has been tracked since 1958 at Mauna Loa observatory in Hawaii. The evidence that climate change was a reality began to emerge in the 1970s, and by the end of the 1980s something approaching a scientific consensus had been reached. In other words, the current generation of political leaders – with the notable exception of Jacques Chirac – first came to power in a world in which climate change was already a pressing political issue.

Nor is there any doubt about the way in which climate change could or should be tackled. No technological fixes or unproven technologies are needed. Cutting carbon emissions means minimising energy use, either through better energy efficiency, lower consumption, or both; and to meet that minimum need, adopting renewable energy generation in place of oil, gas and coal. The main tools would be regulation (for example, mandating levels of energy efficiency, or banning particularly damaging activities such as manufacturing consumer electronics with energy-draining stand-by features); fiscal instruments (a mix of incentives such as subsidies for micro-generation and higher taxes on carbon polluting activities such as air travel); quotas (for example, a low basic tariff on domestic electricity use to avoid fuel poverty, coupled with high marginal prices for those who exceed their quota); and social marketing (advertising and other communications techniques to inform the public about how to avoid carbon emissions, motivate them to act responsibly, and create social norms that become self-policing). In short, a couple of competent civil servants could within a week or two have drawn up a robust plan to deliver the necessary reductions, at any point over the last 15 years – had the political will been there.

Still, 70 years on since the possibility of climate change was first advanced, 30 years since the first hard evidence emerged, and 16 years since the first 'earth summit' at Rio placed it high on the political agenda, the world's leaders are – to judge by their public utterances – at last ready to intervene.

The problem is, the change in rhetoric is not matched by changes in policy. In other words, the world's leaders have adopted the language of the environmentalists about the 'challenge' of climate change without accepting the consequences: the end of the carbon economy; rapid investment in energy efficiency and renewables; genuine burden-sharing with developing countries; and radical social change, particularly away from unsustainable consumerism. The paradox is frustrating; but simplistic explanations of their behaviour – stupidity, greed, or a callous regard for their own interests – stand in the way of a fruitful exploration of this failure of the political system. Conversely, understanding why politicians are, in their own terms, acting rationally offers new insights into the most effective strategies for transforming the climate change debate.

BRITAIN: THE CURRENT LEADERSHIP

Tony Blair displays this paradox in a particularly dramatic way. At the time of writing, he is a political leader in a position to take effective legislative and administrative action, should he have wished to, by virtue of his own position within the Labour Party and the party's majority within Parliament. He is intellectually and imaginatively equipped for understanding climate change in both its practical and emotional dimensions, and in addition has a personal interest in science and technology. He is blessed with considerable leadership skills, particularly in framing moral issues and in building consensus. And despite Iraq, he retains considerable standing in international politics. Further, the country he leads cannot be assumed to be indifferent to climate change. A large section of the population is sensitised to 'green' or environmental issues, particularly animal welfare and protection of the countryside. The UK also has an international outlook, and a strong interest in aid and development. Most of all, Blair has made a personal commitment to tackling climate change, describing it as a threat to the UK equivalent to that of international terrorism, and setting ambitious targets for the reduction of carbon emissions.

Yet the reality is that the response of the UK government, like that of the nation itself, has been entirely inadequate. UK carbon emissions, which were heading downwards up to 1997, have since risen once more. The UK's self-imposed target for reduction will now not be met, and even the Kyoto targets look vulnerable. Economic and physical development remains unsustainable. And touchstone decisions, such as the expansion of Stansted Airport, indicate that narrow or short-term economic considerations still dominate thinking within the government.

In short, we have a leader who could act, and believes he should act decisively to tackle climate change, but has not done so through nine years in power. It is as if the wartime rhetoric of Winston Churchill were combined with the policies of Neville Chamberlain. This gap demands an explanation.

Fortunately explanations, or perhaps allegations, are not in short supply. For convenience, they can be divided up into four broad 'themes'. The first is one of *economic capture*: essentially, that governments pay too much account of the views of business as a whole and certain industries (such as oil companies, airlines and the media) in particular. The second is *inertia*: that governments are unable to act decisively because the political and administrative system is too inflexible or ineffectual. The third is *short-termism*: governments always avoid policies that mean pain today for a gain far in the future. This leads to the fourth, the lack of *public will*: in other words, that people are congenitally short-term (and possibly subject to economic capture and inertia as well), and that governments merely reflect the will – or lack of it – of their citizens.

Each of these themes has an element of truth; the task is to try to understand more about how each one works in isolation and in combination, and this in part must probe the perspective of the decision makers themselves: the politicians and their advisers.

ECONOMIC CAPTURE

Oil companies, being in the main large, financially powerful and operating in a highly strategic and regulated industry, are interested in political outcomes. Those operating in the UK may not be as open or aggressive as their US cousins in seeking to influence the political scene – no significant political donations, and no major political figures with a background in the oil industry – but the closeness is there. For example, David Simon, BP's chief executive, joined the Blair government in 1997 as Minister for Competitiveness, while Anji Hunter left Tony Blair's innermost circle in 2003 to become Head of Public Affairs at BP. Accusations of impropriety or undue influence miss the point: such exchanges are not about individuals joining an uncongenial organisation purely for gain, but about those individuals sharing a common outlook. To New Labour, BP is a British company that leads the world, employs a lot of people, makes a huge contribution to the economy and is run by people whom ministers would feel comfortable sitting next to at dinner. To BP executives, Tony Blair would be a political leader combining strong support for business and a willingness to listen with the common agenda of corporate social responsibility.

More widely, the Blair administration sees itself as combining free-market enterprise and business-like managerial competence. Business leaders are admired; their views are sought; their contribution to working groups and task forces encouraged. The warmth of this relationship breeds the suspicion that as businesses believe that nothing must interfere with profits and growth, and that as climate change threatens both, so they must be working to ensure that all measures to tackle climate change are weakened or delayed. This would include using their influence on government.

As with the role of the oil companies, this view has a lot of truth behind it, but can also be misleading. Certainly, individual businesses and their representative bodies have campaigned hard and effectively against a number of climate-related proposals. Within the European Union, the intensive lobbying over the Emissions Trading Scheme is nothing new. The carbon tax proposed in the early 1990s was shaped to anticipate industry accusations of unfairness and of the impact on competitiveness and growth. By recycling revenue into reductions in national insurance tax (in other words, shifting from a tax on jobs to a tax on pollution), it could be positioned as a contribution to the debate on growth, competitiveness and employment. Nevertheless, those industries with high energy costs and few employees (for example, the chemicals sector, represented by CEFIC, the European Chemical Industry Council) naturally remained hostile, and could draw on the broad sympathy of other business organisations. Whether or not this lobbying was decisive in wrecking the carbon tax, it certainly weakened the hand of the Commission in promoting it in the face of opposition from individual member states.

Businesses have considerable advantages in lobbying on environmental issues. Firstly, they tend to have more money, better organisation and more focus on clear objectives. They are also pivotal in delivering jobs and growth, which remain the touchstone for politicians at a national or international level, and in their own constituencies. The general threat of job losses flowing from political action is powerful at any time: all the more so if it can be linked to a specific plant in a particular region or constituency. Save perhaps for the handful of countries which operate national party lists, the notion that 'all politics is local' holds good.

The fundamental power of business, though, lies in its central role in meeting the objectives that Western governments set themselves, particularly on GDP growth. This measure has a widely recognised distorting effect on policy making. For example, one driver for the growth in childcare under Labour was that parents who care for their own children do not contribute to GDP, unlike those who pay for others to do so. Any increase in economic efficiency appears much greater because the value of childcare within the family is excluded from GDP. Similarly, if the country's capital stock is converted to revenue (for example, by building on an undeveloped site, or extracting minerals) that will increase GDP, even if the country is poorer as a result. And external effects – pollution, social exclusion, loss of amenity, increased insecurity – are ignored.

This all-embracing focus on economic indicators is essentially a twentieth-century phenomenon – caused first by the fiscal and social burdens of two world wars and economic dislocation and unemployment, then cemented in place by years of consumerism. It creates a barrier to dealing effectively with long-term issues: for example, balancing the apparent gains of economic growth now against the social and environmental price to be paid in the future. Can the political system balance current growth rates against the likely costs of the destruction of much of East Anglia in 50 or 100 years? Apparently not. The balance is 'achieved' not through the reality of developing and implementing policies, but through the rhetoric of targets, studies and recycled initiatives.

But governments do not adopt measures in isolation; they do so in large part because they are expected to. If the nation's wealth and power are static, then any attempt for one group or class to gain must come at the expense of others. Growth gives the possibility – or perhaps the illusion – of individuals or groups gaining without others losing out. Rising incomes and increased consumption have generated a culture of contentment and political stability, and the link to social instability and a decline in the quality of life is far harder to quantify or explain than the immediate satisfaction of higher wages or more affordable consumer goods. By its very nature, economic growth contributes to climate change: with growth averaging 3 per cent a year, the energy efficiency with which goods and services are produced would have to be increasing at the same annual rate merely for emissions to remain stable. There are the one-off costs of manufacture and of disposal. Nor do all technological advances lead to 'lean manufacture' or more efficient operation: plasma screen TVs, for example, typically use over twice the electricity of the cathode ray tube sets they replace.

The increase in carbon emissions in the UK since 1997 is largely explained by economic growth, with every activity from industrial output to more travel for business or leisure making a contribution. Economic competence is the rock on which the reputation of the UK government – and of Gordon Brown, the Chancellor of the Exchequer since 1997 and, at the time of writing, the most likely successor to Tony Blair – is based. Abandoning this path, reducing consumption, modifying consumer behaviour or limiting consumer choice through controls or prices, would be the most radical political step the government could make.

Cheap air fares provide an example of this. With the current framework of taxes and subsidies, air travel is predicted to increase steadily over the coming decades. The government's policy is to provide the capacity to meet these predictions. Capping growth through regulation or taxation would face a coalition of airlines, tour operators and other businesses, unions, and passengers (particularly those who have bought second homes near to low-cost destinations). Such a coalition would receive powerful support from the media, which relies on travel advertising for much of its income, and is controlled and staffed by people for whom air travel is a way of life. This illustrates perhaps the strongest card that industry has to play: Western democracies have come to place economic growth at the heart of their policy making, and consumerism as their chief tool for satisfying their voters. This is the prevailing culture. Alternatives – whether in economic analysis or ideology – have to struggle against the inertia in government, the media and the civil service that is generated by that culture.

INERTIA

When presented with new and threatening information, people the world over suffer from the same mental distortions. First comes the comfort of outright denial, often accompanied by anger directed at the bearer of bad news. If the facts start to pile up, rejection turns to procrastination – the evil day is put off by demanding more information or further studies. Then, when the evidence becomes overwhelming, the facts are accepted without any admittance of error and without the internalisation needed to act upon them; this is usually assisted by false comforts such as the belief that 'it might not be that bad' or 'something will turn up'. It may also lead to the conclusion that it is necessary to act, but that regrettably there are no effective tools to hand. This in turn can contribute to the alarming phenomenon whereby those opposed to action on climate change move directly from 'it isn't happening' to 'it is happening, but it's too late to do anything about it'.

Such behaviour is in one sense irrational, if for no other reason than doing nothing until it is too late is usually the worst of all options; but it is not above analysis or explanation. Usually, the underlying psychology of the decision makers is significant: so too is the relationship between the decision makers and those acting as advocates for one or other course of action. In the case of the former, the key psychological process is one whereby information tends to be accepted must readily if it accords with the preconceptions of the recipient. This means that decision makers and their advisers often become wedded to their errors. Fresh information may be ignored, misunderstood, downplayed or discredited so as to protect the 'rightness' of the original decision. The more serious the consequences of that initial error, and the more that decision makers are criticised for it, the more such psychological defence mechanisms are called upon.

Of course, people can change their minds: they tend to do so either at an early stage, when they are not committed to entrenched positions; or where information comes from a trusted source; or in response to new information or experiences of such force that they have no choice but to respond. Sadly, the processes of climate change do not provide a moment of crisis that demands a response: each passing day, concentrations of CO_2 increase without sudden or visible consequences. There is, perhaps, a parallel with extinctions amongst species. Where there is a direct link between human activity and population decline, there is at least a chance that the latter will signal to those responsible before it is too late: as with the current (albeit threatened) moratorium on whaling. But if there is an indirect link – such as the artificial introduction of a predator – then the chances are that the theoretical risks will be ignored, yet the visible decline in numbers will come too late to reverse the original decision: as with the dodo.

Institutional inertia is tied closely to the psychological make-up of the individuals and organisations in whose hands power lies. The civil service does not provide a perfect mirror to reflect the will either of the people or of the politicians they elect. Inevitably, the knowledge, experience, interest and prejudices that officials bring to bear on any question – and even the choice of questions to consider – is determined by their upbringing, their class and educational background, by their working lives and social contacts, and by the political currents in which they swim; and above all, by their psychological profile. By and large, civil servants are averse to risk: administration is not a career that attracts swashbuckling entrepreneurs. But any judgement about relevant risks tends to be made not on the long-term external consequences, but on more immediate criteria, such as the effect on the individual's career of contradicting the settled conclusions of his or her colleagues.

The importance of the civil service is hard to over-estimate, despite its relative decline in the last 25 years. In the UK, government ministers and their political appointees are still outnumbered by 2000 to 1.[2] Individually, officials are often far more progressive than their political masters or mistresses, especially those actually working on environmental issues – yet this is to some extent offset by the pro-business and anti-environmental approach of many officials in the Department of Trade and Industry and in the Treasury. But the collective nature of the civil service, where scientists, specialists and enthusiasts rarely reach the top, tends towards continuity and balance.

Inertia has, ironically, become in many ways more deep-rooted as first Margaret Thatcher and then Tony Blair developed more presidential styles of government. With greater central control, both within the cabinet and in the supervision of departments by the Prime Minister's Office and the Cabinet Office, the chances of individual cabinet ministers having the scope to carve their own path in their own areas of responsibility have diminished. It is remarkable how many Secretaries of State for the Environment have become passionate about the subject: Chris Patten, John Gummer and Michael Meacher have all retained a strong interest in the subject after leaving office. But their ability to make a difference when in post was closely circumscribed by the need first to convince others in Cabinet, and second to overcome the lack of interest or sympathy on the part of the Prime Minister of the day. The interference from the centre affects civil servants too, with advisers in Downing Street and the Treasury seeking at a micro level to oversee and direct the work of the experts in much the same way as Blair and Brown would do at a macro one. Essentially, such interventions are about setting the frame in which policy options are developed. This would include the defining of objectives; the scope for costs to be incurred by government or other interest groups such as business; and the acceptability or otherwise of key policy instruments. The latter is probably the most crucial restraint on the ability of officials responsible for climate change policy – or their ministers – to develop and 'sell' in Whitehall effective mechanisms for tackling the problem.

Many of the tools needed to tackle climate change, and particularly taxation and regulation, are distinctly out of fashion. The proposed EU carbon tax of the early 1990s was based on the principle not of higher taxes but of shifting the tax burden away from employment and on to pollution: the proceeds from the tax would have been used to reduce national insurance contributions. Since then, the idea of 'stealth taxes' has been fostered and extended to cover any innovation in taxation: even though the recent Liberal Democrat proposals to rebalance taxation in favour of environmental measures were supposed to be revenue neutral, they were still presented, and criticised, in much of the media as 'new taxes' or 'tax hikes'. The 1990s saw new 'green' taxes such as those on landfill and aggregates; policy making in the current decade prefers voluntary arrangements and market instruments such as emissions trading. Even a tax on plastic shopping bags, adopted successfully in countries as diverse as Bangladesh and Rwanda, and described by the Irish government as its most successful environmental intervention, has been ruled out for the UK.

Regulation is now seen as the enemy of 'competitiveness'. Deregulation (and its newer incarnation 'better regulation') have created an atmosphere in which proposals for legislative intervention are assumed to be costly and burdensome. The internal bureaucracy of devising 'Regulatory Impact Assessments' for new proposals is itself a disincentive to officials thinking of proposing new regulations;

and the criteria which they use tend to allow economic arguments to prevail. Given that the UK Parliament still produces vast amounts of both primary and secondary legislation each year – more than most comparable countries – the suspicion must be that the process in the UK ends up generating not less regulation, but less effective regulation.

In addition to an acceptance of a neo-liberal agenda whereby regulation is of itself 'bad', the UK suffers from a political climate innately hostile to 'Brussels'. Though the European Union will often provide the most cost-effective way of regulating an industry or process (not least because it provides for some measure of continuity for industries operating across national boundaries), it is particularly disliked as a regulatory forum. Measures such as energy efficiency labelling for refrigerators, washing machines and the like, have been both popular and effective. But heavy industrial lobbying wrecked the EU's similar 'eco-label' scheme in the 1990s, even though it was in the interests of most industries to have a single set of standards covering all member states, rather than each one developing a regime requiring separate testing and registration for any given product. 'Brussels' could then stand accused both of burdening business with eco-labels, and failing to protect businesses from national 'eco-label' schemes. As a result, even simple measures such as requiring 'stand-by' features on consumer electronics to switch off after a set time have still not been adopted, either at EU or national level.

The widespread disinclination to use tools such as taxation and regulation leads policy makers to resort to 'softer' alternatives, notably the use of incentives (especially in energy efficiency) and social marketing (classic public information campaigns, such as reminding people to switch off their televisions overnight and to avoid over-filling their kettles). These alternatives can have some effect. Fiscal incentives are essentially the reverse of punitive taxes: reducing the rate of duty on one fuel (such as bio-diesel) has some of the same effect as raising the duty on another (such as petrol), at least in terms of switching from one alternative to another. It may not reduce the overall amount of fuel bought, or rebalance the relative cost of private motoring compared to public transport, as a tax increase might, but incentives would certainly be part of any effective 'policy mix' to tackle climate change. The problem with incentives or 'tax breaks' is that, from the point of view of those responsible for limiting public expenditure, they are costly; while for those wedded to 'the market', they may also be distorting. Certainly, they can have unforeseen consequences, and may not always be effective; the incentive has to be sufficiently 'eye-catching' to overcome habit or inertia. If pitched too low – for example, the modest differential in UK road fund duty for smaller and less polluting vehicles – the uptake can be embarrassingly small.

Social marketing – essentially, the use of advertising and other marketing techniques to 'sell' ideas such as the need for energy efficiency or behavioural change, such as participation in recycling schemes – are also potentially powerful. For politicians who are unwilling to contemplate regulation or taxation, or to find the money to set up a powerful series of fiscal incentives, persuasion is an attractive alternative. Exhortations such as 'climate change – together we can tackle it' or 'are you doing your bit?' can be effective if pursued vigorously over time and linked closely with straightforward ways for the target audience to put the exhortation into practice. But when deployed without the support of legislation, enforcement or strong tax/price signals, social marketing soon runs up against the constraint of the 'free rider'. For individuals not motivated by altruism, the 'rational' response to such messages is to ignore them. The 'game theory' is simple: if everyone else obeys the command, there is no need for the individual to do so: their contribution is so small that the planet will still be saved. If no one else obeys, there is no point in the individual taking part, as the planet is doomed anyway. If enough people take this approach, then this will send out a signal to those who are taking part that their contribution is in vain: essentially, that they are 'mugs'. Unless their altruism is strong, such signals will convert participants into non-participants, so undermining the effectiveness of collective voluntary action.

The 'free rider' effect is well-understood in policy making. Indeed, governments experience it themselves when considering collective voluntary action at the international level. Kyoto has always suffered from two deep 'free rider' wounds. First, there is the lack of an effective mechanism for 'burden-sharing' that trades off the desirability of emerging nations such as China to keep carbon emissions low with the responsibility of industrialised nations such as those in the EU to make cuts commensurate with their higher per-head emissions and greater wealth. Second, there is the absence of the biggest player of them all – the US. The lack of 'contraction and convergence', together with fears that the US would hitch a free ride, helps explain why all parties to Kyoto were unwilling to adopt ambitious targets: doing so would have risked more than they were willing to lose in relation to other countries, especially in respect of the ill-defined but dearly held concept of 'international competitiveness'.

Within individual states, the 'free rider' factor tends to mean that policies dependent on collective voluntary action will usually fail, or under-deliver, or require immense effort, or only deliver over a long time scale, potentially involving generational changes (in other words, only as an older, less-compliant generation dies off, and a new and more compliant generation emerges, does underlying behaviour shift). Successful schemes require high levels of altruism, or emotional engagement, or civic responsibility. The latter in particular has been in decline for many years (witnessed, for example, by falling turnout in elections), so making the scope for collective voluntary action even more narrow. But such schemes have three great advantages, as far as many politicians are concerned. First, they require no legislation, are quick and comparatively cheap: say £10 million for a high-profile campaign, compared to £100 million to increase differentials to favour lower-pollution cars, or £10 billion for a new rail line to reduce vehicle emissions. Second, TV adverts, poster sites, direct mail and so on are all very visible: even if they do not lead to any change in behaviour, they do give the impression of a government taking the issue seriously. This brings with it the risk that the appearance of action becomes a goal in itself, or even the only goal.

Perhaps the greatest attraction of collective voluntary action for politicians, though, is that it shifts the responsibility away from government and on to the public: a problem shared is a problem halved. And this may not be unreasonable. It is, after all, individuals, not governments, that leave TVs on stand-by, fly around the world and drive to work rather than taking the bus. Governments set the framework or intervene within the market, but they do so in response to signals from the public as well as to achieve their own objectives. If society will not cooperate with efforts to protect the climate, then government intervention is doomed. But, of course, the problem would not arise. Governments usually know enough about public opinion – whether it is the gut instinct of the politician who knows his or her voters, or based on polling, focus groups and other research – to know what they will put up with. 'Putting up with' here translates into votes: essentially, if the public does not think that climate change matters, or is not prepared to support new taxes or regulations, then political parties will be reluctant to propose them. This makes it tempting for politicians to rationalise or justify to themselves their lack of effective action through taxation or regulation and their use of appeals for collective voluntary action as an alternative. The public have no appetite for the former: the latter at least lays much of the responsibility where it truly lies.

SHORT-TERMISM

Such an equation opens up the question of leadership: should politicians attempt to educate, persuade or challenge their followers, or should they instead merely provide what their followers say that they want? The simple answer is that they must do both; but the widespread perception is that politicians increasingly favour the path of least resistance. Various overlapping explanations for this have been advanced, notably the development of political marketing, the absence of significant differences in ideology between competing parties, the role of the media, and the rise of consumerist politics.

Modern political marketing is a subtle and refined business. Resources are increasingly targeted on where they will have the greatest electoral impact: especially on 'floating', 'undecided' or 'switch' voters in marginal electoral areas, whether precincts, states or constituencies. There is nothing particularly sinister in this – though it may have negative effects, such as increasing voter apathy. Applying consumer profiling allows political parties to identify types who may be particularly rewarding to target and then to find individuals who match that type – perhaps because of the car they drive, the supermarket they use or the charities they support. The letter canvassing support can then be addressed to the right householder – and also be tailored with the most effective messages. At the heart of modern political marketing is an acceptance by the main parties that political brands, the identity of the party and its leadership, and political products – that is, individual policies – have to be adapted or even designed not only to attract voters, but to attract those vital swing voters in marginal constituencies.

The implications of this approach – often labelled 'designer politics' – go beyond the traditional practice of political parties each favouring their own people and areas, whether it is the Conservatives targeting health resources on relatively affluent southern England, Fianna Fail favouring the construction industry that helps fund the party, or the Democrats' links to organised labour. It also goes beyond the problem of those seeking the backing of one or other party but whose votes are in the wrong place: in the UK, for example, few fishing communities lie in Labour–Conservative marginals and they have tended to be ignored by both main parties. It even goes beyond the natural effect of the concerns of marginal constituencies having a disproportionate effect on the political agenda: the special place of the British motor industry is not unconnected to the geographical overlap between car plants and West Midlands marginal seats.

Instead, this kind of politics is about designing and marketing political *products* that will appeal to floating voters in marginal seats. In the UK there are, roughly, 800,000 of such individuals out of a total electorate of around 40 million. Individual policies or spending decisions will address their most salient concerns, and also the underlying aspirations and ethos of that group. So if we might characterise marginal floaters as non-political, uncommitted and consumerist, then it is no surprise if political programmes tend to avoid political needs and concentrate on satisfying consumerist wants. If we profile this group, and find (amongst other things) a comparatively high proportion of car ownership, of overseas travel and of aspiration towards private health care, then it is no surprise if the main parties are resolutely focused on exactly these issues. In this sense the claim of 'government by focus group' is misleading: focus groups are only one small part of the array of research tools used by political parties to develop their 'offer' and test it on the key audiences.

Of course, not every policy is designed for the marginals. Parties are expected to govern for all, few people are entirely self-interested, and policies also have to attract and motivate party activists. As an example, Labour has increased overseas aid considerably since 1997 because it accords with the party's traditions and self-image, is popular with Labour Party members, and insofar as it has been noticed by the wider population, they in the main approve. In other words, while overseas aid is not a priority for marginal floaters, it is not something they object to either. In effect, not every policy is designed for this group of 800,000 voters; but they do have a form of veto. If they are against a policy, it will not happen, or if it is seen as essential (as with indirect tax rises) it will be hidden.

This is the crux for climate change policy making in the UK. Those policies which would tackle the problem, from higher fuel costs to road pricing, and from a shift away from a consumerist society to one based on other aspirations and values, would have a disproportionate impact on the marginal floaters. Governments will push on with deeply controversial policies so long as the marginal floaters do not object too much. Iraq might have put 2 million people on

British streets, but they were the 'wrong' 2 million: readers of the *Independent* and the *Guardian*, not of the *Express* or *Daily Mail*. The mishandling of the 2001 foot-and-mouth epidemic and the ban on hunting in 2005 may have alienated 'the countryside', but it was the countryside of Tory voters: it is hard to point to a single seat that Labour lost in 2005 as a consequence.[3] But the fuel protests of 2000 were different: the marginal floaters backed the protesters, not the government, and so the government capitulated. The fuel duty escalator – the most effective tool then in place for combating climate change – was scrapped, and the prospects of it being replaced are minimal.

PUBLIC WILL

Each of these four sets of explanations has something to contribute to an understanding of the failure of the political process to deal effectively with climate change. The exact mix in each country depends on factors ranging from the personalities and preoccupations of individual leaders to the ability of business chiefs to influence the politicians – either by shaping their perspective or funding their campaigns -and from the mindset and methods of the bureaucracy charged with proposing solutions and putting them into effect, to the mechanics of the electoral process.

Despite these variations, there remain three critical issues for campaigners and others seeking a more progressive response from governments. The first is their understanding of how and why decision makers and their advisers behave in relation to issues such as climate change. With a leader such as Tony Blair, the more he is criticised or vilified, and the more that protesters mass outside the gates of Downing Street, the more convinced he becomes that he is taking the right moral course. Germany's Angela Merkel, in contrast, is more pragmatic, more attuned to the construction of social and political alliances that influence electoral dynamics, of which marches and rallies can be a potent demonstration. Similarly, civil servants tend to be suspicious of the emotional dimension to decision making: their psychology and self-image is more overtly dispassionate, making them attracted to economic indicators rather than environmental realities. Yet paradoxically, it is the same emotional self-denial – and the comparative absence of emotional content from the policy-making process – which may make a powerful and targeted emotional appeal all the more effective.

The second issue is the way in which campaigners engage with the wider public, to maximise the extent to which awareness of the dangers of climate change is channelled in positive directions. The danger is that the public may become more aware, yet come to believe that the problem is too large, or the political system too distorted, for them to make an effective contribution. Then they are particularly susceptible to political leaders telling them what they want to hear: that current policies are enough to solve the problem, or that action by one state in isolation is futile. Here, the comparative lack of leadership shown by politicians becomes a vacuum into which others can step; not presenting themselves as helpless critics, but as the ones with the clear, practical and achievable path forward.

The third issue is a recognition by campaigners that individual action will always be undermined by the 'free rider' problem and that, for all its faults, it is politics that will deliver progress on climate change. Politicians are anxious to garner votes from every direction. The more that the public are sensitised to climate change, and linked issues such as recycling or out-of-town development, the more that this can be converted into political signals that politicians and political strategists can read; the more, in turn, they will adopt progressive policies. Climate change and environmental concerns as a whole are becoming more 'salient' to voters: coming to rival more supposedly mainstream concerns such as the economy or education. The media is giving more coverage to the issue, even though the strong pro-consumerist bias of the media means that its overall contribution is still strongly negative. Across Europe, support for the Greens has risen. Politicians initially reacted by changing the rhetoric: but if the pressure is maintained, shifts in policy will follow.

Of course, such shifts are largely based on self-interest. In the UK, Conservative leader David Cameron has played the green card strongly (though as yet with no firm policies). In doing so, he was responding to rising public concern and also recognising how the environment could shift perceptions of the Conservatives from being the pro-business, self-centred and self-styled 'nasty' party towards a more progressive, softer, and more altruistic image. Labour has countered Cameron's impact by giving the equally young and even more thoughtful David Miliband the environment portfolio, and by giving the alternative energy industry much of what it wanted in the latest energy review. But the review also contained the much-trailed move that is authentic Blair: the embrace of nuclear power. It is everything he instinctively turns to: bold, high-tech, and likely to infuriate those he feels furthest from politically; in this case, the Greens and his own anti-nuclear traditional left. As an attempt to split the environmental movement, it has already shown some signs of success – a typical piece of political triangulation. It may also create the most lasting political legacy any leader could wish for: one with a half-life measured in millennia.

But despite the difficulties, an approach that takes account of the mindset of decision makers, allied with a thorough understanding of the attitudes and behaviours of voters and how they might be persuaded to change, and an awareness of how the political process can be used most effectively, provides climate change campaigners with a robust way forward. After all, we have in some ways been here before. In the early 1990s, the threat to the ozone layer led to concerted action by developed and developing nations, including a form of burden-sharing. The Montreal Protocol was not perfect; but it was a shining success compared to the response on climate change. It showed that politicians could respond to public concern, particularly if that concern contained an electoral threat or opportunity – in the case of ozone, the rise in environmental awareness and the surge of support for the Greens in the 1989 European elections. It also showed that if a handful of countries took up progressive positions – including, in that case, the United Kingdom – they could exert considerable leverage within the European Union, and the EU could in turn act more effectively in international negotiations.

Climate change is an even more serious threat, demanding economic and social changes to match. But the current political stalemate is not inevitable. If a few EU member states were to follow Iceland's lead on achieving zero emissions by 2050; if a few thousand voters in Illinois or Florida were to shift allegiance; if the public were to become more aware that pleasant-sounding 'global warming' is a synonym for 'global suffocation', then anything is possible.

NOTES

1. 14 September 2004. The full text of this speech is available at http://www.pm.gov.uk/output/page6333.asp
2. Roughly 250 ministers and special advisers to 500,000 civil servants. Even counting only the Senior Civil Service and Principal or Grade 7 administrators – that is, the policy-making core of the civil service – the proportions remain close to 60 to 1.
3. See Robert Worcester, Roger Mortimore and Paul Baines, *Explaining Labour's Landslip*, London: Politico's, 2005.

Part III

Critical Players

5
First They Blocked, Now Do They Bluff?
Corporations Respond to Climate Change

Melanie Jarman

'There is no system that has not another system concealed within it'
Jeanette Winterson, *Art and Lies*[1]

In his excellent book *The End of Nature*,[2] Bill McKibben writes of how human beings have become 'so large that they altered everything'. We have, he says: 'ended nature as an independent force, something larger than us'. No structure displays this more clearly than the institution through which we conduct much of our lives – the corporation. The corporation repackages the natural world and sells it back to us as our food and water, and as the products that shape our daily lives. Nature gets reduced to something with value only when it has a price. But McKibben describes the 'end of nature' as something more than the way in which we relate to the natural world. It is an actual process he says, beginning with 'concrete changes in the reality around us'. This applies to corporations too, for in the process of amassing global empires their use of fossil fuels has changed the very atmosphere that surrounds us. In a very practical sense, corporations have helped hasten the demise of natural systems as we know them.

Traditionally, corporations have ignored or even blocked actions to curb increasing levels of carbon dioxide and other greenhouse gases in the atmosphere. Digby Jones, Director-General of the Confederation of British Industry, infamously once accused the UK government of 'risking the sacrifice of UK jobs on the altar of green credentials'[3] when it declared measures to tackle climate change. The UK corporate sector was never that keen on the government's Climate Change Levy, and had actively lobbied for a higher amount of emissions allowances in the first round of the EU Emissions Trading Scheme. Yet, in June 2005, an ad hoc alliance of UK corporations made a move that seemed to suggest this stance may be changing. Was this a sign that the corporate world might at last support action on climate change?

123

'We are convinced that we need to take urgent and informed action now if we are to avoid the worst impacts of climate change' wrote 13 of the UK's biggest companies in a public letter to the UK Prime Minister, Tony Blair, in June 2005.[4] 'We want to offer our help' they said, in 'efforts to make progress on climate change'. Welcoming a UK government commitment to a reduction in carbon emissions by 60 per cent by 2050, the corporate leaders said they wanted to help bridge the gap to the 'radically different low-carbon future' that this target implied. The letter's signatories included oil companies BP and Shell, alongside aviation company BAA. Surely these had the most to lose in a future where carbon dioxide emissions and by implication, use of fossil fuels, was severely limited? Still, they continued: 'We need to create a step-change in the development of low-carbon goods and service.' In a bizarre about-turn of surprising humility they even acknowledged that: 'what we have done so far is not nearly sufficient given the size of the challenge facing us'.

WHAT THEY'VE DONE SO FAR

Big business has certainly never shied away from commenting on climate change. Far from it: over 1,000 business lobbyists were present at the landmark signing of the Kyoto Protocol in Japan in 1997.[5] The problem was more that, while the corporate world may have taken part in conferences, discussions and debate on climate change, the position that it took was to oppose effective action. In the run-up to the signing of the Kyoto Protocol, corporate-funded lobby groups used blocking tactics such as trying to discredit the models used to predict climate change. Then, when the scientific consensus for global warming became overwhelming, they switched tactic and put forward economic arguments against action. One of the most prominent industry-funded lobby groups of the 1990s was the US-based Global Climate Coalition, set up by a wide group of professional sceptics from US car, oil and manufacturing industries and by the PR company Burson-Marsteller. The Coalition funded and promoted scientists and 'experts' who denied the very existence of climate change, or its human-induced causes. While the Global Climate Coalition was 'deactivated' in 2001, its approach to climate change lives on today through, for example, the work of the Exxon Mobil oil company.

Some major oil companies – most notably BP and Shell – have changed tactics on climate change. ExxonMobil, however, still follows the old road. Exxon funds think-tanks, media outlets and consumer, religious and even civil rights groups in order to spread scepticism. Such a contrary position feeds directly into the work of the Bush administration, with which the company has strong links. The traffic flows both ways: alumni of the Competitive Enterprise Institute, a lobby group part-funded by Exxon, hold important positions within the Bush administration. Meanwhile, Philip A. Cooney, who was originally a lobbyist for oil industry trade association the American Petroleum Institute, was offered a job at Exxon after resigning as chief of staff for President Bush's environmental policy, in 2005.[6] Cooney's resignation became inevitable when the *New York Times* published documents revealing that he had edited reports in ways that cast doubt on the link between the emission of greenhouse gases and rising temperatures.[7]

Six months after the Cooney controversy, Exxon demonstrated that its stance on climate change caused few problems with its financial bottom line. In January 2006 the company announced a profit of $36.1 billion after tax[8] – the biggest in corporate history. This record figure placed Exxon among the world's biggest economies, equivalent, speculated the *Independent*, to the seventeenth biggest, just behind Russia but well ahead of Taiwan or Sweden.[9] Arguably, while still raking in the money, why should Exxon change its climate-change stance? Lee Raymond, chairman and chief executive at the time, remained bullish. He told the *Wall Street Journal*: 'We're not playing the issue [of climate change] ... I get this question a lot of times: "Why don't you just go spend $50m on solar cells? Charge it off to the public-affairs budget and just say it's like another dry hole?" The answer is: That's not the way we do things.'[10]

SPLITTERS

While that may not be the way that Exxon does things, it has become the way of the two UK-based oil companies that signed the letter to Tony Blair: BP and Shell. Both of these companies have chosen to split with their industry's traditional approach to climate change. Rather than blocking action, both have decided to join in instead with framing the debate on what action to take.

BP has set itself up as the oil company that most prominently declares concern over climate change. As one of the first to leave the Global Climate Coalition, it recognised early on that too-close involvement with climate scepticism could become a PR liability.

In 1997 the company's chief executive, Lord John Browne, broke new ground for an oil company in announcing that: 'The time to consider the policy dimensions of climate change is not when the link between greenhouse gases and climate change is conclusively proven, but when the possibility cannot be discounted and is taken seriously by the society of which we are part. We in BP have reached that point.'[11]

BP's different tack to Exxon included investments in renewable energy and the creation of an internal emissions trading system with a goal of reducing greenhouse gas emissions by 10 per cent from 1990 levels, by 2010. The company image became more nature-inspired, with a kind of flower logo, and a translation of the initials BP into the open-ended slogan 'beyond petroleum'. Chief executive Browne, meanwhile, was armed with some seriously environmentally-minded rhetoric, which he has been scattering liberally ever since. The exercise has certainly changed perception of the company from that of a climate change 'denier' to that of a 'doer': BP came second in *BusinessWeek's* December 2005 survey of Top Companies of the Decade for reaching its 2010 greenhouse gas reduction target in 2001 and for increasing valuation by $650 million through improvements in operating efficiency and energy management.[12] Lord Browne also appeared in *BusinessWeek's* list of Individual Achievers for a 'visionary call for industry action' on climate change and for 'transforming its traditional oil-field culture and drastically shrinking its so-called carbon footprint'.[13]

Shell has followed BP in seeking a piece of the environmental action. Shell left the Global Climate Coalition as global concern over climate change began to develop. It announced investment in renewables and launched an advertising campaign that declared that it was possible to have both profits and principles. Seeming to echo Lord Browne's concern over the effect his company's core product has on the environment, Shell chief executive Jeroen van der Veer told the *Financial Times*, in January 2006, that: 'Unchecked, [the world's increasing energy needs] will result in significantly higher carbon emissions ... The world's energy needs must be met while cutting carbon dioxide emissions'.[14]

'ENVIRONMENT IS IT'

Corporations whose core products cause the greatest contribution to greenhouse gas emissions have not been alone in airing their concerns over climate change. HSBC, another signatory of the UK-based companies' letter to Tony Blair, was the first international bank to declare that it was going 'carbon-neutral'. HSBC plans to offset its emissions through tree planting and carbon trading, and is developing a scheme to rate the carbon-risk exposure of its customers. Despite Exxon digging in its heels on the issue, corporate concern on climate change is clearly gaining PR currency. 'Environment' has become a key branding theme. Bob Sheppard, deputy director for corporate programmes at environmental education organisation Clean Air-Cool Planet said: 'There are a lot of creative types looking for the next big thing ... these days, environment is it.'[15]

To stay with 'it' then, any company worth its salt has to be seen to take a stand on climate change. The UK-based Carbon Trust looked at the implications of this in a 2004 study that examined how brand value for companies in different sectors would be affected by 2010 as a result of their response to climate issues.[16] The Carbon Trust report suggested that climate change could become a mainstream consumer issue in the next five years, with reputational implications for sectors not seen to be addressing the issue appropriately. While some consumers would be prepared to take the steps that would seriously reduce emissions – flying less, for example – the report suggested that, in general, customers do not have easy substitutes for sectors with high, evident carbon dioxide emissions. Given this lack of easy substitutes, customers may focus on relative company performance. 'If you are still determined to fly' questioned the Carbon Trust, 'is there a more carbon responsible airline? If you don't want to cut back on driving, is there a more climate-responsible petrol company from which to buy petrol?' The report speculated that if climate change becomes a major consumer issue and one airline, for example, is significantly behind its peers on this issue, half of the company's value could be at stake. This suggests that those who take on board the 'environment is it' mantra are more likely to have the much-sought-after competitive edge. And there is already clear water between some companies in the very sectors that the Carbon Trust referred to: while aviation company BAA put its name to the Tony Blair letter, chief executive Michael O'Leary of rival Ryanair refuses to support an industry-wide effort to limit carbon dioxide emissions. Asked what he would say to travellers worried about the environment, O'Leary replied: 'I'd say, sell your car and walk.'[17]

While O'Leary's stance may make him an entertaining interviewee, over time it could become as unsustainable for Ryanair's business practice as it is for the planet. For, Carbon Trust research aside, marketing trends are not the only pressure on companies to engage with climate change. With the entry into force of the Kyoto Protocol, and with the European Union Emissions Trading System also operational, the need to comply with emerging carbon policies is becoming increasingly unavoidable. In the US, despite the national government's current lack of decent carbon regulations, the corporate community is increasingly affected by local and state legislation. Rather than backing the Bush administration's intransigence on the issue, some have called for federal regulations as a way to bring stability to an already developing greenhouse gas market. An unprecedented six of the eight leaders of large energy companies that spoke at an April 2006 US Senate hearing on climate change policy were in favour of a cap on greenhouse gas emissions.[18] At a meeting of power company executives the previous November, Jim Rogers, chief executive of US-based Cinergy – whose coal-fired plants put out 1 per cent of annual CO_2 emissions in the US – had predicted that: 'The regulations [on greenhouse gas emissions] will change someday. And if we're not ready, we're in trouble.'[19] Cinergy's plans include looking at its greenhouse gas emissions with a view to ensuring that its operations, particularly its costly power plants with a long lifespan, have a future in an increasingly carbon-constrained world. 'To simply avoid this debate', says the company's chief executive, 'is not an option.'[20]

CHANGING CLIMATE AS THE CLIMATE CHANGES

While some companies are approaching the issue of climate change by trying to stay ahead of related measures, others, like a textbook response in a corporate training exercise, have begun to translate 'the climate threat' into 'the climate opportunity'.

Firstly, what was formerly perceived by the corporate world as a problem – an international agreement to limit greenhouse gas emissions – has become a forum for new property rights and profit potential, with the Kyoto Protocol driving an emissions trade predicted to be worth billions. As part of a 2001 series of presentations titled 'New Markets for a Green Economy', World Bank employee, Ken Newcombe, pushed the idea that to engage with climate issues was essential for any company wanting to get ahead. 'Developing and projecting an efficient greenhouse response', said Newcombe, 'has become an issue of corporate strategic competitiveness.'[21] Newcombe played a key role in setting up the first global carbon fund, the World Bank's Prototype Carbon Fund, which was 'designed to show how a market for carbon emission credits for developing countries can work under the Kyoto Protocol's proposed flexible mechanisms'.[22] The World Bank itself states that its primary interest in such exercises has been in developing a market: 'The World Bank's carbon finance products help grow the market by extending the frontiers of carbon finance to new sectors or countries that have yet to benefit.'[23]

Alongside the rapidly developing market in greenhouse gas emissions, new market opportunities abound in the development of low-emission products. US-based GE, generally known to environmentalists for dragging its feet in the clean-up of chemical spills in New York's Hudson River, is one of the forerunners in this game. While much of GE's business is still in carbon-intensive products, the company has launched a specific programme, Ecoimagination, to pioneer next-generation clean technologies, lower the company's emissions and boost its energy efficiency. 'We will focus our unique energy, technology, manufacturing, and infrastructure capabilities to develop tomorrow's solutions' said Jeffrey Immelt, GE Chair and chief executive.[24] Or, as Jonathan Lash, president of the World Resources Institute, put it: 'Immelt ... believes he is going to operate in a carbon-constrained world and he will have the technologies that the world wants and needs to buy.'[25] Immelt has pledged that by 2010 Ecoimagination's parent company will be spending $1.5 billion on research and development in eco-friendly technologies.[26] While this is no small sum, GE's plans are as much about market development as they are about any kind of environmental enlightenment experienced by key staff. Immelt declared that Ecoimagination was being launched 'not because it is trendy or moral but because it will accelerate our growth and make us more competitive'.[27] When asked by *Forbes* magazine whether Ecoimagination was just a sales pitch Immelt admitted: 'It's primarily that ... In its essence it's a way to sell more products and services.'[28] His position is similar to that of Vivienne Cox, chief executive of BP's gas, power and renewables division, who has said: 'It is good business ... The economy of the future will be a low carbon economy.'[29]

BUSINESS AS USUAL – AS USUAL

So, rather than demonstrating a dramatic shift in the way that business is conducted, it seems that corporations are responding to climate change by sticking to fairly usual parameters – responding to regulatory and PR trends, and making the most of new market opportunities in order to get ahead. 'Far from breaking the bank,' says *BusinessWeek*, 'cutting energy use and greenhouse emissions can actually fatten the bottom line and create new business opportunities, while simultaneously greening up companies' reputations.'[30] Does this mean that Amanda Griscom Little, writing for *Grist* magazine, was right to say: 'if Immelt can merge altruism and profitability by selling technical fixes for the many challenges posed by global warming, more power to him'?[31] If this corporate response adds up to less greenhouse gases entering the atmosphere, then does it matter if business as usual continues?

Well, yes it does matter, for business as usual runs counter to the kind of action that is actually needed to tackle climate change. Firstly, the current corporate response can only go a limited distance towards cutting the energy use that *BusinessWeek* so neatly links to a fattened bottom line. Energy efficiency measures and products may be able to cut energy use from what might have been without those particular measures and products. But, if these cuts take place within a context of continued overall growth, then they are not contributing to what actually needs to happen – cutting energy use and greenhouse emissions from where we are at right now. Immelt, as he has said himself, still wants to keep producing and selling more stuff. When *Grist* magazine pressed him to clarify his stance on policies geared towards shifting to a low-carbon economy – would he endorse a federal Renewable Portfolio Standard requiring that a certain percentage of the nation's electricity come from renewable sources? Does he support a cap-and-trade emissions programme? – he was found to be 'adamantly vague'.[32]

Secondly, much of the current corporate response to climate change consists of a dollop of rhetoric and a token green gesture alongside a main dish of business as usual when it comes to the use of fossil fuels. Despite their advertising hype and their signatures on the letter to Tony Blair calling for a 'step-change' towards a low-carbon world,[33] BP and Shell remain oil companies. Indeed, Shell chief executive Jeroen van der Veer's vision is for something that is surely an oxymoron – 'green fossil fuels'.[34] Van der Veer has in mind the fledgling technology whereby CO_2 from fossil fuels is captured and then injected underground. The US Department of Energy has praised this technology for having the potential to boost its oil reserves four-fold[35] – a vision that is surely a world away from the most effective 'step-change' that would move towards a low-carbon world – leaving fossil fuels in the ground to start with, and focusing on reduced consumption, efficiency and renewables.

For BP, the 'beyond petroleum' re-branding exercise was so successful in terms of public relations that it won a *PRWeek* 2001 award for Campaign of the Year.[36] Yet in terms of BP's practice, its £750 million investment in photovoltaics company Solarex, in 1998, amounted to just 0.8 per cent of an oil-and-gas buying spree that took place around that time.[37] BP spent £67 billion on Amoco in 1998; £16 billion on ARCO and £1 billion on Mobil Europe's downstream assets in 1999. In 2000 it also spent £3 billion on Burmah Castrol and £600 million on a stake in PetroChina. The split that BP practised then between a public display of concern over climate change and continued business as usual is still very present today. Just two days after the letter of support for action on climate change was delivered to Tony Blair, it emerged that signatory BP had been privately lobbying in Washington to block a more stringent set of regulations on climate change in the US, which would have introduced a mandatory curb on greenhouse gases.[38]

The business as usual pattern of continued fossil fuel use is not even challenged by the Kyoto Protocol, the treaty that should be the main driver of global agreements on the aforesaid step-change. The Corporate Europe Observatory has speculated that the Kyoto Protocol, 'the most corporate-friendly environmental treaty in history',[39] may result in a net increase of greenhouse gas emissions. According to Larry Lohmann of The Corner House, the Kyoto Protocol and EU Emissions Trading Scheme markets 'do not create the right conditions for the structural change needed to tackle global warming. On the contrary, they shore up the fossil fuel status quo while blocking constructive alternatives ... Kyoto's Clean Development Mechanism and other project-based credit markets merely help perpetuate the fatal flow of fossil carbon out of the ground.'[40]

The World Rainforest Movement has found that the contributions from the corporations Mitsui, BP, Mitsubishi, Deutsche Bank, Gaz de France, RWE, and Statoil to the World Bank's Prototype Carbon Fund – credits from which can be used against obligations in the Kyoto Protocol – for carbon market projects in 1999–2004 were approximately $45 million.[41] Yet the support these corporations received from the World Bank for fossil fuel projects in 1992–2002 amounted to $3,834,600 million.[42] In many cases, investors in the Prototype Carbon Fund are receiving emission reduction credits from projects in countries where they are simultaneously developing fossil fuel projects supported by the World Bank. The World Rainforest Movement describes these as 'projects which will help lock those countries into a fossil-fuelled energy path and lead to emissions of greater orders of magnitude than the Prototype Carbon Fund projects claim to be reducing'.[43] It appears that, rather than moving towards a low-carbon world, Kyoto's emissions trading markets merely add a 'green' edge to the existing carbon-intensive one.

CUCKOOS IN THE NEST

Despite this gloomy prognosis for change, pressure on corporations to do something about climate issues is mounting from within their own ranks. The insurance industry, faced with record-breaking pay-outs due to unpredictable weather patterns, may yet force the rest of the corporate world to take the threat seriously. In May 2005, US and European institutional investors with over $3 trillion of assets under management issued a call for US companies, Wall Street firms and the Securities and Exchange Commission to intensify efforts to provide investors with comprehensive analysis and disclosure about the financial risks presented by climate change.[44] Alongside that call, the Carbon Disclosure Project has mobilised institutional investors with over $20 trillion under management to improve disclosure of data on climate change risks and opportunities from the world's leading 500 companies.[45] It seems that climate change is growing as a factor in the analysis of corporate and investment risk profiles. According to Jennifer Hall Thornton of the merchant banking group Climate Change Capital: 'There is no doubt that climate change is now firmly on the corporate agenda, and that institutional investors are increasingly aware of its potential impact on business and on financial returns.'[46]

Similarly, shareholders – that force traditionally said to drive the corporate hunger for profits – may yet pressure the corporate world to take climate change more seriously. Michael J. Johnston, executive vice president of a money management firm, claims that 'Shareholders are pressuring everyone to disclose what they are doing in the environmental arena.'[47] While some of this is about avoiding unnecessary risks, shareholders also understand the language of cost savings. US-based International Paper Company changed its practices in order to cut both CO_2 output and energy costs. Vice president of environmental affairs David Struhs said: 'It doesn't matter whether carbon emission reductions are mandated or not ... Everything we're doing makes sense to our shareholders and to our board, regardless of what direction the government takes.'[48]

Finally, energy efficiency and diversification are becoming increasingly desirable to corporations regardless of the climate issue. As illustrated by the US Department of Energy's excitement over the potential of carbon-storage technologies to squeeze more oil from less accessible oilfields, fossil fuels are increasingly expensive to extract, with demand likely to outstrip supply in the not too distant future. Stuart L. Hart of Cornell University had a bleak warning in Worldwatch's *State of the World 2006* for companies that treat environmental issues as a new marketing angle, rather than as a call to reinvent their business models: 'for [businesses that are at the very root unsustainable], continued blind adherence to yesterday's technology could spell doom, not just a missed opportunity'.[49]

OF PENGUINS AND PSYCHOPATHS

When their resource base is threatened, most species in the animal kingdom limit their population size. This tends to happen on an involuntary basis, through lack of food or habitat. Some commentators have speculated it happens on a voluntary basis too. Wilder speculations include the idea that penguins, for example, turn homosexual in order to limit reproduction and thus ensure that the limited resource base stretches further and existing young are properly cared for. Though these changes may add up to the same thing – readjusting the population size in response to outside factors – working out what is behind such behavioural changes is clearly far from an exact science. According to Joel Bakan, author of *The Corporation*, the way in which the corporate form behaves is slightly more transparent. The corporation, says Bakan, behaves like a psychopath.[50] It will 'pursue, relentlessly and without exception, its own self-interest, regardless of the often harmful consequences it might cause to others'.[51] Yet even though driven by self-interest, the corporate world may yet find itself doing something that works for the good of the society within which it operates. According to *Spectrum* magazine, US Congressional support for revived tax incentives for the wind industry may be happening because of the work of GE's lobbyists.[52] Despite their self-interested motivation of having new products to promote, GE executives may be due some credit for pushing clean energy closer to the mainstream in the US. It may just be possible that lower rates of growth in greenhouse gas emissions will result from measures taken because a corporation wants to exploit a new opportunity.

However, although a January 2006 survey in the *McKinsey Quarterly* found that 84 per cent of the corporate executives who replied agreed that high returns to shareholders should be combined with 'contributions to the broader public good',[53] this combination only takes place when these two factors happen to coincide. The primary responsibility of the corporation is to generate profits: it can only act in society's best interest when this gives the corporation a commercial advantage. In the case of effective action on climate change – which requires consumption patterns to reduce from their current levels, posing a fundamental challenge to the doctrine of economic growth – this isn't likely to happen to any great extent. While corporations can only go so far as their profit motive allows them, they cannot be trusted as a driving vehicle for effective action on climate change. In making an offer of 'a partnership between business and the UK Government',[54] the ad hoc grouping that wrote to Tony Blair in June 2005 is problematic not just because its ideas for a low-carbon society are based in an almost religious belief that technology will get us there, but because they are lining themselves up to jointly create the rules for the low-carbon society.

Corporations will not leave the climate debate. Indeed, with control over such massive resources they will inevitably have a substantial influence: it is not an idle question to ask whether Toyota's decision to build the hybrid Prius car in China will have a greater impact on global carbon emissions than the Kyoto Protocol. To ignore such clout and pretend that corporate action on climate change is not important would be a very blinkered approach. However, while they may yet have to rethink their structure and focus due to changing energy patterns, in the meantime corporations cannot be allowed to define the parameters of the climate debate. This, according to Carbon Trade Watch, would leave us with limited parameters of 'price forecasts and carbon derivatives'.[55] Decision making over action on climate change must include the voices of those who have no economic power – yet are often most harshly affected by a changing climate. It must include an understanding that there are limits to what the natural world can cope with from human activity. Only then will it be relevant to the depth of the crisis.

NOTES

1. Jeanette Winterson, *Art and Lies*, Vintage, 1995.
2. Bill McKibben, *The End of Nature*, Bloomsbury Publishing, 2003.
3. 'UK industry braced for carbon fallout damage', *Daily Telegraph*, 23 February 2004.
4. http://www.cpi.cam.ac.uk/bep/downloads/CLG_pressrelease_letter.pdf
5. 'Greenhouse market mania: UN climate talks corrupted by corporate pseudo-solutions', *Corporate Europe Observatory*, November 2000.
6. 'Cooney Lands Job With Exxon', Center for Media and Democracy, http://www.prwatch.org/node/3759
7. 'Bush aide softened greenhouse gas links to global warming', *New York Times*, 8 June 2005.
8. 'Exxon makes history with $36bn profit', *Independent*, 31 January 2006.
9. Ibid.
10. 'Oil chiefs disagree on issue of climate change', *Financial Times*, 6 July 2005.
11. http://www.bp.com/genericarticle.do?categoryId=98&contentId=2000427
12. http://www.businessweek.com/magazine/content/05_50/b3963415.htm
13. http://www.businessweek.com/magazine/content/05_50/b3963417.htm
14. 'Vision for meeting energy needs beyond oil', *Financial Times*, 24 January 2006.
15. 'Saving the environment, one quarterly earnings report at a time', *New York Times*, 22 November 2005.
16. 'Brand value at risk from climate change', work carried out by Lippincott Mercer on behalf of the Carbon Trust, autumn 2004, http://www.carbontrust.co.uk/carbon/PrivateSector/brand value.htm
17. 'Worried about airline pollution? Sell your car, says Ryanair boss', *Guardian*, 22 June 2005.
18. 'Cap of Good Hope', *Grist* magazine, www.grist.org, 6 April 2006.
19. http://businessweek.com/magazine/content/05_50/b3963401.htm
20. http://www.businessweek.com/magazine/content/05_50/b3963413.htm
21. Presentation to the Katoomba Working Group III, titled 'New markets for a green economy', 23 March 2001.
22. http://siteresources.worldbank.org/INTCC/Miscellaneous/20733920/EnvStrategyAnnexF2001.pdf
23. 'Carbon finance at the World Bank: Questions and Answers', http://siteresources.worldbank.org/ESSDNETWORK/NewsAndEvents/20546024/CarbonFinanceQA.pdf
24. '"Natural Capital" investment or higher costs and lower profits', UNEP News Release 2005/36, 12 July 2005
25. 'It was just my Ecomagination', *Grist* magazine, www.grist.org, 10 May 2005.
26. Ibid.

27. 'The greening of GE', *Spectrum Online*, July 2005 issue.
28. 'GE turns green', Forbes.com, 15 August 2005, http://www.forbes.com/home/free_forbes/2005/0815/080.html
29. http://www.bp.com/genericarticle.do?categoryId=98&contentId=7012404
30. http://businessweek.com/magazine/content/05_50/b3963401.htm
31. 'It Was Just My Ecomagination', *Grist* magazine, www.grist.org
32. Ibid.
33. http://www.cpi.cam.ac.uk/bep/downloads/CLG_pressrelease_letter.pdf
34. 'A vision for meeting energy needs beyond oil', *Financial Times*, 25 January 2006.
35. 'US Says CO_2 Injection Could Quadruple Oil Reserves', *Red Orbit*, 3 March 2006.
36. http://www.ogilvypr.com/about-ogilvy-pr/awards.cfm
37. 'Branded a liar ... How BP uses the threat of climate change to assist company profitability', *Corporate Watch* magazine, issue 11, summer 2000.
38. 'BP shows two faces as it fights US bill to cut CO_2 emissions', *Independent on Sunday*, 12 June 2005.
39. 'Greenhouse market mania', Corporate Europe Observatory.
40. 'Climate politics after Montreal: time for a change', *Foreign Policy in Focus* commentary, 10 January 2006.
41. 'The World Bank's role in the creation of the carbon market: helping the rich become richer, and the poor grow poorer as fossil fuel subsidies keep flowing', World Rainforest Movement Bulletin, Issue Number 93, April 2005.
42. Ibid.
43. Ibid.
44. 'U.S. & European investors tackle climate change risks and opportunities at the UN', Ceres Press Release, 10 May 2005.
45. 'The Carbon 100: quantifying the carbon emissions', *Henderson Global Investors*, June 2005.
46. http://www.climatechangecapital.com/pages/newsdetail.asp?ID=78
47. 'Saving the environment', *New York Times*, 22 November 2005.
48. http://businessweek.com/magazine/content/05_50/b3963401.htm
49. 'Transforming Corporations', Chapter 10, *State of the World 2006*, Worldwatch Institute 2006.
50. Joel Bakan, *The Corporation: the Pathological Pursuit of Profit and Power*, Constable & Robinson, 2004.
51. Ibid.
52. 'The Greening of GE', Spectrum Online.
53. 'The frustrated will to act for public good', *Financial Times*, 25 January 2006.
54. http://www.cpi.cam.ac.uk/bep/downloads/CLG_pressrelease_letter.pdf
55. 'Hoodwinked in the hothouse: the G8, climate change and free-market environmentalism', Transnational Institute briefing series No. 2005/3, Carbon Trade Watch, June 2005.

6

Mostly Missing the Point:
Business Responses to Climate Change

David Ballard

Few would argue that the response of businesses to the massive challenge posed by climate change is currently adequate, but the same might be said of other groups in society. For example, while by no means a sufficient response, trends in UK energy efficiency in the business sector over recent decades have been far better than in people's domestic lives.[1] Is it realistic to consider that the business community might play an important role in creating a sustainable society in carbon terms? To the extent that it is, what lies behind current difficulties and what work needs to be done to enable higher quality responses by business people?

Some argue that it is unrealistic to look to the business community for genuine leadership in tackling the problem of climate change. For instance, some argue that there is an explicit anti-environment conspiracy currently active at senior levels in some US corporations.[2] Others have argued that the responsible management approach promoted by business leaders, as at the Rio convention, can be seen as a deliberate attempt to subvert the emerging agenda.[3] The evidence that this is the case for some people within the business community is strong.

But can we generalise from these extreme, perhaps even sociopathic, cases to the whole business community? I suggest not. To draw another parallel with the domestic sector, the UK fuel protests of September 2000 could be seen as a successful populist attempt to undermine a key environmental policy (carbon taxation) of a duly elected government, but no one seriously argues that civil society is therefore a sworn enemy of a sustainable society. We rather recognise that civil society is complex, that people think and behave in different ways, not always consistently, that they often do not use their power with appropriate understanding of the wider consequences of their actions.

An archer once explained to me that the colloquial English term 'cock-up' refers to the directionless and weak progress of an arrow wrongly inserted into a bow with the single 'cock' feather uppermost. I suggest that this is a good analogy for business activity on climate change; that 'cock-up', caused by businesses mostly missing the point is at least as strong a narrative as 'conspiracy', and that it leads to more hopeful strategies for change.

I have worked on environmental issues for many years in the business sector and have not encountered any overt hostility to environmental work at all, certainly not in my various encounters at boardroom level. On the other hand, I have encountered a lot of doubt as to whether an issue such as climate change has anything to do with business, doubt which I see as symptomatic of a serious failure of understanding in relation to the situation. For instance, the environment director of one company once told me, in all seriousness, that managing issues like climate change was no different to managing health and safety.

Again, however, such failures of understanding are by no means limited to the business community. In my work outside the business world, similar doubts are raised by academics, by senior managers in local authorities, by ordinary citizens, even by some environmental activists.

My purpose in this chapter is not to draw conclusions as to the motives of senior business people but rather to explore the evidence that the business community is mostly missing the point and so failing to grasp the issues adequately. I will then move on to discuss some of the ways in which this might be addressed.

THE DOMINANT 'BUSINESS AS USUAL' ASSUMPTION OF THE CORPORATE WORLD

1. The late 1980s: environmental concerns change the context of business

Three tragedies of the 1980s had a major effect on environmental practice in businesses. The first of these, the Chernobyl nuclear accident of April 1986, was not properly speaking a business tragedy at all, occurring as it did within the old USSR. Nonetheless, the impact on the context of business was very significant: the public mood on environmental issues changed significantly for a while, with the relative success of the Green Party in the European elections of 1989, and the more general rise in support for environmental pressure groups around that time arguably having been significantly facilitated by that event.

Directly in the business world, the terrible death toll that resulted from releases of methyl isocyanate at the Union Carbide plant in Bhopal, India, in 1984, was followed a few months later by further (though happily not, on this occasion, lethal) toxic releases at the company's West Virginia plant. These incidents led directly to the adoption of the Toxic Release Inventory in the USA.

The Exxon Valdez oil spill, in 1989, led to the adoption of the Ceres Principles for good corporate governance of environmental issues.[4]

The potentially beneficial side-effects of these three otherwise shocking tragedies was reinforced by other events. The Brundtland report of 1987 brought the phrase 'sustainable development' into professional discourse. In 1988, UK Prime Minister Margaret Thatcher's Royal Society speech brought the issue of climate change into the mainstream political agenda. The negotiation of the 1987 Montreal Protocol for the reduction and then elimination of ozone-depleting substances such as chlorofluorocarbons (CFCs) from industrial processes and consumer products was completed at around the same time.

2. Bringing the environment into 'business as usual': the early 1990s

The United Nations Conference on Environment and Development (UNCED) held in Rio in 1992, which was attended by 108 heads of state, showed how significant the issue was becoming. The outputs included the UN Framework Convention on Climate Change (UNFCCC) which eventually led to the Kyoto Protocol for the control of carbon emissions.

Faced with what might have been the emergence of a radically new agenda, and stimulated to some extent, no doubt, by the business sector tragedies above, business leaders participated in the Rio conference with, on the face of it at least, some energy. Indeed, the predecessor to the World Business Council for Sustainable Development (WBCSD) was formed specifically to promote participation by business, alongside other sectors of society. The primary message of leaders of the business community at Rio was, you can trust us: we know how to manage things, these new challenges can be brought under managerial control.

Following the Rio Conference, practices broadly along the lines of the Ceres Principles quickly became the foundation of managerial responses. These included processes such as measurement, reporting, stakeholder engagement, allocation of responsibility at board level, clear delegation to managers below and adoption of environmental management systems such as ISO14001. These measures can be seen as extending mainstream management practice to the environmental agenda.

LOCK-IN AND THE HUGE MANAGERIAL CHALLENGE OF TRANSITION

So the response of the business community has basically been one of 'business as usual'. In the change theories of leading organisational thinkers, such as Chris Argyris and Donald Schön, this is sometimes known as a 'level one' response – one that applies the same 'mindset' or set of taken-for-granted assumptions to resolve an issue, thereby tending to block significant change. An example of a level one response would be a stressed executive who takes up jogging as a way of relaxing but is soon training hard to run marathons competitively: the behaviour is still conditioned by the same assumptions. But climate change requires that many underlying assumptions be questioned in 'level two' and higher responses so as potentially to allow responses to address the root causes of the issue.[5]

To demonstrate this point, it is worth considering briefly the crucial role that the technical and economic infrastructure of business plays in the interactions between human beings and the environment.

Climate sceptics sometimes say that it is crazy to imagine that mere humans could have a significant impact on the great planetary systems that regulate the climate. And were we to consider humans simply as social beings, that might perhaps be true. Deforestation, which is a major contributor to climate change, has been happening since the beginning of agriculture, but the capacity of a single human being or small group to clear land with their bare hands or with axes is quite limited. Add the chainsaw and the bulldozer to the picture, however, and organise people into large corporate systems, with economic incentives to clear land, to manufacture and sell equipment, to keep processes supplied with usable energy, and the potential for destruction becomes magnified many times.

With industrialisation, massive economic, technological, legal and sociological systems have quickly become dependent on each other and have imprisoned us as we have become dependent on them. To take an example, building roads leads to offices and shops being situated near them, increasingly on the periphery of towns rather than in town centres. This stimulates the market for cars: most of us know from experience that public transport works much better to and from city centres than between points on a periphery. Cars last for many years: even in the UK the total fleet is still rising.[6] This means that people are increasingly able to decouple themselves from their communities by travelling further to work. This then drives the need for more roads. People's livelihoods – their needs as well as their greeds – become dependent on road building, car manufacture, petroleum extraction, distribution, and so on.

In turn shareholders and lenders want a profit on their investments, individual citizens come to depend on these profits to finance their retirement, and governments depend on them to finance social services, build hospitals, train teachers, and bring a police officer to the scene of a crime. Indeed, without the prospect of a profit for someone, even the investment needed to maintain our current systems – social as well as economic and technical – will not be forthcoming. But as these profits are in turn reinvested, these intertwined economic, technical and social systems become more and more complicated.

Such economic activity is dependent on use of fossil fuels to an extent that is rarely appreciated. For instance there is a very strong correlation between economic growth and the amount of work as measured by physicists – basically moving things from place to place – required in an economy.[7] More economic growth, more physical work. Since the basic laws of physics set limits to the efficiency with which free energy can be converted into physical work, more economic growth implies an increasing consumption of free energy. But the energy flows that are central to our economy are, of course, still largely sourced from fossil fuels. The International Energy Agency has projected an average 1.7 per cent annual increase in energy use to 2030, with over 90 per cent of the increased demand being met by fossil fuels.[8]

It doesn't take much of an interruption to that flow of energy to have a major impact on economic activity: the OPEC (Organisation of Petroleum Exporting Countries) embargo of the early 1970s caused economic mayhem, and yet the flow of oil to the USA only fell by 5 per cent.[9]

So what are the assumptions that need to be challenged? These technical-economic systems have become 'locked in', self-perpetuating, ever more complex, becoming ever more destructive. There is a very strong argument that continued growth in physical work, and therefore in economic activity, is not a realistic goal if climate stability is to be achieved. But the whole basis of current economic and business planning, completely and – I would say

– unthinkingly assumes the opposite. So there is an immediate and huge challenge to the assumptions of the current economic model, in which the business community is completely entwined alongside government and the ordinary citizen.

THE STRATEGIC IMPLICATIONS OF CLIMATE CHANGE FOR BUSINESS

If this example is typical of the wider context, what are the particular points that the people I encounter in business might be missing when they see climate change as largely irrelevant? This is not the place to 'prove' the scientific consensus on climate change but rather to summarise the key points and then to consider how the climate change agenda poses specific strategic risks (and perhaps opportunities) to businesses around the world.[10]

To summarise before looking in more detail, the physical infrastructure of the business world will be significantly affected by climate change and this will impact upon businesses' costs and competitive position as it is strengthened and renewed, or as it fails. This is known as the adaptation agenda. In addition, as described above, the energy systems on which the current business model depends need to change very significantly and very quickly if there is to be any hope of bringing climate change under control and if completely unmanageable impacts are to be avoided. This is known as the mitigation agenda. Added to this, major diversion of financial capital and free energy will be required actually to make that transition, and this will also indirectly but very significantly affect the market for goods and services.

Note that both adaptation and mitigation actions are central to climate responses: they should not be considered to be in opposition to each other. Delays in the climate system (e.g. between hopefully rapidly reduced emissions of greenhouse gases and the impact on climate change some decades later) mean that climate impacts are bound to become more serious: adaptation is a necessity. On the other hand, unless we cut greenhouse gas emissions, impacts will spiral right out of control and threaten the very survival of our species amongst others: mitigation is a *vital* necessity.

IMMEDIATE ADAPTATION PRESSURES

The UK has done significant work on what climate impacts are likely to mean in practice.[11] For instance:

- One of the main impacts of climate change will be on rainfall. While the effects of this will differ around the world, in a country like the UK we are likely to see less rain in the summer, which will lead to more droughts.
- As a consequence of droughts, the ground is likely to become less absorbent. When rain does fall, it is likely to be more tropical in nature with sudden downpours which can then not easily be absorbed by the dry ground.
- This will lead to more flooding both from swollen rivers and from inadequate storm drainage. A third form of flooding will result from increasing sea levels as the sea warms and expands and – in due course – as land ice near the polar regions melts.
- Another impact is likely to be increased wind speed. When this occurs alongside heavy rain, a phenomenon known as 'driving rain' occurs: this has great capacity to penetrate building cladding.[12]
- There will also be an increasing number of significant heat stresses: the summer 2003 high temperatures across Europe, which killed 30,000 people in Europe, blocked river and road transportation, disrupted essential services such as hospitals and which led to nuclear power stations having to close down, could be attributed to climate change with some statistical confidence that this was not a chance event.[13]

While impacts in other countries will be somewhat different in some respects, nonetheless, they are likely to be just as significant. For instance, hurricane activity is being studied carefully and, although it is too early to say that any single incident – such as Katrina or the 2004 hurricane season – is related to climate change and not just the result of natural variation, a greater number of such events is both expected and observed.

These will only be relatively early 'discomfort and damage' impacts, which will occur, say the Intergovernmental Panel on Climate Change (IPCC), if temperature rises do not exceed 2° C. If temperature rises go beyond this, however, then we will move into the 'disaster' zone, with much increased likelihood of extreme weather events with 'disastrous consequences for some'. If still unchecked, then we will eventually find ourselves in the 'catastrophic' zone, with 'irreversible damage to global ecosystems'.[14] These scenarios will not look any more comfortable for investors than for the rest of us.

People often talk of the corresponding economic benefits that might accrue from climate change, at least in the short term. These are not complete fantasy: for instance, a successful UK wine producer has tracked temperatures over some years and puts his vineyard's economic viability down to the extended warming effect of climate change.[15] But these can be exaggerated. Again, the impact of higher temperatures on UK tourism patterns is seen as an opportunity, but the evidence was reviewed in a recent study and no link between changes in weather and holiday plans could be identified. In addition, the impact on the landscape will be great and costs seem likely to rise, for instance, to counter the erosion impact of torrential rain on footpaths.[16]

It seems clear that economic impacts will be significant and that they potentially affect all areas of the economy. Indeed, in its excellent Governance advice on climate change, Ceres stressed that all sectors of the US economy are potentially at risk.[17]

EARLY SIGNS OF THE COST OF IMPACTS

Such predictions are already being supported by the observations of major reinsurance firms such as Swiss Re and Munich Re, two companies who demonstrate through their analysis over many years that the business community is not altogether 'missing the plot', and that the best business minds can contribute to the great endeavour of responding to climate change. Analysis by Munich Re makes particularly sobering reading.[18] Climate-related economic losses are on an exponentially rising trend. Dominated by extreme weather events, 2004 was the costliest year yet for the insurance industry with losses that exceeded $41 billion (this was before Hurricane Katrina, where the losses appear likely to be far greater). There are other factors besides climate change at play behind these numbers, including changes in settlement patterns, but the rising trend in extreme weather events is entirely consistent with the IPCC's warnings.[19]

Businesses' ability to insure against catastrophic financial losses is already reducing as insurers become less willing to offer cover to assets in potential flood plains. And yet the UK's Carbon Trust has identified that many of the financial risks can be significantly reduced, provided that timely action is taken.[20] The development of a competent insurance market that is skilled not only in assessing exposure to risks but also in assessing a management team's ability to respond to them is, therefore, of strategic importance to the business sector.

THE REQUIRED MITIGATION ACTIONS

The possible points at which climate impact transitions shift from 'discomfort and damage' to 'disaster' and beyond are not yet clear. However, it is widely agreed that if climate change is to be contained at anything like a safe level, then major cuts in greenhouse gas emissions are required. The UK target is to cut emissions by 60 per cent by 2050, which was said by the UK's Royal Commission on Environmental Pollution in 2000 to be consistent with a contraction and convergence approach to stabilising atmospheric CO_2 at 550 ppmv.[21] While such a reduction would be far beyond Kyoto, recent scientific advice is that stabilisation at well below that level will be required to prevent major impacts and that much more aggressive reductions are required.[22]

A 2005 study by the UK's Tyndall Centre for Climate Change Research showed that it is feasible in principle to make 60 per cent cuts in carbon use in the UK's economy. Indeed a variety of routes are possible to this end, including more aggressive investment in low carbon sources and in carbon capture and storage or, by contrast, a high-energy efficiency route with less investment in low carbon generation. It seems possible that these approaches could be combined to achieve greater savings than 60 per cent and it seems likely that other nations could also potentially make large savings. This implies that the climate change dice are not yet finally cast.

But the choices required to make even these transitions are not easy. In the UK, for instance, rapid rises in carbon dioxide from air and ship transportation mean that these sectors could potentially use almost all of the carbon dioxide emissions from a 40 per cent economy, and yet there is currently no governmental or inter-governmental mechanism for the control of emissions from either. To the extent that this problem remains unaddressed, the reductions required for the rest of the economy move from challenging but possible to extremely punishing. If it is addressed, however, the impact on corporate supply chains in a globalised economy will surely be huge.[23]

IMPLICATIONS FOR CONSUMER SPENDING

In addition, actually making these transitions will not be easy. A considerable investment of financial capital will be needed to finance any transition. For example, the lifetime of a new aircraft from manufacture to disposal is several decades, longer if the design lead time is taken into account. Even if a new much lower-carbon aircraft were to be feasible (not a current likelihood), a massive flow of financial capital would be needed to retrofit or replace the existing fleet. Even energy efficiency measures and adaptation measures require financial investment, particularly when retrofitted.

There will also need to be a flow of free energy: a windmill produces four times as much energy as it uses over its life but the investment comes before the savings; the same is true of energy efficiency measures: we must invest energy as well as capital if we are to save carbon. This investment of energy must occur as the economy as a whole cuts its use of carbon-based energy very dramatically. Energy and economy specialists Malcolm Slesser and Jane King, for instance, have calculated that the transition to a low carbon economy requires a huge diversion of energy from use for consumption (e.g. on consumer goods) to the creation of infrastructure.[24]

The implication is that the pattern of consumer spending will be significantly affected with knock-on consequences for markets in goods and services.

Taken together, the various aspects of climate change clearly pose radical challenges to the competitive environment of many, if not most, businesses. Neither the adaptation nor the mitigation agendas look good for investors, nor for the business executives whose job it will be to keep them happy in years to come. And yet the consequences of ignoring them seem much worse.

ASSESSING HOW FAR LEADING BUSINESSES GRASP THE AGENDA

My direct experience suggests strongly that very few people in business (as elsewhere) grasp the scale of the challenge. I wondered how to test this, to move beyond personal experience to third party sources. I decided that this could be most straightforwardly done by focusing on businesses that are regarded by their peers and by external critics as doing relatively well on corporate responsibility and environmental issues. If even these companies miss the point, it is surely fair to conclude that the laggards will be far worse.[25]

I chose a sample of businesses that had been awarded, or short-listed for, significant environmental or sustainability prizes in 2004, or 2005. In the UK I chose businesses that had been awarded prizes by Business in the Community, a group of companies 'committed to improving their positive impact on society', in 2005, or which had been short-listed for awards for their environmental or sustain-ability reporting by ACCA (the Association of Chartered Certified Accountants) in 2005. In the USA I selected from businesses that had been short-listed for similar awards by ACCA and Ceres, in 2004, and from those that had scored well (above 70 out of 100) for their governance on climate change issues by Ceres. This produced a list of companies that is skewed towards the USA and the UK but, nonetheless, contained others from a wider range of countries, including Germany, Canada, Japan and Australia.

I then looked at their corporate position on climate change. This was facilitated by the sterling efforts of Paul Dickinson and his team at the Carbon Disclosure Project (CDP), in the UK. This is an organisation that acts on behalf of institutional investors (pension funds and others) with total assets currently in excess of $31 trillion. Each year it sends a simple questionnaire to leading companies worldwide – in fact to 500 in 2005. Company responses to the nine questions offer an insight into their grasp of these issues.

Not every leading business responded to the CDP 2005 survey. In selecting the companies, I left non-respondents out of my analysis, thereby further skewing my analysis towards businesses that are likely to perform relatively well. I added a further two businesses (Tesco and Barclays) that had not met the other criteria but which are well-known and which come from under-represented sectors (food retailing and banking). This left me looking at 20 companies from a range of sectors.

The companies I looked at emit around 230 million tonnes of carbon dioxide per annum from direct operations; the figure would be much higher if their supply chain impacts (for instance Tesco), or the impact of their products in use (for instance, the oil company Statoil) were included.

ASSESSING THEIR STRATEGIC UNDERSTANDING OF CLIMATE CHANGE

With this deliberately overwhelming skew of my sample in favour of businesses that might be expected to perform well, and with the scale of the use of carbon of some of them, it is surely fair to conclude that if many of these businesses do not have a strategic grasp of the climate change agenda, then the business community as a whole is 'mostly missing the point'.

As a minimum, I was looking for these businesses to show that they considered the practical implications of climate change impacts and climate change mitigation measures on their current business model. The CDP survey makes this relatively easy. For instance, the first question invites managers to say whether they perceive that climate change itself, the policy responses to it, and/or adaptation responses to climate change represent commercial risks or opportunities to the company.

Corporate strategy processes often include a review of contextual trends that are captured in the mnemonic 'PESTLE': Political, Economic, Social, Technical, Legal and Environmental.[26] The brief overview above suggests that climate change might easily affect most of these trends, and so really ought to be picked up and assessed by a strategically competent organisation. This simple question is, therefore, a strong test of a company's wider strategic grasp. I was looking for evidence, both from this question and from their responses to other questions, that they grasped the agenda.

Adaptation

Looking to the specifics, what about adaptation to climate impacts? The situation is clearly generally poor. Work by experts in the UK, in 2003, found that there is a significant risk of building collapse with consequent loss of life and yet that climate adaptation hardly featured on the corporate agenda in the construction sector, neither among clients nor among building contractors. My own work in the construction sector, carried out in parallel at the same time, came to exactly the same conclusion: the importance of climate impacts is very rarely recognised.[27]

The 20 businesses that I looked at were hardly any better, with eleven of them not even mentioning climate impacts as a potential risk. These included DuPont, despite its substantial interests, for instance, in building design and construction. DuPont's Chairman and CEO, Chad Holliday, said, in 2005, that he 'believes that there is a need for prudent action'.[28] While his speech is impressive on the mitigation side, the climate change adaptation agenda does not get a mention.

Norwegian energy company Statoil did not mention the impact agenda, despite vital facilities such as its Mongstad and Kalundborg refineries being near sea-level and therefore potentially vulnerable to flooding. Neither did food retailer Tesco, despite likely massive climate impacts on the production and distribution of food. Metals company Alcoa, despite its statement that 'the issue is serious and that urgent action is required now', did not see the need to assess the risks to its own facilities, many of which are near rivers.

Only nine of the 20 mentioned impacts. At the better end, British Telecom and National Grid Transco obviously had at least some grasp of the operational implications, particularly of wind on cable networks. However, most of the nine mentioned adaptation to impacts only superficially, often parking the issue in the 'too hard' tray. For instance, Barclays mentioned that 'the challenge of climate change is to interpret the impact on the whole range of businesses we support', but there is no sign that it has actually done so, beyond the most general levels. And yet a bank's assets are secured by the future asset values of the businesses in which they invest. Those by a river are obviously less secure in terms of asset values than those in a spot secluded from the wind on higher ground. Bankers Citigroup do appear to grasp the generic risks but not to have worked through the detail.

In the metals sector, the 'potential impacts of actual changes in the climate on Alcan's business have not been quantified and without better information on the likely local impacts of changed weather it would be very difficult to do so'. This is highly questionable: making sense of uncertain futures is exactly what scenario planning was created to address and in any event one can reasonably easily assess a plant's or product line's exposure to known risks such as flooding, water shortages and high wind without necessarily having the whole picture. Bayer of Germany recognises that there will be risks and opportunities but does not analyse them.

Mitigation

So the strategic grasp of the adaptation agenda appears weak, even for these leading companies. On the face of it, the picture on reduction of carbon emissions is much better: all 20 businesses had quantified carbon emissions to at least some extent.

Indeed a few clearly grasp that this is a strategic issue. Four businesses stand out in particular. German company Bayer 'is working on the assumption that the requirements for reducing greenhouse gas emissions will be tightened even further' and aims to lower emissions by 50 per cent from 1990 levels, by 2010. DuPont had reduced its CO_2 emissions by 72 per cent from 1990 levels by 2003, and is clearly planning for a radical change in energy use by business. British Telecom has a similarly impressive record, 'actively pursuing emissions reductions strategies' including much greater production and use of renewables. Statoil is 'preparing for a carbon-constrained economy and is engaging in the development of non-fossil energy sources and carriers. ... climate change strategy is an integral part of our business strategy'.

Three other businesses, all heavily dependent on energy, are showing encouraging signs of assessing the strategic agenda. Aluminium manufacturer Alcoa states that it sees the importance of climate change, had achieved a reduction of over 25 per cent from 1990 levels by 2003, and plans to maintain this despite planning a 40 per cent increase in production by 2010. Toyota also recognises that the marketplace is changing and commits to become a 'leader and driving force'. Mining company Anglo-American recently surveyed the significant risks and opportunities that it acknowledges will face it in a carbon-constrained world. While most surely have far to go, at least these companies seem to recognise that this is a major issue.

However although mitigation is to some extent on each of the remaining 13 companies' agendas, even here the lack of strategic grip is usually only too apparent. Food retailer Tesco, for instance, has clearly taken a number of steps to help reduce incidental energy use, setting up travel clubs for staff, and trying to make use of space on empty lorries. But the food sector is the third biggest energy user in the UK economy, with supermarket refrigeration alone accounting for a whopping 5 per cent of UK electrical energy consumption. This means that Tesco faces major strategic challenges if the 40 per cent (or less) UK carbon economy becomes a reality.[29] There is not a hint of this in its response to CDP's questions.

National Grid Transco has achieved good reductions, but the implications for its transmission networks of the various options for low carbon electricity generation is not mentioned either as risk or opportunity. Alcan sees the risks to its business model as being increased costs (aluminium is one of the most energy intensive of all sectors) but its targets for reduction are modest and the more fundamental question of how it might gain access to the energy that its current business model takes for granted in a significantly carbon-constrained world is not discussed. Neither bankers Citigroup nor Barclays seem to recognise that the profitability of the businesses and projects in which they invest will be significantly impacted by the move to a much lower carbon economy. And so on.

CONCLUSIONS: MOSTLY MISSING THE POINT

It is good to acknowledge that at least some businesses do seem to get the plot and appear to be engaging with the issue in a thought-through way. British Telecom appears to have a grasp of both the adaptation and mitigation agendas. Others, particularly DuPont, Bayer and Statoil, grasp the mitigation agenda. National Grid Transco seems to understand the adaptation agenda reasonably well. There is good practice on one or the other dimension in some of the other 15 businesses, including, but not limited to, those mentioned above.

However, the analysis clearly shows that most companies, even at this level, do not really recognise that 'business as usual' is not a dish that is on the strategic menu any longer. If any companies 'get it', these 20 surely should. But the majority are still framing the issue in a vaguely corporate-socially responsible way and do not see the issue in its strategic gravity. While they are all applying the sound management techniques introduced after the Rio convention – they routinely measure, report, have management systems, engage with communities, have board level sponsorship, and so on – even these practices, far ahead of many, do not seem to help them grapple with an issue of this magnitude and urgency. Indeed, it may be that these processes do not help at all, but rather hinder, insofar as they might give the illusion of control and of adequately engaging with the tremendous challenges that we face. Both adaptation and mitigation have the potential to stop the economic show; neither can be seen as optional, but few companies seem really to grasp this, with grasp of the adaptation agenda being particularly weak.

Japanese office equipment supplier Ricoh puts it bluntly: 'We do not think that climate change represents commercial risks in terms of business activities.' Unfortunately, Ricoh's analysis ignores the vulnerability of its operations to impacts altogether. While no doubt competent in its operations, the company positions carbon reductions as being attractive to customers, rather than as a survival necessity, but makes no effort to prove the point.

The broader business community

If this is the position of 20 of the world's leading companies, what of the mainstream business community? While the UK's Confederation of British Industry (CBI) published statements in 2005 supporting the national target of 60 per cent carbon reductions, the emphasis of its comments is towards security of energy supply, avoidance of cost penalties and of what it regards as over-regulation. The tone is of supporting the general good rather than focusing the government's attention on what it regards as a major and pressing strategic priority. It argues that the business community is a relatively low direct emitter of carbon.[30] Its evidence to the UK's Stern Committee on climate change economics at around the same time barely mentions the cost of climate change adaptation, and when it does mention climate impacts it does so in terms of the highly questionable potential benefits rather than the considerable costs.

Putting this in context: broader public grasp of climate change

This should not surprise us too much. Businesses are made up of ordinary people, and the vast majority of the population, in the UK at least, would perform just as badly – indeed probably much worse. While almost everyone has heard of climate change, 85 per cent think it is happening and 71 per cent think that humans are causing it, only around 15 per cent see it as a pressing danger that needs to be dealt with now, by our generation (2001 figures).[31] Putting it this way, it is clear that businesses can usefully be seen as made up of people who are broadly like the rest of us.

Implication: the business sector is not yet ready to lead

The implications are obvious. We cannot rely on the business community to lead transformation, even to be able to offer meaningful advice to government or each other, if their understanding of the agenda is as limited as it appears to be. Stakeholder-led processes are unlikely to work if the stakeholders do not grasp the agenda, even at the very top of the tree. Do not expect businesses to drive change down supply chains if even those at the top do not really understand what is going on. Beware of advice from business leaders unless you are sure that they are among the few who have grasped what is going on. When speaking to members of the business community never take their understanding for granted. For they are no other than the ordinary person in the street.

The as-yet unrealised potential of the business community

While this analysis should dispel any fond delusions that the business community yet has the capacity to lead responses, I still believe that it is potentially a great place for change agents to work on the climate change agenda. The transition to a low carbon economy surely cannot happen without business people. And their support may be closer than previously. For instance, in June 2006, as part of a wider consortium, Tesco did approach the UK Prime Minister Tony Blair, suggesting seven areas for government action on climate change.[32]

A later chapter in this volume, by Susan Ballard and myself, presents a research-based summary of what we see as the vital elements of human change in response to climate change. The notion of 'agency' or the ability to do something personally meaningful in response to what is a massive, overwhelming agenda is key. We argue that how people define 'agency' changes as they engage more fully with the agenda. Early in the engagement process, agency is defined in terms of meeting other objectives that an individual sees as meaningful, whether this be increasing sales or reducing costs, gaining a knighthood for good works, protecting one's investment or maintaining services to the community (such as hospital or education services) about which one cares deeply.

As a person's engagement deepens, with consequent increases in awareness, 'agency' (doing what is personally meaningful) is increasingly defined in terms of making an appreciable impact on the issue of climate change itself. But however it is defined, without a sense of 'agency', of being able to engage in a way that they find personally meaningful, people will not engage.[33]

There are very good reasons why 'agency' interpreted in both ways is unusually present in the business community. At the entry level the adaptation agenda potentially provides a clear set of easy-to-understand challenges to the bottom line and to services. Steve Rayner, Professor of Science and Society at Oxford University and a sociologist who has written extensively on environmental issues, explained this to me when I met him in 2002: if you are responsible for a new project – say a new hospital or a new factory – it is relatively easy to assess risks of flooding, of high winds, driving rain, and the like. If these issues are thought through, they can usually be addressed, at least for the lifetime of the building. This means that services can be provided, investment values don't collapse, profits can be maintained. This offers very clear agency at the entry level.

If you are a hospital administrator and are building a hospital with potential climate risks, you will probably only encounter this agenda once in your career but if you work in business, for instance, in the construction sector, you encounter it again and again. Not only can your own climate risks be reduced but it is also possible to help your client organisations, as a commercial service, to recognise them and address them. This means that the business community can potentially create the conditions for deeper change.

To focus on adaptation runs the risk, of course, that people might become complacent, that they might ignore the need for mitigation, but Steve Rayner argued, and my experience in working with his advice has been consistent, that the opposite can also be true if the process is well designed and supported. As people explore what climate change might mean for an investment, they improve their understanding of its broader implications. They find that they have some albeit limited agency, that they can do something meaningful in response. That potentially opens the floodgates of awareness – and these are hard to close again. As engagement deepens, the search for agency can easily shift to the mitigation agenda. My own experience supports Steve Rayner's conclusions.

At this deeper level of mitigation agency, there is a difficulty: if total carbon emissions were 7.2 billion tonnes in 2004 (figures from Vital Signs 2005), and if emissions from an economy such as the UK's were only around 2 per cent of that figure, how can any single project offer meaningful reductions? The search for agency on climate change itself is much more daunting; significant scale is needed and this needs a multiplier effect from change initiatives.

Here again the business world offers significant possibilities for agency and, therefore, for change. It is a paradoxical truth that it is just when the largest damage is possible that the greatest possibility to do something meaningful in response to climate change can be found. Engineers can already design and build structures with very low carbon footprints indeed: the Velux company's UK headquarters in Kettering, for instance, was built with around 20 per cent of the carbon footprint of a typical building, was built quickly and more cheaply than a typical design and has very high occupancy satisfaction measured in terms of absenteeism.[34]

The change agent who works in business is in a potentially key role, able to bring these options to the scoping discussions at the framing of the project and to do so over and over again. Such projects are not just potentially meaningful in terms of the direct carbon savings but can also offer the taste of agency and of association with other people to a wide stakeholder group.[35] If supported in action through a difficult transition, the people involved in such processes often become champions who work to limit and reverse climate change. In time – and it takes time, for this is a complex agenda – some of these champions will gain the depth of understanding that will enable them to become truly effective. This implies that the process of major investment can potentially act as the crucible of much wider social change.

This is a credible strategy for social change, and the business community could be central to it. And yet the analysis earlier in the chapter suggests that the number of business people who have the capacity to lead such processes remains very small.

How might this potential be realised, how might this hypothesis be tested? Due diligence and risk management processes during the investment process may be the way in, with the financial sector being key. If the Barclays and the Citigroups of this world are exposed to unassessed risks, but basically understand how to investigate risk and manage it, then this is potentially a rewarding place for change agents to focus attention. Let them ask their clients whether they have assessed climate risks and whether they have managed them; let them ask searching questions about companies' resilience to a low carbon economy and call for this capacity to be enhanced as a condition of investment. Let the wider change community in the governmental sector, in NGOs, in education, and more widely, focus awareness efforts particularly on such moments when action is easy, working with the pragmatism of the business community rather than against business people.

NOTES

1. UK Department of Trade and Industry Energy Consumption Tables, Table 1.4: Final energy consumption by final user (1) 1970 to 2005, http://www.dti.gov.uk/energy/statistics/publications/energy-consumption/overall-tables/page17954.html
2. Robert F. Kennedy Jr, *Crimes Against Nature*, London: Penguin, 2004.
3. See Nick Mayhew, 'Fading to grey: the use and abuse of corporate executives' "representational power"', in R. Wellford, ed., *Hijacking Environmentalism: Corporate Responses to Sustainable Development*, London: Earthscan, 1997, pp. 63–95.
4. www.ceres.org. Ceres is a national network of investment funds, environmental organisations and other public interest groups working to advance environmental stewardship on the part of businesses.
5. More on level-two change can be found in Chris Argyris and Donald A. Schön, *Organisational Learning II: Theory, Method and Practice*, Reading, MA: Addison Wesley, 1995.
6. The number of cars on the UK's roads increased by 68 per cent from 1980 to 32 million in 2004, with the rise being steady throughout, apart from a brief period of stability during the early 1990s. This shows that even more than a century after the first cars came onto the UK market, end-

of-life withdrawals from the car population are still below the number of new cars being produced each year. See Department of Transport, UK, 'Transport Trends', 2005 edition, p. 13.

7. Malcolm Slesser and Jane King, *Not by Money Alone: Economics as Nature Intended*, Charlbury: Jon Carpenter Books, 2002, p. 64 and Appendix 2.

8. *International Energy Outlook* 2002, quoted in *Vital Signs 2003–2004*, Worldwatch Institute, p. 34.

9. James Howard Kunstler, *The Long Emergency*, Atlantic Books: London, 2005, p. 46.

10. See the UK Government's Stern Review of the Economics of Climate Change, 2006 discussion paper, 'What is the Economics of Climate Change?' and associated technical annex for a good overview of climate change and of its economic impact, at http://www.hmtreasury.gov.uk/independent_reviews/stern_review_economics_climate_change/sternreview_index.cfm. A critique by Ian Byatt and others which summarises some of the most common sceptical arguments is also available on this site, as is Sir Nicholas Stern's crisp response. The overwhelming extent of the scientific consensus is summarised in Naomi Oreskes, 'The Scientific Consensus on Climate Change, *Science*, 306, 3 December 2004, p. 1686.

11. This work is co-ordinated by the government-funded UK Climate Impacts Programme, http://www.ukcip.org.uk

12. See Chris H. Sanders and M.C. Phillipson, 'UK adaptation strategy and technical measures: the impact of climate change on buildings', *Building Research and Information,* Special Edition, July 2003, for detailed assessment on the likely impact of climate change on UK buildings.

13. Sir David King, UK Government Chief Scientific Adviser, speaking at the Greenpeace Business Lecture, 2004. Available on http://www.greenpeace.org.uk/contentlookup.cfm?CFID=5264391&CFTOKEN=79794930&ucid param=20041013100519 with slides available from http://www.ost.gov.uk/about_ost/csa.htm

14. See Michael Grubb, 'The climate change challenge: scientific evidence and implications', The Carbon Trust, 2005, p. 17, which summarises the IPCC view on future scenarios. Available on http://www.carbontrust.co.uk/publications/publicationdetail?productid=CTC502

15. Talk by the proprietor of the Camel Valley vineyard, Cornwall, UK, August 2005.

16. D. McEvoy et al., 'Climate change and the visitor economy: challenges and opportunities for England's Northwest'. Sustainability Northwest (Manchester) and UKCIP (Oxford), 2006, http://www.snw.org.uk/tourism/downloads/CCVE_challenges_And_Opportunities.pdf

17. Douglas G. Cogan, 'Corporate governance and climate change: making the connection', 2006. Available on http://www.ceres.org/pub/

18. Response available on http://www.cdproject.net/response_list.asp?id=3&letter=M

19. Data from *Vital Signs 2005*, p. 51. Total losses, including those uninsured, were the second highest ever at almost US$105 billion.

20. Carbon Trust report on Business and Climate Change, http://www.carbontrust.co.uk/Publications/

21. 'Energy: the changing climate', Royal Commission on Environmental Pollution, 22nd Report (2000), Available on http://www.rcep.org.uk/newenergy.htm

22. See findings of the UK's Met Office, international scientific conference, Exeter, February 2005, available on http://www.defra.gov.uk/environment/climatechange/internat/dangerous-cc.htm

23. See http://www.tyndall.ac.uk/media/news/tyndall_decarbonising_the_uk.pdf

24. Slesser and King, *Not by Money Alone*, especially chapter 10.

25. Research published in Dexter Dunphy et al., *Organisational Change for Corporate Sustainability*, London: Routledge, 2003.

26. See http://www.strategy.gov.uk/downloads/survivalguide/skills/s_pestle.htm for further explanation.

27. See Sanders and Phillipson, 'UK Adaptation Strategy'. Also D.I. Ballard, 'Using learning processes to promote change for sustainable development', *Action Research*, 3(2) 2005, pp. 135–56.

28. http://ap.stop.dupont.com/Media_Center/en_US/speeches/holliday_09_17_05.html

29. Estimate by Doug Marriott, UK retail energy expert, details from MarriottUK@aol.com

30. 'Powering the future: enabling the UK energy market to deliver', CBI, November 2005, http://www.cbi.org.uk/pdf/energybriefnov05.pdf

31. Defra, 'Survey of Public Attitudes to Quality of Life and to the Environment', Department of the Environment, Food and Rural Affairs, London, 2001.

32. See letter from the Corporate Leaders Group on Climate Change, available at http://www.cpi.cam.ac.uk/bep/clgcc/downloads/pressrelease_2006.pdf. Note that this letter concentrates entirely on the mitigation agenda, misses most of the macro-economic risks and does not mention the adaptation agenda at all.

33. This has been observed by many researchers. The best summary of the argument is perhaps given in P. Macnaghten, R. Grove-White, M. Jacobs and B. Wynne, *Public Perceptions and Sustainability in Lancashire*, Lancaster: Lancashire County Council, 1995.

34. The performance data were given by Preben Gramstrup, Head of Group Facility Management at VKR Holding A/S (Velux's parent company) in a presentation at the University of Bath in December 2003. Further information on this innovative project may be obtained from the *RIBA Journal*, April 2002 and in the *Architects Journal*, May 2002.

35. The Awareness, Agency and Association-based model of change is summarised in this volume in Susan and David Ballard, 'Clearing the Pathways to Transformation', and in D.I. Ballard, 'Using Learning Processes'.

7
The Mass Media, Climate Change, and How Things Might Be

John Theobald and Marianne McKiggan

The corporate mass media are, predominantly, still presenting human-induced climate change as a basic argument between 'believers' and 'unbelievers'. The debate is stalled at square one. Experts present media consumers with contradictory statistics and projections. The impression is conveyed of a complex scientific issue, beyond ordinary people.

While some experts are reported as telling us that the planet is past the point of no return, and that nothing can be done, others are portrayed as split between 'technical fixers' and 'primitives'. Technical fixers maintain that science will come up with the answers in the context of 'business as usual'. Primitives are presented as advocates of windmills and abolishing cheap air travel. In the UK, the government and mainstream media are using climate change as an argument for resurrecting nuclear energy, and as a factor in military planning for the future: 'In a grim first intervention in the climate-change debate, the Defence Secretary issued a bleak forecast that violence and political conflict would become more likely in the next 20–30 years as climate change turned land into desert, melted ice fields and poisoned water supplies.'[1]

The mass media give space to the issues, but frame them in such a way as to paralyse consumers. We have the freedom of choice as to why we do nothing. We may sink into depression induced by doom-filled prophecy. We may just 'leave it to the experts'. We may feel repelled by a new parsimonious lifestyle. Or at best we may indulge in small-scale individual actions like cycling to work and recycling our rubbish, which will massage our consciences, but seem insignificant compared with the size of the problem.

No wonder most of us dismiss the subject and get on with the more pressing business of work, consumption and distraction. After all, especially for the UK, visions evoked in the media of sun-drenched beaches, flamingos on our riverbanks and vineyards on our hillsides in a globally warmed world seem quite attractive. If, as a result of climate change, our green and pleasant land can become agreeably warmer and drier, do we have to concern ourselves with flooding, desertification and consequent mass death and disease elsewhere? What is more, robust defenders of the mainstream media argue, the complainers protest too much. Clearly the media *have* now launched a massive public debate. There is a huge increase in public awareness of climate change. The mass media are precisely fulfilling their appointed function in democratic societies, informing the public in an accessible way of all sides of a complex issue.

In the US, climate sceptics – those with interests in the maintenance of the status quo and thus denying the climate crisis – continue their campaign to discredit climate science, and 'professional journalism' practices of both newspapers and wire services facilitate these efforts.[2] For example in the US prestige press, adherence to 'balance' has been found to result in systematic bias and confusion in research into climate coverage.[3] The mass media tend to present the issue in terms of 'controversial science' with the depth of the scientific consensus rarely articulated, or in terms of political conflict. Understandings of links between extreme weather events – a notable example being Hurricane Katrina which devastated New Orleans in August 2005 – and climate change are seldom presented. Where they are, uncertainty or scientific dispute are emphasised.[4] In mid 2006, the release of Al Gore's film and book *An Inconvenient Truth*, a documentary on climate change, produced a flurry of US press coverage, much of which focused on political conflict: Gore 'lays out basic facts ignored by blinkered government' whilst 'Bush has been silent on the link between oil and global warming'.[5] US commentators may look to the UK and Europe for better climate coverage, but the mainstream media are everywhere constrained by the same corporate interests.

So what *is* happening? The first part of this chapter demonstrates how the news media are actually behaving, and why. It bases its findings on an analysis of UK mass media coverage of a pivotal event in the UK, in early 2005, the scientific conference *Stabilisation 2005: Avoiding Dangerous Climate Change*. Drawing on this, the second part of the chapter speculates on how, in a more truthful and democratic media context, significant public sphere debate and decisive activity on climate change might develop.

'AVOIDING DANGEROUS CLIMATE CHANGE' IN THE MASS MEDIA

A three-day 'international symposium on the stabilisation of greenhouse gases', *Stabilisation 2005*, was held in Exeter, UK, in February 2005. Called by British Prime Minister Tony Blair, to coincide with the UK government's 2005 G8 and EU presidencies, it took its cue from Article 2 of the United Nations Framework Convention on Climate Change which set out its ultimate objective as the 'stabilisation of greenhouse gas concentrations in the atmosphere at a level that would prevent dangerous anthropogenic interference with the climate system'.[6] The conference, attended by more than 200 participants, mainly scientists, from 30 countries,

discussed the long-term implications of different levels of climate change for different sectors and the world as a whole. Major themes included key vulnerabilities of the climate system and climate thresholds, socio-economic effects, both globally and regionally, emissions pathways to climate stabilisation and technological options available to achieve stabilisation levels.[7]

The conference established that since the Intergovernmental Panel on Climate Change (IPCC) last reported in 2001, there is now 'greater clarity and reduced uncertainty about the impacts of climate change' and that 'in many cases the risks are more serious than previously thought'. 'Impacts of climate change are already being observed' and 'serious risk of large scale, irreversible system disruption' is more likely above a 3 degree Celsius increase, which is 'well within the range of climate change projections for the century'.[8] Dominant themes picked up on in the media coverage were the 'potentially disturbing' 'new impacts' identified at the conference,[9] impacts on the Antarctic, the Gulf Stream and ocean acidification, whilst coverage of options for stabilisation centred on technological fixes.

The press: from sceptics, to inevitable doom, to salvation by technology

During the week of the conference, UK national newspapers produced 139 articles mentioning 'climate change' or 'global warming' (http://web.lexis-nexis.com/professional/ Search: January 31–February 6, 2005). Thirty-four of these were directly linked to the conference. Of these, the left-liberal up-market press carried the most articles; eight each in the *Independent* and *Guardian*, whilst the right-wing *Financial Times*, *Daily Telegraph* and *The Times* produced five, four and two articles respectively. Mid and down-market titles included one article each in the *Mirror* and *Daily Mail*, and three in the *Express*, including a diatribe against the scientific consensus from renowned climate contrarian, David Bellamy.[10]

Headlines in the *Daily Telegraph*, *Guardian* and *Independent* demonstrate the media's tendency to frame climate change as an environmental story, devoid of human agency or suffering, as if humans are not part of nature. 'Polar bears "already doomed" by pollution in the air',[11] 'Hotter world may freeze Britain: fifty-fifty chance the Gulf Stream may be halted',[12] 'Dramatic change in West Antarctic ice could produce 16ft rise in sea levels'[13] and 'Scientists warn growing acidity of oceans will kill reefs, and fish suppers will be just jellyfish and chips'.[14] What are we to make of these pronouncements? 'Already doomed' means it is too late to do anything, whilst 'pollution in the air' sounds as though it is some other factor, discrete from climate change, afflicting the bears. That global warming 'may' freeze Britain or 'could' lead to a dramatic increase in sea-level signifies uncertainty. How are readers to discern the risks? The final headline implies that ocean acidification is only being 'warned' about by scientists, whilst 'jellyfish and chips' quotes Carol Turley who presented the findings on ocean acidification at the conference. The phrase was cited in a number of press articles and served to trivialise grave findings: 'In cartoon form, you could say that people should change their tastes from cod and chips to jellyfish and chips.'[15] Thus victims of the climate crisis are, in media coverage, limited to cod, coral and polar bears.

Beyond the headlines these titles largely framed the conference outcomes as 'valid science',[16] providing a degree of explanation of the findings. There were no overtly sceptical articles such as that in the *Express*, yet discussion of scepticism and uncertainty was pervasive. The *Guardian* stated: 'Although most of the scientists at the conference believed that climate change was a risk to the welfare of the human race and the natural world [an economic adviser to Russian President Putin] refused to accept that current warming was any more than a variation in the natural climate.'[17] The article's author, Paul Brown, made no attempt to disqualify this opinion for the fabrication that it is.[18] By saying 'most scientists', he puts the economist in the same category as climate scientists, and 'believed' suggests that some act of faith is required. Doubt is emphasised by phrases such as: 'Of course, the scientists cannot be certain that signs of melting they now see [in the West Antarctic ice sheet] are not an aberration', and by stating that the findings add to the 'growing litany of scare stories',[19] as if all this was merely a 'scare story'. Whilst small paragraphs at the end of otherwise valid science-framed articles may at first seem inconsequential, *en masse* the result is to mislead, undermine the science and reinforce mythical ideas leading to inaction.

Reflecting dominant elite discourses, not least those of the conference organisers, media coverage centred on technological fixes in discussing what could be done about climate change. For example: 'A new generation of safe nuclear power plants and coal-fired stations that capture their carbon emissions could solve the problem of global warming, Prof. Sir David King, the Government's chief scientist, said yesterday.'[20] Carbon capture and storage, politically popular and hailed as a solution that will allow business as usual, ranked amongst the most widely cited 'solutions' even though, as King pointed out, 'None of us know whether carbon sequestration is feasible', and tellingly went on 'but if it is, it is a way of using coal reserves all over the world'.[21] There was no questioning of nuclear safety. The solutions offered evade challenges to levels of consumption or economic growth. Of the articles on the conference, none mentioned 'Contraction and Convergence' or 'behaviour change'. This confirms Anabela Carvalho's finding that 'the "quality" press's analysis of the governance of climate change remained within the broad ideological parameters of free-market capitalism and neo-liberalism'.[22]

The predominant tone was to present climate change as inescapable, for example: '"I believe that most of the warming we are expecting over the next few decades is now virtually inevitable, and even in this time frame we may expect a significant impact", [UK Environment Secretary] Margaret Beckett said'.[23] Implicit in this text is that severe global destruction is now unavoidable. This leads to a sense of despair, ultimately engendering passivity. In reality, whilst emissions past and present mean that some warming is indeed 'inevitable', a lot can be done to prevent the magnitude of future devastation as projected on the basis of continuing business as usual.

Of the UK national newspapers, the *Independent* provides the most prominent climate coverage, engaging readers during March 2006 in a climate change debate, 'Your World. Your Say'.[24] Yet despite an increasing sense of urgency, and a questioning of 'business as usual', the framing and content confirm that it has still not moved past the first base of 'debate'. Similarly, analysis of its performance on the 2005 conference suggests that, while it went further than other titles, fundamental issues, notably any critique of society's blind faith in growth, remained absent. Nevertheless, the most comprehensive article on the outcomes of the conference, 'Apocalypse now: How mankind is sleepwalking to the end of the earth', was published in the *Independent on Sunday*, in which Geoffrey Lean catalogued impacts, pointed to action which could be taken, and was critical of the UK government's position.[25]

An *Independent* comment piece was the only article published during the conference that linked corporate lobbying to climate sceptics:

There is legitimate dispute about the extent of climate change, but – as one climatologist told me off the record – 'find me a scientist who denies the link between the actions of man and the changes in the climate, and I'll find you money from the oil, gas and energy companies'.[26]

These articles are exceptions to the rule and on the whole 'there are few serious attempts to explore the identity and motives of corporate opponents to action on climate change, or to draw attention to the true significance of their folly'.[27] The UK government's position is often presented as benign, trying to get the USA on side. Another common frame includes 'the problem of developing world growth' while virtually excluding critique of domestic policies on energy, transport, aviation, or the UK's motivation for waging war in Iraq and other resource wars.

Broadcasting: the BBC's Radio 4 *Today* programme, setting complacency on the agenda

On Monday we were told temperatures throughout the year would be rising by 11 degrees, on Tuesday the warning was of a mini ice-age as the Gulf Stream reversed, even that couldn't save the polar bears that were doomed on Wednesday, and by Thursday all aquatic life was in trouble as the oceans turned to acid.

Those have been the dire predictions from climate scientists who have been meeting in Exeter this week, and vying with each other to come up with the scariest forecasts. But behind all the hype there was some serious science, and some serious questions about how long we can continue to churn out carbon dioxide and other greenhouse gases.[28]

This was the opening to a summary of the conference as presented by BBC Radio 4's influential current affairs programme *Today*. From the outset, the 'On Monday ... on Tuesday' structure suggests constant self-contradiction and that each proposition is unrelated to the preceding ones, whilst reference to polar bears and aquatic life detracts from both human agency and impacts on humans. It discredits climate scientists' findings, suggesting that the science is unreliable. Whilst the text goes on to mention 'dire' predictions, they are undermined both by the previous sentence and by the context that scientists are 'vying with each other to come up with the scariest forecasts'. There were only *some* serious questions' and *some* serious science', the rest being 'hype'. What are listeners to make of this? That we should not concern ourselves with this 'hype', that only polar bears and aquatic life will be affected? The fact that dreadful consequences are already underway goes unmentioned. The scientists were not engaged in some sort of scariness competition, but presented wide-ranging evidence on the consequences of human-induced climate change. Outcomes were deeply worrying, with discussions of increased drought, hunger, rising sea-levels, population displacement, species extinctions and the collapse of crucial ecosystems.

This opening sabotaged the conference overview that followed and an interview with former IPCC chair, Sir John Houghton. He said that 150 million extra refugees from rising sea-levels, floods and droughts by 2050 was a 'fairly conservative' estimate, that this would cause insecurity and human misery, and that the 'urgency to act now is really very strong'.[29] The overall impact of the BBC's quizzical tone is a concentration on scientific uncertainty and questionable futures, detracting from impacts that are already underway.

During 1–5 February, 14 hours of *Today* programme broadcasting, climate change and the conference were given 33 minutes of airtime over three days – scant attention considering it opened the issue by quoting Sir David King and Tony Blair on the severity of the problem: 'a greater threat than terrorism' and 'an enormous threat to civilisation' respectively.[30]

In an example of the BBC's penchant for artificially 'balancing' its coverage by inviting industry-funded sceptics to comment, a three-way debate was set up between left and right think-tank representatives and a Liberal Democrat environment spokesperson. Julian Morris, director of the free market think-tank the International Policy Network, was introduced as such but listeners were not made aware of the Network's agenda or funding. In 2004 it received $115,000 from ExxonMobil and published a report claiming that climate change was a 'myth'.[31] Sceptics' interests are rarely made explicit.

Throughout the week *Today* presented findings from the conference, an item on domestic energy efficiency, discussions and interviews; yet still, as the opener to Saturday's programme highlighted, it repeatedly cast doubt on the ever increasing body of research which concludes that climate change must be taken seriously and acted upon.

Broadcasting: television news lets out a barely audible growl

The worst disasters ... happen on time scales that defy television's relentless dailiness ... The only points of entry for the story are heat waves and new scientific studies, and so this behemoth of stories pops up from time to time and lets out a growl. But we need to hear it roar.[32]

During February 2005, a period which included the coming into force of the Kyoto Protocol, the publicly funded BBC1's *Six O'Clock News* and commercial station Channel 4's News at 7 p.m. dedicated just 1.33 and 2.45 per cent of total airtime respectively to climate change. During the conference neither programme devoted their top stories to it. Instead, both led with items on terror suspects, incapacity benefit, migrant labour and high-profile court cases.

BBC 1's *Six O'Clock News*, the UK's most popular news programme, presented no coverage of the conference. Instead, one item, a three-minute 'special report' on ocean acidification, was shown but not explicitly linked to the conference and narrowly framed the issue as a 'threat to coral reefs' story with no mention of fundamental connections to climate change.[33] In this instance BBC News clearly failed to live up to its self-proclaimed aim 'to provide access to the information and ideas everyone needs to make sense of an increasingly complex world, providing background and context to the news'.[34]

Channel 4 News did at least cover the conference on two consecutive days. The first item presented the conference's aims, emphasising that scientists have provided the information policy makers need to act on. However, the report exaggerated the divergences and downplayed the consensus. Describing scientific uncertainty surrounding the stability of the thermohaline conveyor, the correspondent stated:

It is an obvious contradiction that typifies why it is so hard for scientists to conclude what the risks of climate change are. This current lack of consensus leaves them open to criticism. Just last week saw a meeting in London of scientists sceptical of climate change predictions to pre-empt today's summit. They attempt to blow holes in theories like those on sea-level rise.[35]

Informed viewers will have identified attendees of the Scientific Alliance meeting as a handful of sceptics notorious for their systematic obfuscation and links to corporate-funded think-tanks.[36] To most, however, the pictures showed a scientific event which looked as legitimate as the Exeter conference.

The following day Channel 4 presented an item on carbon capture and storage.[37] It did not question the problematic nature of the technology, presented as enabling more oil or gas to be extracted from current North Sea reserves. This was doubtless because it explained the technology using a 'promotional video', identified on screen as such, from Statoil, a Norwegian oil company.

Following the conference, the *Independent*'s environment editor, Michael McCarthy, wrote in the Catholic newspaper *The Tablet* that the conference findings were more serious than previously thought. After highlighting World Energy Outlook predictions of a 62 per cent increase in global emissions over the next 25 years, he described a conversation with *Guardian* journalist Paul Brown on the way back to London from Exeter: '"The earth is finished." Paul said: "It is, Yes." ... And what will our children make of our generation, who let this planet, so lovingly created, go to waste?'[38]

We can only respond to this by noting that excessive consumption is blatantly encouraged by the papers that both he and Brown write for – stuffed full of advertising for airlines, cars, consumer goods, and corporate greenwash from oil companies. These newspapers and other mainstream media quite self-evidently contribute to the maintenance of a system that could indeed 'finish' the earth.

This snapshot supports previous critical analysis of media performance on climate change, such as that of Robert Babe who suggests that, despite 'smatterings of ecologically-sound reporting and opinion, by far the major thrust of the press is to promote hedonism and consumption'.[39] Structural, institutional and ideological constraints keep debate within the bounds of acceptable premises, through the selection of topics, distribution of concerns, framing of issues, emphasis and omission, resulting in systematic bias.[40] Notable omissions include the identification of responsible actors, those who benefit most from the maintenance of the status quo, serious consideration of impacts, and crucially, positive visions for alternate futures.

HOW THINGS MIGHT BE

An imagined positive future can only be achieved through the awareness of a majority of citizens that they should use their power – an easy dictum, rarely achieved. It is a concept that used to be known as 'democracy' before the mass media contorted the word into a synonym for willing passive conformity, or at best inconclusive chatter, within the safe spectrum of elite-approved ideas. Empowerment is the last thing that today's mass media intend to inspire in their consumers. Instead, critical citizens will have to defy mainstream media output, defining their needs and responsibilities through their own thought, and dialogue with the counter-currents of radical debate. A new wave of such activity is already swelling as solidarities emerge between the developing world and Western countercultures. Indeed this is occurring to a greater extent than the mainstream media would have us believe (for example, go to http://www.zmag.org, http://www.medialens.org, or http://www.fifth-estate-online.co.uk, and surf on from the links provided there). But it is still in the subculture, pulled forward by networks of activists and thinkers, and supported by a diverse multitude of sympathisers. Numbers increase with the urgency of the issues, but they are still a small minority.

Power elites can as yet adequately drown out new visions, whether by hegemonic control, propaganda, intimidation or force. The idea of subversion being successful can thus seem implausible. Termites are not aware when the tree they and their ancestors have spent their lives burrowing through alongside many unseen others will, despite an external appearance of solidity, disintegrate. To understand this, we only need to imagine ourselves back a generation and remember the *impossibility* of the collapse of the Soviet Bloc, let alone the rise of mass popular resistance to neo-liberalism and neo-conservatism. It can be argued credibly that one crucial reason for the collapse of the Soviet Union and its satellites was that most of their people had ceased to believe their media. Instead, they were following other agendas which led them into huge frustration and unquenchable desire to see their system and way of life overthrown or radically reformed. As we can observe today, they escaped the bonds of one kind of domination only to be invaded by another. Today's lesson from that is that, to be successful, positive popular visions of radical change need to be forged in great practical detail, and with robust popular solidarity to prevent their destruction by seductive, but unscrupulous, predators. We can see just such a struggle in today's Latin America where, for example, one means of resisting reactionary forces in Venezuela, Bolivia and Brazil is the setting up of alternative popular mass media structures, exemplified by the radical television station *Telesur*.

In the context of climate change politics in 'developed' countries, this chapter has already offered a critique of mainstream media practice. Such analysis rightly provokes the demand for a constructive alternative – even if today's mass media are structurally and ideologically incapable of providing it.

Explicit in the critique is the idea that a *genuine* fourth estate would *reject* what the current mass media are doing: blinding their publics with confusing data, false debates, despair-inducing reporting, depressing future scenarios, and pathetically inadequate notions for individual action – a package leading to virtual inactivity on the vital issues, and temptation to indulge while there is still time.

Functions that *radicalised, democratic* mass media have the potential to perform in an accurate and constructive coverage of climate change are envisaged here under three headings:

- Clear and constant naming and shaming of the human agents of dangerous climate change, setting out the implications of their present actions for future life and societies.
- Detailed development and dissemination of a positive philosophy and attractive images of sustainable lifestyles.
- Tracing a coherent set of linked actions, from the global to the personal, which develop equitable means of getting from where we are to where we want to be.

POINTING THE FINGER

It falls to alternative media outlets, principally the growing network of websites, to reveal the omissions and distractions in the mainstream. The Web is overtaking newspapers and challenging television as the main source of information, especially for the young in rich countries. It is also becoming available to many in parts of the world which previously had almost no access to printed or electronic information sources. It is still mostly a free space for genuine public sphere activity. As individuals joining virtual communities become increasingly aware through search engines, hyperlinks and messaging of where information can be found, so facts and updates about the human agents of climate change can traverse the world and reach millions in a few minutes. Instantaneous regional and global mobilisation is now a reality, where publics are tuned in and receptive, and not only the will, but also the hope for change are present. These are big prerequisites in a world with so many other passions and priorities, but it is a truism that the power of valid argument and information cannot operate if effective dissemination does not take place.

No one knows this better than the corporations responsible for dangerous climate change, and they have more resources to control media outlets and disseminate counter-information than a multitude of citizens' initiatives. Without doubt the greater the success in naming and shaming them, and publishing the consequences of their acts, the greater will be the tidal wave of greenwash, refutation and disinformation. History warns that just as power elites have taken over the press, radio and television, successively snuffing out ideas and initiatives for popular control and radical content, so the current window of relative Internet freedom will be progressively closed as power elites come to perceive it as a threat. The negative scenario is familiar and credible.

A more positive scenario is, however, there to be realised. History also reveals that publics *have* successfully turned on elites, and that seemingly robust structures *can*, given propitious conditions, collapse without violence or undergo radical reshaping in the face of overwhelming resistance. The naming and shaming process will thus not just consist of the spreading of information. This would be merely the catalyst for consciousness raising and campaigning activity. The more success these have, the greater will be the penetration of internal doubts, and conversions to alternative policies, into ever higher echelons of corporations and governments.

In this process, as the history of the collapse of empires, governments and socio-economic structures shows, the rot can quite suddenly be revealed as terminal. Loyal employees and experts emerge as long-term sceptics. It becomes for them more expedient to declare their opposition than to cling to the old corporate or party line. The same card-carriers, managers and technocrats who have spent half a career pursuing one goal will now work with equal energy towards a new one. In this scenario, yesterday's heresy and whistle-blowing quickly become today's dominant discourse and democratic response to a changed situation.

POSITIVE FUTURE IMAGES[41]

There will, however, be no sea change in public support without positive future images. Media bosses and their elite friends know well that doom scenarios, prospects of future deprivation and contradictory expert conclusions just cause collective mental traffic jams which ultimately preserve the status quo. People actually shift their goals when they glimpse a future which looks better than the present. The current climate change debate is failing to provide this.

Positive future visions do not need to assume publics which are self-interested in terms of class, wealth or geographical location, and prepared to ignore disaster for others as long as their own well-being is preserved. The existence of deep social and survival instincts across the planet make it possible to believe that people will work together for the fulfilment of a greater aim; and what greater aim can be imagined than the harmonious survival and development of the place that sustains our existence? At one level humans may wish, or be manipulated into protecting, local identities, vested interests and privileged lifestyles, but at a deeper level, they may also yearn for the growth of a popular planetary consciousness. It is simple to understand that the earth has finite resources which current human activity is despoiling in a way which cannot continue. It is elementary logic that we need, while there is time, to develop a relationship with our environment which balances resource use, recycling and regeneration, and creates a connected, self-sustaining perpetual process of life-respecting resource distribution. However, this does not have to convert into unexciting images of diminished lifestyles and thwarted aspirations.

Constructive media coverage of climate change would therefore clearly distinguish 'happiness' from 'consumerism'. It would reject the promotion of unsustainable pursuit of possessions, compensatory self-indulgence, and high-speed leisure travel as crude propaganda for surrogate utopias and relentlessly marketed individualistic fantasies, spinning dreams of satisfaction in the interests of corporate profits. It would set out instead alternative aspirations and lifestyles, well-known but less heard in the clamour for status-linked acquisition, reminding that respect, giving, interconnectedness, creativity and social action are better catalysts for happiness. It would demonstrate that a simpler, more reflective, lower-impact life is actually more enjoyable than one driven by the current stresses and inevitabilities which many find to be negative elements in their lives and provoke the appetite for escape. Such messages would be far less open to accusations of manipulation than the propaganda thrust on the public by current mass media practice.

To promote such a paradigm change would indeed be inconceivable for today's mass media, but the ideas sustaining it are already present as seeds in many minds. They are old thoughts which are being reformulated by contemporary thinkers in the constantly renewed search for meaning. Writers such as Fritjof Capra, David Suzuki and Vandana Shiva synthesise the ideas of many others in scientific, philosophical, ecological and religious thinking.[42] Their formulations involve a shift from macho exploitative individualist hedonism to a more feminised and networked integration of the individual with social consciousness and the natural environment. Capra's understanding, for example, using a Western appropriation of Taoist categories, is that the overstressed 'yang' of capitalist accumulation of surplus wealth requires a transformative balancing with the 'yin', which emphasises interdependency and sharing with others and the web of life.

From such culture-changing visions flow a whole set of perspectives which can filter through economic, social and political systems and into the lives of communities and individuals. It will be up to alternative media networks to broaden the dissemination process and the accompanying public debate and activity so that such ideas come to resonate with most people in the form of practicable, attractive life models. New media networks can be the channels for this paradigm change to permeate society. By this means practical consequences which appear as constraints or deprivations from the perspective of the lush uplands of current rich-world consumer lifestyles will re-emerge as normal aspects of sustainable living. Experience will show that overall the satisfactions and advantages of the new outlook outweigh any reduction of wasteful gadgets and objects of artificially aroused desire. Preventing dangerous climate change in this context will be an automatic priority, but it will also be an automatic effect.

SIGNPOSTING THE WAY

Speculative vistas are all very well, but making them real is an adventure, and if the mainstream media will not recognise the goal, they will not provide reliable guidance on reaching it. They will always, for example, prioritise technical fixes over reductions in consumption. Practical strategies and action plans such as Contraction and Convergence have great difficulty in obtaining serious consideration, let alone credence, in the mainstream media, since they do not fit corporate interests. The rehabilitation of nuclear energy receives voluminous coverage, unlike renewable energy which is belittled.

Ironically, the very market forces that maintain it may soon force the mainstream press into structural changes which will reduce its influence and profligacy. Given the long-term decline of newspaper circulation, significant reduction in the number of titles is foreseen, with the Web becoming an even more significant news source. This would be welcome, both in terms of democratic media development and in terms of sustainable economy. Beyond this, a genuinely free press – a press free from business, as Marx put it – would reduce its current wasteful paper consumption by at least 80 per cent and eliminate corporate control. Sensibly managed, the UK press, for example, could easily produce the same range of news and comment on important issues while reducing its number of titles by half and the number of pages in the remainder by 60 per cent. Given the expansion of the electronic media, there would be no loss of diversity, and greater opportunities for free expression and public sphere activity.

With the decline of print media, it will be increasingly for alternative media networks to take the opportunity to promote public debate on the means of making *real* progress away from the disastrous consequences of human-induced climate change. Although today the project is certainly underway, the sense of urgency is still only reaching a small minority.

Media independent of corporate interests, which gave attention to the issue of climate change that was proportionate to the scientific community's estimation of the primacy of the issue, could only turn their constant attention towards practical policies for real change. History shows that, for good or evil, when the media so wish, they can provide blanket coverage of a single dominant issue for weeks and months on end. No technique is neglected in the framing of the issue in such a way as to bring majority public opinion around to a particular desired standpoint. The mass media know how to do this, particularly when there is an issue deemed to be of overwhelming importance. Media behaviour in wartime is a clear example.[43] Where national survival is said to be at stake, the country is ceaselessly exhorted to put aside internal differences and pull together in the overriding cause. Government, industry, the workforce, the education system, voluntary groups and individual citizens are called upon to change lifestyles, accept extraordinary measures, endure hardship and pay the price for the struggle. Moreover, these calls are heeded. The two world wars of the twentieth century successfully required of societies and citizens on all sides of the conflicts immeasurably more in terms of 'sacrifice' than will be required to reverse human-induced climate change. In those two wars, hundreds of millions went to their deaths, were bereaved or permanently disabled – sacrifices proclaimed worthwhile for the conquering of an evil enemy and creation of a better world. The reversal of dangerous climate change is in fact of greater importance, since the viability of a life-sustaining planet is at stake, but the 'sacrifices' are, by comparison, small. The prospect is of saving and preserving life, not destroying it, and of a long-term sustainable future. From this perspective, a democratic media's task of explaining this to the public would be elementary compared with past extravaganzas of the unfree media.

CONCLUSION

Progressive, ecologically aware, alternative media are still very far from having the resources or reach of the mainstream media, and for them to achieve a comparable influence within a short time scale may seem unrealistic. After all, in many minds, climate change is just one issue clamouring for media and public attention in a world that is exploding with injustice, suffering, inequality, violent conflict, disease, disaster, corporate greed and resource wars.

The early part of this chapter demonstrated how the corporate mass media misrepresent the climate change issue, both framing it falsely and inducing public paralysis in the interests of corporate business as usual. The later part speculated on how democratic media might behave differently. In doing so, it has shown the depth of the abyss between where we are and where we would need to be to provoke an adequate response to the climate change crisis.

The alternative media are as yet only a fragile bridge between the two. They can give us hope, but, to paraphrase the Czech dissident of the 1980s and eventual Czech President, Václav Havel, hope is a dimension of the soul which does not depend on our analysis of the facts or our assessment of the situation. It is not the conviction that things will turn out all right in the end, but the conviction that the struggle has a purpose, whatever direction events take.

Havel's career reminds us that empires do end, systems do change and resistance does have an effect. We can also remind ourselves, when looking at current elite structures, of the mythical elephant which remained standing for ten days after it had been shot dead. The climate change issue may be the shot that kills the beast. It is up to us to prevent the mainstream media from keeping it standing beyond its demise.

NOTES

1. *Independent*, 28 February 2006, p. 2.
2. L. Antilla, 'Climate of scepticism: US newspaper coverage of the science of climate change', *Global Environmental Change*, 15, 2005, pp. 338–52.
3. M.T. Boykoff and J.M. Boykoff, 'Balance as bias: global warming and the US prestige press', *Global Environmental Change*, 14, 2004, pp. 125–36.
4. J. Schwartz, '2 studies link global warming to greater power of hurricanes', *New York Times*, 31 May 2006.
5. S. Mallaby, 'Al Gore's unlikely helpers', *Washington Post*, 22 May 2006.
6. United Nations Framework Convention on Climate Change, Full Text, 1992: http://unfccc.int/not_assigned/b/items/1417.php
7. D. Tirpak, J. Ashton, Z. Dadi, and others, 'Report of the International Scientific Steering Committee', May 2005, *Avoiding Dangerous Climate Change, February 1–3, 2005*, Exeter, UK Met Office: http://www. stabilisation2005.com/Steering_Commitee_Report.pdf
8. Ibid., pp. 5–6.
9. Ibid.
10. D. Bellamy, 'The global warming scaremongers are just full of hot air', *Express*, 3 February 2005.
11. C. Clover, 'Polar bears "already doomed" by pollution in the air', *Daily Telegraph*, 2 February 2005, p. 6.
12. P. Brown, 'Climate change: hotter world may freeze Britain: fifty-fifty chance the warm Gulf Stream may be halted', *Guardian*, 2 February 2005, p. 9.
13. M. McCarthy, 'Dramatic change in West Antarctic ice could produce 16ft rise in sea levels', *Independent*, 2 February 2005, p. 12.
14. P. Brown, 'Scientists warn that growing acidity of oceans will kill reefs, and fish suppers will be just jellyfish and chips', *Guardian*, 4 February 2005, p. 5.
15. C. Turley, cited in C. Clover, 'Acid seas "will kill off coral within 70 years"', *Daily Telegraph*, 4 February 2005, p. 6.
16. Antilla, 'Climate of scepticism'.
17. P. Brown, 'CO_2 gases may be buried at sea', *Guardian*, 3 February 2005, p. 2.
18. D. Wallace and J. Houghton, 'A guide to the facts and fictions about climate change', London: The Royal Society, 2005: http://www.royalsoc. ac.uk/downloaddoc.asp?id=1630
19. *Independent*, 'Icy warning', 2 February 2005, p. 28.
20. C. Clover, 'Capturing carbon may be answer to global warming', *Daily Telegraph*, 3 February 2005, p. 11.
21. Ibid.
22. A. Carvalho, 'Representing the politics of the greenhouse effect: Discursive strategies in the British media', *Critical Discourse Studies*, 2 (1), 2005, pp. 1–29.
23. McCarthy, 'Dramatic change in West Antarctic ice'.
24. *Independent*, 'Global warming: have your say', *Independent Online*, April 1, 2006: http://news.independent.co.uk/environment/article354121.ece

25. G. Lean, 'Global warming: Apocalypse Now: how mankind is sleepwalking to the end of the earth', *Independent on Sunday*, 6 February 2005, p. 10.
26. J. Hari, 'The climate crisis is here and now – but the US president has nothing to say about it', *Independent*, 4 February 2005, p. 31.
27. D. Edwards and D. Cromwell, *Guardians of Power: The Myth of the Liberal Media*, London: Pluto Press, 2006, p. 155.
28. *Today* programme, BBC Radio 4, Broadcasts, 1–4 February 2005, 6–9 a.m. and 5 February 2005, 7–9 a.m. Audio archives available: http://www.bbc.co.uk/radio4/today/listenagain/listenagain_archive.shtml
29. Ibid.
30. Ibid.
31. Source Watch, 'International Policy Network', Last updated: October, 2005, Madison, Wisconsin: Center for Media and Democracy: http://www.sourcewatch.org/index.php?title=International_Policy_Network
32. B. McKibben, *The Age of Missing Information*, New York: Plume, 1993, pp. 156–7.
33. *Six O'Clock News*, 'Special Report: greenhouse gases impacts on sea and coral', BBC1, 1 February 2005, 6 p.m. Report available online via BBC News Player: http://news.bbc.co.uk/1/hi/sci/tech/4226917.stm
34. H. Boaden, 'This is BBC News', *BBC Newswatch*, 18 November 2004: http://news.bbc.co.uk/newswatch/ukfs/hi/newsid_3970000/newsid_3975900/3975913
35. Channel 4 News, 'Warming warnings', Channel 4, 1 February 2005.
36. Source Watch, 'Scientific Alliance', last updated November, 2005: http://www.sourcewatch.org/index.php?title=Scientific_Alliance
37. Channel 4 News, 'Buried at Sea?', Channel 4, 2 February 2005.
38. M. McCarthy, 'Slouching towards disaster', *The Tablet*, 12 February 2005: http://www.gci.org.uk/articles/Tablet.pdf
39. R. Babe, 'The media on the environment', in J. Klaehn, ed., *Filtering the News*, Montreal: Black Rose, 2005, p. 187.
40. E. S. Herman and N. Chomsky, *Manufacturing Consent, the Political Economy of the Mass Media*, London: Vintage, 1994, p. 2.
41. J. Theobald, *The Media and the Making of History*, Aldershot: Ashgate, 2004, pp. 203–8.
42. F. Capra, *The Hidden Connections*, New York: Doubleday, 2002. D. Suzuki and A. McConnell, *The Sacred Balance. Rediscovering Our Place in Nature*, Vancouver: Greystone Books, 1997. V. Shiva, *Biopiracy*, Boston: South End Press, 1997.
43. Theobald, *The Media and the Making of History*, pp. 67–203.

8
Having the Information, but What Do You Then Do With It? The Scientific and Academic Communities

Jonathan Ward

A scientific consensus on global warming, and its general impact upon the planet, has been with us now for the best part of two decades. Yet it seems to have taken large parts of the academic community by surprise. Whilst highly significant advances have been made by UK university research groups – such as the Tyndall Centre – in the observation, recording and prediction of the problem,[1] the academic community as a whole has failed to take on board its wider implications. It has done little to find solutions to the crisis that threatens to envelop us in the twenty-first century; outside, that is, of much vaunted technological innovations. In the absence of governmental leadership there is, moreover, an overall incoherence in the direction and purpose of academic research as geared to the broad realities of anthropogenic climate change.

This issue raises fundamental questions about the role we expect of universities and academics, and conversely the role that they perceive for themselves in an era of impending crisis. Now is a time for questions. Asking the right questions first might help us focus in on the problems and what might be their solutions.

HIGHER EDUCATION – WHAT IS IT FOR AND HOW DOES IT RELATE TO GLOBAL WARMING?

In attempting to understand the subject of this chapter, it may be best, initially, to ask what the role of a university is and what, indeed, education means to us. With the current government's aim of reaching a target of enrolling 50 per cent of school leavers in higher education, what happens in universities affects half of the population of each generation. There were, in total, 2,423,590 further education

(FE) and higher education (HE) students studying in the UK during 2004–05 within a country of 59.8 million people.[2] Crudely speaking (foreign students aside), 5 per cent of the country at any one time is studying at these institutions. Thus, given that people are passing through them every few years, it is plain to see that a very significant number of the population attend and learn from these institutions. So what messages such institutions convey, internally and externally, is of the utmost importance to society as a whole.

Today, most of us would regard universities and FE colleges as either places of teaching, or centres of excellence in research. It would pay to delve deeper, even to some historical origins. 'Education', for instance, is derived from the Latin *educare* meaning 'to raise', 'to bring up', 'to train', 'to rear'. In recent times, however, there has been an attempt to link it to a different verb: *educere*, meaning 'to lead out' or 'to lead forth'. This reveals one of the theories behind the function of modern education – 'of developing innate abilities and expanding horizons'.[3]

A quick definition of 'university' from an online dictionary reads 'noun (pl. universities): a high-level educational institution in which students study for degrees and academic research is done; origin, Latin universitas "the whole", later "guild", from universus (see UNIVERSE)'.[4] Thus, one might assume, perhaps naively, that universities not only look at everything, but at the 'whole'; and so – combined with the 'leading out' of education – can enable students away from the increasingly spoon-fed, constrained and narrowly focused curricula of the state school system to become a next generation of leaders, workers, campaigners, mothers, fathers, friends and citizens suitably equipped to face the challenge of acute climate change. Most aptly this would mean that at a minimum they all knew at least something of how the earth is affected by natural and anthropogenic systems and activities, and of how these are fundamentally interconnected. One might also hope, as a follow-through, that they would know something of James Lovelock's *Gaia* theory of global interconnectedness,[5] explaining how 'Nature' is an interconnected network of systems in which the 'whole' can regulate the overall behaviour of these systems.

Certainly, we know that universities have spent centuries trying to further our knowledge about everything within our universe. Yet, when it comes to an all-embracing crisis such as global warming, something has been lost sight of. The problem, of course, goes deeper. During my own experience of campus life as a student, I was struck by the absence of a social or environmental conscience within the student body. The overriding feeling was not one of solidarity, but of competition: in sport, fashion, drinking, social standing and graduate jobs. This, of course, reflects the swing away from an earlier radical generation, eager to question the world around them, towards a more comfortable materialistically based individualism in which career, social and earning prospects are to the fore.

The continuing marginalisation of the more historically grounded premise that university may be the last chance for young people to become truly informed, and to criticise and debate what life and peers offer up to them, is evident in student groups involved in environmental or political campaigning. Jibes based on flimsy stereotypes – 'tree-huggers' and 'left-wing greenies' – are common fare for environmentally conscious students. But the derogatory labels aside, all this should be of concern for two reasons. First, this is still occurring at a time when the headlines are increasingly dominated by news on the worsening crisis that is global warming. Awareness of the issues driving the crisis has never been higher; it's inescapable. For students not to comprehend these issues is beyond belief. Second, the generation that is moving through the ranks of HE now will have to deal with the consequences, whether it be an actual drastic change in the climate, or dealing with the social and cultural changes necessary for a low carbon economy. For these people, on whom so much may rest, to see action upon environmental issues as the property of a curious minority is a disaster.

How much is this, then, the fault of universities themselves? As we have already noted, at these very same institutions researchers are at the forefront of reporting on what is quite probably the greatest crisis ever faced by the human species. Yet, millions of intelligent young minds pass through these institutions without coming face to face with either the researchers or their findings. Most will leave knowing no more than anyone who has access to a newspaper, the Internet or television. One could hope that in an ideal world, the students would press for and seek out more information and more action. Unfortunately, this happens all too rarely; unsurprisingly perhaps, given the myriad pressures – not least financial – on today's generation of students.

What is particularly missing is the study of global warming in the curricula. It should, without doubt, be present across almost the entire spectrum of university teaching. No other educational opportunity like this presents itself. Before these students depart to their careers in whichever field they have chosen, it is fundamental that they realise what role that field plays in humankind's contribution towards the changing of the planet's climate. The economist must be armed with the knowledge of the dangers of a fossil-fuelled capitalist system and the dangers of growth as the primary driving force behind decision making. The engineer must be aware of the impact of the combustion engine, and of the alternatives towards which we must work. The agriculturalist must be educated not only as to our over-reliance on fossil fuel-based intensive farming, but also as to what crops will be suitable for a changing climate in different latitudes and ecological systems.

Even the much maligned 'media studies' student should be able to leave the hallowed confines of academe recognising the schizophrenic discrepancy between newspapers' promotion of rampant greenhouse gas consumerism on one side of a page, and articles proclaiming that our way of life is leading to dangerous global warming, on the other. In university life, too, they ought to learn the techniques and nuances through which the media extends influence upon society's cultural, economic and political ideals. Armed with such information, they could be at the forefront of the cultural shift that will be essential to mitigating the impact of global warming. A more informed and discerning public as a result is also more likely to be better psychologically prepared when crisis hits. This, after all, is the one crisis we can ill afford to merely react to, but on the contrary, is the one demanding that we be hugely proactive.

All this should point to the application in general university policy and practice of a philosophy already well established in the medical sciences – the precautionary principle:

The precautionary principle states that if there are reasonable scientific grounds for believing that a new process or product may not be safe, it should not be introduced until we have convincing evidence that the risks are small and are outweighed by the benefits.[6]

This principle has been applied to existing technologies whenever new evidence appears suggesting that they are more dangerous than we had previously thought (as in the case of cigarettes, chlorofluorocarbons, greenhouse gases and genetically modified organisms). In cases of a new technology the same precautionary principle applies: further research to better assess the risk, and, where the dangers are considered serious enough, to a withdrawal of the intended product or the imposition of a ban or a moratorium on further use.[7]

Of course, in the case of global warming, an application of the precautionary principle cannot be isolated to a single technology or product and, indeed, requires far more than mere knowledge of the chemical processes, or the anthropogenic sources of greenhouse gas emissions involved. Here the principle encompasses an understanding of how our political and economic systems, our culture, societal structure, our very psychology all contribute towards the demand for fossil fuels, the principal source of greenhouse gases. Yet the paradox lies in the universality of the threat. Arguably, only in the 'universe' of universities can such complexity be both cautiously analysed and imparted, in the latter case to be both meaningful to students for their studies but also for their later life. 'Education' is the key. So why are universities so clearly failing in this all-important task? Perhaps the answer lies in the nature of an inherited system.

THE STRUCTURE OF UNIVERSITIES AND THEIR RELATIONSHIP TO GOVERNMENT AND BUSINESS

The structure of academia and the HE system is a labyrinth. At the very top we have the government acting through both the Department for Education and Skills (DfES), as led by a Secretary of State, and the Department of Trade and Industry (DTI). Then there are Non-Departmental Public Bodies (NDPBs), which include a plethora of funding bodies, HEFCE, EPSRC, NERC and others.[8] Another layer down and we find intra-university organisations, and other organisations that make up the umbrella of HE.

As for a typical university itself, it comprises a council, senate, court, convocation, faculties, schools and departments. Key personnel within the university include the Chancellor (normally a ceremonial head who presides over official functions); Vice-Chancellor (academic leader and chief executive of the university); Pro-Vice-Chancellors (responsibility for particular faculties and policy areas) and the Registrar (responsible for all the university's professional and support services). Further layers exist in the form of Deans, Heads of Departments, Group Leaders and so on.

The humble researcher may lie a long way down in the pecking order and possess little influence within her/his institution unless elected or co-opted to a decision-making locus of internal power. By contrast, the government is a key actor, with the power to make radical changes. For instance, in his foreword to *The Future of Higher Education*, a January 2003 White Paper, Charles Clarke MP, then

Secretary of State for Education, proudly declared the government's 'intention to take the tough decisions on higher education'.[9]

Yet examination of this White Paper reveals no mention of 'global warming', 'climate change' or the 'environment'. Traditionally, one might not expect an 'education' document to include any consideration of the environment. Now, though, with a government that claims climate change as a top priority, why is there no consideration of either the effect of the education system upon how we tackle global warming or how it will affect our education system? One might draw several different conclusions. Perhaps the government isn't really as concerned as it claims to be, and only wishes to treat the crisis in more obvious areas such as transport or energy. More likely, however, is that it has been slow to understand both the size and complexity of the problem, and therefore, too, the scale of the work needed to find solutions.

Superficially, the Higher Education Funding Council for England (HEFCE), in its most recent policy document on higher education and sustainability, would appear to be more promising. HEFCE declares a desire:

to make sustainable development a central part of [its] strategy for the future development of the higher education sector ... [its] vision is that, within the next ten years, the ... sector in England will be recognised as a major contributor to society's efforts to achieve sustainability – through the skills and knowledge that its graduates learn and put into practice, and through its own strategies and operations.[10]

Yet these fine words do not seem to carry through to efforts to reduce emissions of greenhouse gases or to instigate research that might mitigate or allow us to adapt to global warming. The strategic plan for the period 2003–08 (revised 2004) – itself a response to the framework and structure laid down by the government White Paper – is recent enough that one might imagine it would at least include a mention of the climate threat, or the way HEFCE proposes to meet the challenge by marshalling facilities and expertise in academia to do so. Its mission statement, offered at the beginning of this strategic plan, does trumpet that: 'Working in partnership, we promote and fund high-quality, cost-effective teaching and research, meeting the diverse needs of students, the economy and society.'[11] But for the next 41 pages of the report, to its very end, there is not a single mention of either climate change or global warming. Would it then be disingenuous to imagine that by not mentioning these issues HEFCE is not only *not* 'meeting the diverse needs of students, the economy and society', but does not consider action on global warming to be part of its remit?

This is no small matter given that elsewhere in the document, under 'strategic vision and role', HEFCE confirms the hugely influential position the HE sector has in defining the direction of the future of our society and economy, and, equally crucially, the necessity for efficient and effective knowledge transfer.[12] It repeatedly invokes how such transfer can generate 'economic and social benefits to the whole community' and be 'the engine of economic and social regeneration for the regions, and the driver of business and institutional innovation'.[13] Yet, surely, when it proclaims that sustainable development is 'about achieving economic, social and environmental objectives simultaneously, ensuring that our actions do not prejudice the needs of future generations'[14] – without even mentioning the biggest threat to our society – the assertion becomes nothing less than risible.

At least the Russell Group, a collective of self-appointed, high-achieving universities, and hence a prime contender for instigating change in our HE system, has the honesty to claim complete disinterest in the issue. In researching this chapter I approached Michael Carr, the Russell Group's Executive Director, with a series of questions designed to find out if there was any coherence in university policy on the environment and climate change. Carr responded: 'The Russell Group is an organisation of universities which work together over specific issues. Climate change is not something upon which Russell Group universities work together collectively and therefore I am not in a position to answer your questions.'[15] Neither could he comment upon the impact of global warming on the running and planning of Russell Group institutions. Can we therefore safely assume that a university cartel which in 2003/04 'accounted for over 60 per cent (£1.7 billion) of UK universities' research grant and contract income, approximately 55 per cent of all UK doctorates awarded, and over 30 per cent of all students studying in this country from outside the EU'[16] does not consider global warming to be important enough to be relevant to its operation and future at an institutional level?

There is, of course, one other critical indicator as to why universities are not pulling the stops out in favour of concerted climate change action. In any capitalist society, it is inevitable that corporations will have widespread influence on every facet of life. Universities are no exception. As we move into an era of education markets and governments that favour increasing corporate–public partnerships, universities are finding it hard to keep corporate influence at bay. There have long been links between industry and universities, particularly in the sciences and in engineering, where research and development (R&D) is essential for industrial growth but involves skills, knowledge and equipment best achieved through specialist collaboration.

One area where such collaboration has been close is in the energy industry; more particularly fossil fuel extraction, delivery and byproduct processing. In fact, these ties have grown with the encouragement of government bodies such as the PILOT taskforce which supports the growth of the oil industry. Key points of its vision include:

- £3 billion per annum industry investment
- Prolonged self-sufficiency in oil and gas
- Up to 100,000 more jobs
- 50 per cent increase in exports (to 2005)
- £1 billion per annum additional revenue for new business.[17]

This does *not* sound like the actions of a government striving to reduce a nation's fossil fuel consumption and associated greenhouse gas emissions. On the contrary, it indicates a commitment to a substantial investment in R&D and recruitment of graduates into this primary carbon sector.

A report by a coalition of grassroots groups, PLATFORM, Corporate Watch and the New Economics Foundation (NEF) well illustrates this point: '[Fossil fuel] companies ... have succeeded in "capturing" the allegiance of some of Britain's leading universities, through sponsoring new buildings, equipment, professorships and research posts.'[18] It goes on:

Universities are encouraging oil companies to steer the research agenda, tailoring courses to meet corporate personnel demands and awarding high profile positions to oil executives. In May 2001, for example, British Petroleum established its own institute at Cambridge University with a £25 million endowment. The Institute's full time director is one of the company's senior managers.[19]

Corporate influence over curricula is particularly pervasive in some institutions. At Heriot-Watt University's Institute of Petroleum Engineering they make no attempt to hide such influence, quite the opposite in fact. Courses are 'tailored to the needs of the petroleum industry and place considerable importance on the maintenance of close links with industry'.[20] At a time when we desperately need to be investing in developing renewable energy technology, it is worrying to find that 'over 50 per cent of oil and gas R&D projects in higher education institutions are fully paid for by the taxpayer, and a further 23 per cent receive part public funding'. Indeed, 'the direct public subsidy is estimated at £36 million per year'.[21]

Once again, if one might hope that research councils would at least be free from this sort of corporate influence, think again. Oil companies, for instance, are well represented in the EPSRC's peer review council.[22] Nigel Woodcock, a Cambridge University geologist, has related the paradoxical situation thus:

Geologists ... of all people, should be able to spot the threat of a slow catastrophe beginning to happen; to see the climate modellers' writing on the greenhouse wall ... [Yet] we keep our eyes on the ground, and more often under it. We are disinclined to focus upwards on the atmospheric consequences of using these resources. There are many geological jobs in finding fossil fuels so we are therefore reluctant to admit the link between fossil fuels and global warming. People in glasshouses don't throw stones.[23]

All this is doubly paradoxical given that the only reason we know global warming is happening, and that it is an immensely dangerous and imminent crisis, is through the work of university researchers and affiliated groups. So why is it that those with the finger on the pulse in the HE world have not realised, or possibly not accepted, the seriousness of the issue? Indeed, what message does it send out to the public at large if the very institutions which describe the ever worsening impact of anthropogenic emissions, who sanction further work on global warming and have access to all the results and interpretations, don't then appear to be too concerned? Is the fault ultimately to do with a vacuum of leadership, a lack of resources, or some peculiar culture of academic inertia?

THE CULTURE OF UNIVERSITIES AND OBSTACLES TO CHANGE

As a result of a steady increase in degree-awarding institutions within the UK during the past half-century, the HE market has become increasingly competitive. Faced with the prospect of falling numbers of undergraduate applicants and a reduction in funding, universities are moving towards business models akin to those of corporations. Compounding this situation is the advent of fee-paying students.

The HE sector, in terms of teaching at least, is now a customer-based, competitive market. With fees likely to increase from their present levels, students will rightly be more demanding of universities and will exercise their right to choose more carefully.

One result could be a situation where institutions reduce numbers of undergraduate courses with notably high overheads. These would traditionally include areas such as medicine, engineering and the sciences. A more obvious trend, however, especially if an institution wishes to remain a large teaching institution, is to maximise income from its research activities. This is now *de rigueur* to such a point among Humanities and Social Science departments that almost their entire collective effort is dedicated to achieving the highest possible score in HEFCE's supposedly quinquennial Research Assessment Exercise (RAE), thereby entitling them to a higher proportion of HEFCE's limited funds, relative to other comparable departments.[24] If this in itself might suggest why the crisis of global warming never seems to have percolated down to considerable areas of academic existence, the big money anyway lies in government-promoted industrial and corporate partnerships.

As we have already seen, this funding framework clearly does not favour renewable R&D when compared with long-established fossil-fuel heavyweights.[25] As a result, universities under financial pressure are likelier to move their core research base towards activities associated with emissions of greenhouse gases than towards research which studies and seeks to prevent global warming. And, however short-sighted this may seem on one level, the issue is simply that universities are now, in many respects, run as businesses and though the bottom line may not be profit, it is certainly one of averting financial crises.

That said, the very nature of these institutions and the philosophy upon which they are based makes it difficult to argue a case for the work of one area dictating the running, the direction and detail of all. Universities promote and undertake cutting-edge learning and research in a huge number of disciplines and subjects. If they were to radically change their policies on the advice of environmentalists, climatologists and others investigating global warming and its possible impacts, would we not see a substantial curtailment in the activities of other departments, particularly those that currently specialise in areas that contribute significantly to greenhouse gas emissions and the intensive use of fossil fuels? Institutions which were top-heavy in this way might risk signing their own death warrants if they were to undertake a serious appraisal of their future viability. At the very least they would most likely need to overhaul the direction of their work in a paradigm shift towards a goal of carbon neutrality.

So where can we find signs of positive action towards this goal? I posed a number of questions to Martin Wiles, Energy and Environment Manager at the University of Bristol, where I work, regarding its environmental policy and performance. This encompasses both the gathering and distribution of information on global warming and how it features in the university's planning and educational curricula.

The response on being asked whether the university takes on board information from research groups that work in areas related to global warming, was 'Where appropriate, but limited.' Another two-fold question was whether the university had begun to incorporate its research on the causes and extent of global warming into politics, economics and other social science curricula and, inversely, to what extent was it backing research on the impact of political and economic systems *on* global warming and how these might be changed to negate such problems? The response was limited to noting that 'a new unit on sustainable development open to undergraduates is being run this year for the first time, so teaching is focusing on this issue'.

On asking who does the university look to for leadership in global warming issues and policy, the reply was that he was 'not sure it does look to anyone. It may compare itself with others.' This reveals, at the very least, that the university is not aware of any central leadership on the issue of global warming and emissions reduction. Finally, I asked what role the university considered it had in tackling global warming in the UK and beyond? Wiles' response, again, was that he was not sure, but added that his unit through 'doing what we are doing in terms of energy management ... are managing the estate in a good business way. I feel we are making a significant contribution and that lots of other FE and HE institutions are, the £200 million spent on energy alone makes it worth while.'[26]

These answers suggest that Bristol University sees itself neither as a leader in tackling or promoting awareness of global warming nor as following any other leadership on the matter. Even if this is actually incorrect, it still, nevertheless, paints a worrying picture of isolation. It might be crass to invoke the cliché of the ivory tower, but it would appear to any outsider that this institution, when it comes to this critical issue, *is* insular. Under no pressure to change other than that exerted by itself, or by competitors in the education market, in turn, it exerts no pressure on its employees (at most we are politely reminded of our duty to turn the lights off when we leave), its competitors, the government, or the surrounding community.

Yet, this institution *is* at the forefront of global warming research, most obviously through the Bristol Research Initiative for the Dynamic Global Environment (BRIDGE) which encompasses multi-disciplinary teams drawn from across the University and with links to the Hadley Centre, British Antarctic Survey, UK Met Office, Defra, the Environment Agency, and the Centre for Global Atmospheric Modelling and the oil industry. The group's aim is to 'improve the understanding of natural climate and environmental variability and to use this knowledge to predict future changes more accurately and assess its impact on all aspects of human society ... [to] provide information to the Intergovernmental Panel on Climate Change and ultimately feed into the government's policy considerations'.[27]

Not only is the existence of this group an extremely welcome step forward but, linked to other developments within the university, it is evidence that the potential for real change exists. The university is moving forward with its emissions targets and carbon trading scheme, whilst also liaising with student groups in the establishment of an 'Environment Week'.[28] There is a university environmental newsletter, too, which suggests environmentally friendly actions ranging from energy-saving mantras such as turning off lights, PCs and appliances, to encouraging the use of local farm schemes, and recycling food waste and Christmas trees.

The problem is that none of this goes nearly far enough in the direction in which we must be heading. The language on environmental issues is constantly watered down, and despite soaring energy bills and the massive savings which could be made from a really rigorous energy reduction and recycling programme, resource wastage goes on being approached in that softly-softly way so maddeningly typical of a throwaway British culture as a whole. There is certainly little evidence of any collective sense of social responsibility around the country's campuses. Moreover, the good work that is being done comes primarily from pressure from within, and almost never through government directive.

INCREMENTAL SHIFTS AND BIG IDEAS

One institutional sector which is having to grapple with energy usage and carbon emission targets is that of university estates. Often large, sprawling collections of a few nice older buildings, and a generic mass of concrete eyesores, many campuses are suffering from the legacy of large-scale developments from the 1950s to the 1970s, in which little thought was given towards long-lasting sustainability or energy efficiency. Now, many institutions are left managing criminally inefficient buildings stretched beyond their original purpose and often life span. The headache is compounded by the often energy-intensive nature of research, irregular working hours, and changing demands upon the estate.

Bristol, again, as an example, suggests some of the problems – and successes. The university is in the midst of modernising its estate, that is either improving existing stock or carrying forward to a series of new building projects. To this end, the estates office is operating to industry standards set by BREEAM (Building Research Establishment Environmental Assessment Method) whose assessment considers management of the project, energy use, health and well-being, pollution, transport, land use, ecology, materials used and water consumption to arrive at an overall rating of buildings on the basis of Pass, Good, Very Good and Excellent.[29]

The university aim is to work towards attaining a Good or Very Good level for its current buildings and to achieve an Excellent assessment in some of its new estate. Equally, its Environment and Energy Unit aims to reduce CO_2 emissions per square metre by 20 per cent,[30] or even up to 50 per cent, in the longer term. Actually the university is already obligated under the EU Emissions Trading Scheme (EU ETS), in conjunction with Defra, to make a 10 per cent reduction in CO_2 emissions; that is 3,804 tonnes, by December 2007, compared with the base year of 2003.[31] Under EU ETS, the university must also hold a greenhouse gas permit in order to operate its 140 boilers on the campus, each of whose emissions must be monitored and reported.

The current state of play is that the university does admit experiencing a number of problems in this area – not least given that its CO_2 emissions actually *rose* last year by 10 per cent to 39,000 tonnes.[32] At least, though, it acknowledges that its 'operations naturally have a significant local, national, and global environment impact' and through its Energy Efficiency Monitoring Unit, formed in 2002, is seeking 'to *try* and reduce this impact and where possible save the University resources and money'[33] (my italics). It is important to note the use of language in university environmental policy documents. Words such as 'try' imply good intentions, but betray the fact that there is no particular pressure or urgency to actually achieve positive results. Language such as this incorporates room for failure, which in the case of global warming may simply not be an option.

That said, the fact that the Monitoring Unit is as much driven by the need to make energy savings as simply for the environment's sake, should not be discounted. A future plan, for instance, is to install and run a 'combined heat and power' (CHP) unit, with heat and power (electricity) generated in a single process, for a variety of purposes, including water and space heating. CHP is particularly beneficial to the university as the electricity can be generated at a lower cost than it can be purchased, with CO_2 emissions reduced by over 30 per cent, by comparison with separate generation from the grid. While the project will reduce the university's CO_2 emissions by 540 tonnes, its economic saving will be £300,000 per annum.[34] Could this be the real goad behind universities adopting low carbon and energy efficient measures? However, at a cost of £2.7 million and with no payback for several years, this is exactly the kind of large-scale investment that requires universities to be on a sure footing in terms of long-term funding.

Bristol University's efforts represent a small potential, at the level of micro-management. By contrast, Harvard, the premier Ivy League university, in a critical scoping document on HE, seems to have correctly identified what many institutions in Britain have not. Namely, that the majority of those who currently sit in influential and prominent positions in society are likely to have studied at university, just as will be the case in any future generation. Harvard Green Campus Initiative thus proposes that 'by fostering their appreciation for the problem [global warming] now, they will be more likely to help mitigate it in the coming decades'.[35]

The Harvard document proposals, however, go considerably further. Not only have the authors accepted that there is a 'special responsibility' placed upon the peoples of the West, as the major source of human-made CO_2 emissions to date, but because of the unique position in these societies that universities occupy this makes them ideal candidates for taking up the challenge. On the one hand, this means that they need to tackle their own considerable contribution to the greenhouse gases 'that are at the root of the problem'; on the other, 'if colleges and universities are to expect their students to assume a sense of social responsibility, then they are *obliged* to lead by example'[36] (my italics). This point has been made even more succinctly by the Initiative's Director, Leith Sharp:

'If a university can't meet its profound responsibility as a member of a global community, then who will?'[37]

Thus, the document continues:

Institutions of higher education are in an ideal position for developing innovative greenhouse gas reduction programs because of their focus of learning. Many have faculty whose research aligns with the study of global warming or the many social, ecological and economic problems that surround it. Students are ideal candidates for research and data collection projects. By tapping the energy and knowledge of their academic personnel, colleges and universities may be able to identify ways of addressing global warming locally and on a national scale.[38]

THE WAY FORWARD?

The Harvard Green Campus Initiative seems to have got the measure of the problem. It recognises that reducing the threat of global warming will take coordinated action on the part of governments, industry, communities and individuals. But it also proposes that because of the particularly prominent role in society that academic institutions play in countries with a strong emphasis on HE, these are critically positioned 'to inform people about global warming and enable them to address this critical threat in all areas of their lives'.[39]

Of course, with a combined operating budget in 2001 of 'more than $250 billion – 2.8 per cent of US GNP and more than the GDP of all but 20 countries',[40] US universities and colleges have awesome economic muscle hardly imaginable to the rest of us. And Harvard still has to turn the fine words into practical action. Yet it has set the right tone, taking on board the principle that because universities have a special (tax-free) status, plus government resources 'in exchange for their contribution to the health and well-being of society through the creation and dissemination of knowledge and values',[41] this also confers upon them a special mission not only to 'teach students about their significant role in the problem' but also to educate them on the disastrous consequences that global warming will bring for people around the world.[42]

By contrast, most British universities seem to be behaving in ways that can be best described as muddled, or, more cynically, as hypocritical. Through the media, they feed the public with the dangers of global warming, identifying in the process the sources of emissions which threaten to exacerbate the situation, whilst dithering over cutting back their own. Meanwhile, the overriding message from the universities, their funding bodies and the government would appear to be that global warming is not nearly so serious as to demand coherent, immediate and urgent action.

Is it not time that universities regained their historic focus on the 'whole' and in so doing, on how it all fits together? Global warming *is* global. It touches everything; and with an impact, therefore, which will be universal on the spectrum of human activities. And that is merely a matter of its impacts. What of the solutions we must surely find to avert the worst of what is predicted? How will each solution affect us and everything which we do? Even if we can arrive at a sustainable way of life, how does a national community undertake such a colossal culture change?

Even small incremental steps towards universities playing their necessary role have yet to be properly considered, let alone undertaken. Comprehensive environmental audits for each and every institution, involving a proper assessment of those research areas which contribute most significantly to greenhouse gas emissions, might appear to be a complicated and financially unrewarding process, especially given the usual short-term planning regime. Yet without them how else are we to determine which research areas contribute most significantly to greenhouse gas emissions, and which we know, beyond reasonable doubt, are not leading to a worsening of the projected impact of global warming?

Endorsement and incentives for such a scheme could only realistically originate from the government. Not least, given that resistance to such change would not only come from senior management within universities but from funding bodies and more particularly a number of powerful sponsoring corporations who have contributed to the creation of entire university departments and whose influence should not be underestimated. In other words, this would be a critical test of the government's stated aims of moving to a low carbon economy.

A consequent shift in the volume of funding from fossil fuel industries towards renewable energies might also offer a fillip to those in universities, including significant numbers of staff and students, who have felt increasingly marginalised and alienated by the direction academe has taken in recent years. The problem has been cultural as well as political. The RAE, far from enabling interdisciplinarity, has only served to push research activity further down the road to atomisation. One of the results has been that one knows of the work of other researchers in one's own narrow field, scattered across the globe, but not the groundbreaking news of the next department, or that along the corridor.

In an age of acute climate change another small step towards the re-engagement of academics in the 'whole' would be a clear push from government towards open-access journals and broader academic output freely available on the Web.[43] Again, this is crucial in order to create the sort of free-flowing and open exchange of knowledge and ideas that global warming research needs. One welcome step would be the standard use of Wiki publishing[44] by which academics could be enabled to refine findings in other researchers' papers, rather than having to publish competing or separate papers usually involving considerable time-lags. This endemic problem, in particular, runs counter to the vital need now for rapidly updated, accessible information on climate change at a time when strong climate feedback mechanisms are beginning to take hold, producing greater changes than previously expected, and on a shorter timescale. Whilst the provision of strict criteria for the publishing of data and papers in this way will be of utmost importance, resistance is most likely to come from a multi-billion dollar publishing industry with a virtual monopoly on key prestige journals, though opposition may also come from a significant stratum of academics who have used this *ancien régime*-backed system to win tenure, promotion or a research grant.[45]

Dismantling this redundant framework in favour of a transparent and open exchange of ideas, backed up, that is, by experimental evidence, as the route to scientific progress – the original notion of the Royal Society in the seventeenth century no less – may sound revolutionary, but the urgency of the situation with regards to global warming does not allow room for 'business as usual' scenarios. And that, ultimately, is the nettle universities are going to have to grasp. It is not that they are doing nothing. Some valuable developments are emerging, in the form of dedicated policy units, emissions trading, cross-disciplinary groups and tougher building regulations. Staff are 'encouraged' to be environmentally friendly. But all this remains half-hearted and without conviction.

Now is a time for action. A time for delivering and forcing through changes to make academia work once more towards the benefit of society as a whole; and, indeed, as explicit in Contraction and Convergence, towards the benefit of all humankind. It will take a simultaneous and unprecedented transition across the entire sector for this to be achieved, and more importantly, quickly, to be achieved before disaster overwhelms us. What is the solution? Increased government funding linked to a radical rethinking of research priorities. Funding should be delivered not only through the research councils but through a wider range of sources including the DTI and other public bodies. A government truly committed to the challenge imposed by global warming *will* find the requisite resources and funding mechanisms, and, in so doing, ensure that universities are providing not only the necessary knowledge on climate change but the sort of thinking which might enable us all to transcend it.

NOTES

1. See Tyndall Centre for Climate Change Research: http://www.tyndall. ac.uk
2. Office of National Statistics – table 0a – institution0405.xls: http://www. statistics.gov.uk
3. http://www.askoxford.com/concise_oed/university?view=uk
4. Answers.com. 'Education' definition from http://www.answers.com/ topic/education
5. For more information see Gaia theory (science) – Wikipedia at http:// en.wikipedia.org/wiki/Gaia_theory_(science)
6. Institute of Science in Society (ISIS) 'Use and abuse of the precautionary principle': http://www.i-sis.org.uk/prec.php
7. Ibid.
8. Higher Education Funding Council for England; Engineering and Physical Sciences Research Council; Natural Environment Research Council.
9. DfES – White Paper – *The Future of Higher Education.* Available at http:// www.dfes.gov.uk/hegateway/uploads/White%20Pape.pdf
10. HEFCE, 'Sustainable development in higher education', statement of policy on promoting sustainable development in HE – Vision Statement, p. 5, para. 20, 2005. Available at http://www.hefce.ac.uk/pubs/hefce/2005/05 28/05 28.pdf
11. HEFCE, 'HEFCE strategic plan 2003–08 (Revised April 2004)', Mission Statement, p. 4: http://www.hefce.ac.uk/pubs/hefce/2004/04_17/04_ 17.pdf
12. Ibid. pp. 5–6, paras 7 and 12.
13. Ibid.
14. Ibid., p. 38, para. 18.
15. Correspondence with Michael Carr, Registrar, University of Liverpool, 23 January 2006.
16. See the Russell Group homepage: http://www.russellgroup.ac.uk/index1. html
17. PILOT Taskforce – 'About PILOT – What is PILOT': http://www.pilot-taskforce.co.uk/data/pvision.cfm. 'PILOT is a joint programme involving the Government and the UK oil & gas Industry Operators, Contractors, Suppliers, Trade Unions and SME's aiming to secure the long-term

future of the Industry in the UK': http://www.pilottaskforce.co.uk/data/aboutpilot.cfm

18. PLATFORM, 'Degrees of Capture', Corporate Watch and the New Economics Foundation, March 2003. Available at http://www.carbonweb.org/degreesofcapture.htm

19. Ibid, 'The oil industry and Britain's universities: how many degrees of capture?'

20. Institute of Petroleum Engineering, Heriot-Watt University Edinburgh, Courses section, 'Why Us?': http://www.pet.hw.ac.uk/courses/studying/why.htm

21. 'Degrees of Capture', Chapter 3 – 'Extracting intelligence – Research and development for the oil and gas industry'.

22. EPSRC Peer Review College 2006–09 – available at: http://www.epsrc.ac.uk/CMSWeb/Downloads/Other/CollegeMembers0609.pdf

23. Quoted in 'Degrees of Capture', Chapter 7, 'Intellectual Pollution'. Original source: N.H. Woodcock, 'Geologists and global warming', *Geoscientist*, 1(6), 1991, pp. 8–11.

24. For the RAE2008 see http://www.rae.ac.uk

25. Thus, in response to a 4 March 2003 letter from Gregg Muffitt of PLATFORM to the DfES requesting that the government 'review the funding of energy R&D by the Research Councils (mainly NERC and EPSRC), by the DTI itself, and by other government bodies, with a view to phasing out all subsidies for fossil fuel R&D, with the exception of those which directly relate to mitigating the negative environmental and safety impacts of operations', Dr Chris Hensall for HEFCE responded (29 April 2003) that such funds 'are allocated selectively by a funding formula according to the quality and volume of the research work carried out in the universities'. See http://www.platformlondon.org/carbonweb/documents/todti.pdf

26. Email from Martin Wiles, Energy and Environment Manager, University of Bristol, 4 January 2006.

27. University of Bristol, School of Geographical Sciences. About BRIDGE: http://www.bridge.bris.ac.uk/about

28. University of Bristol Union: Environment – Events: http://www.ubu.org.uk/main/welfare/misc/environment

29. University of Bristol Energy and Environmental Management Unit (hereafter EEMU), The Built Environment: http://www.bris.ac.uk/environment/built_environment/

30. University of Bristol policy document, EEMU: http://www.bris.ac.uk/environment/policy/env_policy.pdf

31. University of Bristol, EEMU, Emissions Trading: http://www.bris.ac.uk/environment/energy/eutrading.html

32. Q&A session, University of Bristol, 'Environment Week – Project Nucleus', comments from John Brenton, EEMU.

33. Bristol University, EEMU homepage: http://www.bristol.ac.uk/environment/

34. From University of Bristol, 'Environment News' newsletter, December 2005: http://www.bristol.ac.uk/environment/forum/ef_newsletter_1205.pdf

35. The Campus Green Team Resource, 'Universities and future leaders: will the blind keep us blind?: chapter 1, 'Background and context, the role of higher education': http://www.greencampus.harvard.edu/greenteams/academia.php
36. Ibid., Universities and Consumption: 'Walking the talk'.
37. Alex L. Pasternack, 'Harvard pushes energy reduction', *The Crimson*, 3 May 2002: http://www.thecrimson.com/article.aspx?ref=214574
38. Campus Green Team Resource, 'Universities and Innovation: Will They?', http://www.greencampus.harvard.edu/greenteams/academia.php
39. Ibid., chapter 1, 'Background and context'.
40. Anthony D. Cortese, 'The critical role of higher education in creating a sustainable future', Association for the Advancement of Sustainability in Higher Education, May 2003, p. 19: http://www.efswest.org/resource_center/pdf/pspr/phecortese.pdf
41. Anthony D. Cortese, 'Education for sustainability: the need for a new human perspective', 1999 Article from think-tank *Second Nature*, p. 8: http://www.secondnature.org/pdf/snwritings/articles/humanpersp.pdf
42. Campus Green Team Resource, 'Universities and future leaders'.
43. Thus, the House of Commons Science and Technology Committee has recommended that 'all UK higher education institutions establish institutional repositories on which their published output can be stored and from which it can be read, free of charge, online. It also recommends that Research Councils and other Government funders mandate their funded researchers to deposit a copy of all of their articles in this way.' See Summary – Science and Technology – Tenth Report – House of Commons, published 7 July 2004: http://www.publications.parliament.uk/pa/cm200304/cmselect/cmsctech/399/39902.htm
44. Wiki publishing: http://academia.wikia.com/wiki/Wiki_publishing
45. 'Scientific publishing is having to change rapidly to respond to growing pressure for free access to published research', *The Economist*, 5 August 2004.

9
Asleep On Their Watch: Where Were the NGOs?

George Marshall

In November 2000 I attended the Conference of Parties to the Framework Convention on Climate Change in The Hague as a registered non-governmental organisation (NGO) 'observer'. I noticed that entire sectors of the NGO world were absent. Of all the hundreds of thousands of NGOs concerned with development, human rights and progressive social change, scarcely a handful were represented. I also saw that many of the organisations claiming NGO status represented specific industry interests including several that aimed to actively undermine the negotiations.

These observations raise one core question, which this chapter seeks to answer: how had the vast issue of climate change become so detached from the agenda of progressive concern that most NGOs had abandoned it to environmentalists and business groups?

WHAT ARE NGOS AND WHAT DO THEY DO?

The term 'non-governmental organisation' came into use with the establishment of the United Nations in 1945 and the need to define a role for international organisations and agencies which worked in the UN's areas of concern. Provisions in Article 71 of Chapter 10 of the United Nations (UN) Charter define NGOs under three main criteria – they are not-for-profit organisations; they are not set up by a government or affiliated to political parties; and they do not advocate violence.

The development of NGOs runs parallel to the development of civil society as a 'third force' and intermediary between the private sphere and the state. One definition, widely accepted in the public understanding of NGOs, is of 'citizens acting collectively in a public sphere to express their interests, passions, and ideas, exchange information, achieve mutual goals, make demands on the state, and hold state officials accountable'.[1] Such independent organisations had been a growing part of the political and civil discourse for the past 200 years. The anti-slavery movement, founded in England in the late eighteenth century, gave rise to many such organisations. The mid nineteenth century saw the formation of the World Alliance of YMCAs and the International Committee of the Red Cross (ICRC). Trade unions emerged as a leading force in the NGO movement later in the century.[2] This history plays a major role in the definition of NGOs as advocates for the vulnerable or powerless; what Kofi Annan, former Secretary-General of the UN, called 'the conscience of humanity'.[3] The World Bank defines NGOs as 'private organizations that pursue activities to relieve suffering, promote the interests of the poor, protect the environment, provide basic social services, or undertake community development'.[4]

Academic analysis of the role of NGOs in global governance also stresses the role of NGOs in supporting and facilitating government decisions; for example, providing expert advice and analysis, monitoring compliance, and legitimising global-scale decision-making mechanisms by 'improving the quality, authoritativeness, and legitimacy of the policy choices of international organizations'.[5] Former UN Secretary-General Boutros Boutros-Ghali affirmed that NGOs 'are an indispensable part of the legitimacy' of the UN.[6]

THE GROWTH OF NGOS

Originally, the UN only recognised NGOs working in three or more countries, but with the recognition of smaller national NGOs accreditation increased rapidly throughout the 1980s and 1990s. From 1990 until 2004 (the period during which climate change has been a major issue), the number of NGOs registered for UN consultative status rose from 893 to 2,531.[7]

The figures for UN involvement are only an indicator of the vastly greater number of 'civil society' organisations which sit outside any UN process. The USA, for example, has between 1 million and 2 million NGOs. By the mid 1990s, about 1 million NGOs were operating in India, 210,000 in Brazil and 96,000 in the Philippines.[8] At this time an estimated 100,000 NGOs around the world were working as advocates for environmental protection.[9]

The growth of NGOs also fuelled increasing sums of bilateral and multilateral aid. Donors saw funding NGOs in the South as a means to project implementation and mobilise community participation (or the appearance of it). By 2002, more than US$7 billion in private and government aid to developing countries flowed through NGOs, compared to US$1 billion in 1970.[10]

ACRONYM SOUP

The original definition of 'NGO' was so broad that it has become a catch-all for non-state and non-profit organisations. As numbers of NGOs have grown, academics and agencies have come to distinguish between NGOs on the basis of different acronym formations. There are now INGOs, BINGOs, RINGOs, ENGOs, GONGOs, QUANGOs, DONGOs, GRINGOs and PANGOs.[11] This is an undoubted gift to anyone wishing to write a rap song about the definition of civil society groups.

Many of these sub-categories reveal a growing trend for organisations with strong political, government and business ties to claim NGO status – and to set up accordingly. As a result traditional NGOs, concerned that their privileged status has been weakened, have sought a redefinition creating a greater separation between different interests. Many NGOs now prefer the term 'private voluntary organisation' (PVO), or 'private development organisation' (PDO). Other terms seek to define NGOs by activities such as 'interest group', 'pressure group' and 'lobby group'. Peter Willetts argues against these attempts to differentiate between different kinds of NGO:

All pressure groups or voluntary organisations have some interests to protect ... In practice, it is impossible to agree any general terms to distinguish praiseworthy from unacceptable groups, either in domestic politics, or in global politics, because such a distinction is a subjective choice made on the basis of each observer's own value preferences.[12]

From an NGO perspective, Willetts' argument is frustrating. Clearly there is a substantial difference, which should be made explicit, between an environmental organisation with a broad public constituency and one formed by commercial interests with the sole purpose of intervening in the political process. However, the argument here is a reasonable summary of the official UN position, happy as it remains to maintain the catch-all term 'NGOs', however unsatisfactory, rather than court controversy with exclusionary definitions.

NGOs AND THE CLIMATE NEGOTIATIONS

The United Nations Framework Convention on Climate Change (UNFCCC), signed in Rio in 1992, provided the structure for all subsequent climate negotiations, including the Kyoto Protocol of 1997. There are currently 753 NGOs with observer status registered with the UNFCCC to attend the climate negotiations.[13] This list only gives an indication of the organisations *interested* in following the negotiations – the number regularly attending the meetings is far lower. Table 1 gives an approximate breakdown by category.

Table 1 Categories of Organisations Registered with the Secretariat of the Framework Convention on Climate Change as 'Non-Governmental Organisations' with Observer Status[14]

NGO Type	Number Registered
Environment	199
Research and academic	156
Business	133
Other	125
Energy	46
Development	16
Labour and unions	16
Governmental	15
Law	15
Indigenous	9
Health	6
Faith	6
Youth	5
Women	4
Foundations	2
Total	753

I must confess that this breakdown is approximate and far from authoritative.[15] Despite this caveat, some conclusions can be made with confidence. Firstly, the UNFCCC is using the widest possible definition of NGO and therefore includes a large number of organisations that represent and are entirely funded by business interests, often referred to as BINGOs. Most of these are umbrella organisations representing broad commercial interests (for example, the Business Council of Australia), or specific sectors (for example, the Japan Electrical Manufacturers' Association). Although some BINGOs are concerned with climate change, or the development of renewable technologies, the majority represent industries that are either primary sources of greenhouse gases (oil, coal, gas, cement, livestock), or large consumers of energy (cars, aluminium, aviation).

A substantial component of NGO engagement in the UNFCCC process, therefore, is from organisations seeking to minimise the extent and cost of climate mitigation measures. Some go further and actively undermine the scientific consensus. In May 2006, one NGO observer, the Competitive Enterprise Institute, launched a high-profile US advertising campaign under the slogan: 'Carbon Dioxide: They call it Pollution. We call it Life'. The aim of this campaign was to persuade the US public that CO_2 was a benign gas that should not be legislated against. In *Carbon War*, a devastating account of the climate negotiations, Jeremy Leggett describes in detail the direct influence such organisations exerted on the positions of the Middle Eastern countries, and the various ways that they successfully undermined the Kyoto Protocol negotiations.[16]

Secondly, and drawing from this point, only a minority of the organisations accredited as NGOs can be considered to be true civil society organisations with a public mandate for progressive change. Of these the largest category is that of environmental NGOs, who have varied motives for attending the negotiations. All of these recognise the importance of a binding intergovernmental agreement to deal with a problem that is global in both cause and impact. NGOs followed the lead up to the Kyoto Protocol because, to quote the UK negotiator, John Prescott, 'it is the only game in town'.[17] However, few of them have had the direct access to negotiators necessary to following a sophisticated and long-term insider strategy. To achieve greater influence the smaller NGOs tend to group together in networks or coalitions, the largest and most influential being the Climate Action Network (CAN), which has 300 members and meets daily during UNFCCC negotiations.[18]

However, CAN's direct contribution to the negotiations is still very limited. It is allowed to make two formal presentations in each plenary – one from the North, one from the South – but remains excluded from the closed-door sessions in which most negotiations take place.[19] In fact, despite all their efforts to maintain a sophisticated and proactive strategy, CAN and the environmental NGOs have been forced to expend most of their energy fighting a rearguard campaign to salvage the international agreement. Inevitably, this has led to substantial compromises. CAN originally pushed for a protocol containing strong compliance and review mechanisms requiring the industrialised countries to reduce emissions by 20 per cent by 2005. They were forced to relinquish each of their demands in turn and by 2000 were concentrating most of their efforts on plugging the gaping loopholes opening up in a protocol that set a far lower target of 5.2 per cent, and remained very weak on compliance, or review.[20]

In March 2001, when President George W. Bush withdrew the US from the Kyoto Protocol, the struggle to save the international process and obtain ratification from the other signatories became these NGOs' overwhelming priority. This led to even greater concessions, especially on sinks and emissions trading.

INTRODUCING THE MISSING NGOs – MiNGOs

There is another category of NGOs that does not appear in any conventional analysis of climate change – the missing NGOs. Entire sections of the NGO community have absented themselves from the climate negotiations from the outset. Following the conventions of NGO acronyms I will call them the 'MiNGOs'.

Looking again at Table 1, we notice that women, youth, faith and indigenous interests are all poorly represented. These are all major areas of activity for the UN with correspondingly high levels of NGO involvement. To take just one example, the 1995 World Conference on Women in Beijing attracted 2,600 NGOs to the inter-governmental negotiations and 35,000 NGO representatives to the parallel forum.[21] Yet, combined, they account for scarcely 5 per cent of the accredited NGOs at UNFCCC. Development organisations are also poorly represented. Most of those attending are small specialist organisations concerned with sustainable development or technology transfer. Only three of the larger international development NGOs have been accredited: Oxfam GB, Tear Fund and CARE Canada.

There is not, to the best of my knowledge, a single organisation specialising in international human rights accredited to the UNFCCC, even though 27 per cent of all the NGOs accredited to the UN have a human rights focus, whereas environment accounts for just 14 per cent.[22] All in all, it is worth noting that the MiNGOs include almost all of the largest and best funded members of the NGO community, including those with the greatest influence and experience in international negotiations.

There is a superficial explanation for this absence: the climate negotiations concerned an environmental issue and were, therefore, outside the area of expertise of NGOs working in other sectors. Certainly, this is the explanation given by the MiNGOs. Amnesty International, for example, despite a level of UN experience that few others can match, considers itself poorly informed on environmental issues generally and unable to contribute usefully in the field of climate change.[23] A second and related explanation is that the MiNGOs believed that the issue was being well handled and did not require further intervention. The impression among development groups during the 1990s was that the climate change issue was following a similar pathway to the ozone depletion issue five years earlier and was moving rapidly to a binding international agreement.[24]

There is a third explanation, which this chapter will explore in greater detail; namely, that very few NGOs outside the environmental sphere have absorbed or accepted the scale and urgency of climate change, or the overwhelming significance that it will soon have for all aspects of human activity – their specialist sectors included.

THE RELEVANCE OF CLIMATE CHANGE TO NON-ENVIRONMENTAL NGOs

Let us take a step back and start from first principles. Let us assume that climate change has a cause that defies conventional classification – a meteor strike, for example. Because it does not fit within the remit of any organisation, all NGOs are forced to look in detail at the implications for their own area of concern and reach their own conclusions about whether it merits attention and organisational resources. As part of their analysis they look at the substantial scientific analysis of the impacts of climate change in three areas of major concern – refugees, health and water. From even this limited analysis it is immediately apparent that climate change cannot be regarded as a purely environmental issue, and that its impacts alone should make it an issue of leading concern to any organisation concerned with development, social welfare or conflict.

Refugees

In 2005, the UN University Institute for Environment and Human Security, in Bonn, stated that there are already 20 million environmental refugees worldwide, more than the number displaced by conflict. The Institute estimates that the number will have grown to 50 million by 2010.[25] The world disasters report, published annually by the International Federation of Red Cross and Red Crescent Societies, says there are 5,000 new environmental refugees every day.[26] Both sources identify climate change as the leading factor behind this growth in numbers. The Intergovernmental Panel on Climate Change (IPCC) estimates that climate change could have created 150 million refugees by 2050.[27] The local impacts will be even more significant. In Bangladesh alone, 20–40 million people will be displaced over the next 100 years by a rise in sea-levels.[28]

Water

Climate change will lead to a major redistribution of precipitation in ways that are often hard to predict. Generally speaking, it is likely to exacerbate existing extremes; dry areas are likely to become drier, many marginal areas will become uninhabitable. Some major rivers will lose a large part of their flow within the next 100 years: the Indus half of its annual flow; the River Niger a third; and the Nile a fifth. Le Paz, Lima and Quito, capitals of Bolivia, Peru and Ecuador respectively, all depend on Andean glaciers for water and hydroelectric power. Due to the rapid shrinking of the Andean glaciers, all three cities could find themselves severely short of water by the middle of this century.[29] In February 2006, the then UK Secretary for Defence, John Reid, warned that water shortages created by climate change will become a major cause of future conflict especially in the Middle East where 5 per cent of the world's population depends on scarcely 1 per cent of its water. He noted that: 'the lack of water and agricultural land is a significant contributory factor to the tragic conflict we see unfolding in Darfur. We should see this as a warning sign.'[30]

Health

The World Health Organisation (WHO) estimates that increases in infectious diseases directly attributable to climate change are already responsible for 150,000 additional deaths per year. It says that this number could double by 2030.[31] Paul Epstein, Associate Director of the Harvard Center for Health and Global Environment, warns that the impacts of climate change on rates of disease could cause 'overwhelming damage' in developing countries. The Center warns that rising temperatures will greatly expand the area within which the malarial mosquito can live, leading to 50–80 million additional cases of malaria per year. Warmer temperatures, reduced water supplies, and proliferating micro-organisms will also lead to a higher incidence of cholera, salmonellosis, and other such infections.[32]

COMPARATIVE WORD SEARCH OF WEBSITES

Given these growing climate change impacts we would expect that the attention given by NGOs to it would be proportionate. For example, we would expect that an NGO concerned with refugees would also be actively engaged from the outset with any climate change-induced cause of forced migration. To measure this supposition I conducted a search[33] for every mention of the phrase 'climate change', and the keywords 'refugee', 'water' and 'health', on the websites of leading organisations from five non-environmental sectors: human rights, development, women's issues, indigenous rights and labour. The names were drawn from an NGO directory developed by Duke University Perkins Library.[34] The main criteria for selection were size, profile and specialism.

On large websites there is always a chance that any word or phrase may appear at random. Therefore, for the purposes of comparison, I also searched for a term of no relevance to the core activities of these organisations ('ice cream') and one of very marginal relevance ('donkey'). The results are given in Table 2.

ANALYSIS OF RESULTS

Of the 20 organisations only eight give more mention to climate change than to ice cream. Indeed, even a small ice cream company with a superficial awareness of current environmental issues gives more coverage to climate change on its website than the largest international aid and development organisations.

To pick out a few examples: Amnesty International, an organisation with a staff of over 300, gives not one mention to an issue which both the Ministry of Defence and the US Pentagon have identified as a major source of future conflict.[35] Refugees International, the leading advocacy NGO on refugee rights issues, gives just four mentions to climate change. It has a very large website which gives over 64,000 mentions to the issues of refugees, health and water – all, as I have suggested above, issues inextricably linked to climate change. The website of the European Council on Refugees and Exiles, an umbrella organisation of 80 refugee-assisting agencies, gives only three mentions, suggesting that the entire refugee sector is failing to engage with climate change.

As I will discuss below, human rights and refugee organisations have numerous internal challenges in taking on board an issue which has been defined as environmental. The YWCA should have no such obstacles. Its website declares that 'the environment is a global priority for the World YWCA movement' and states that 'social equity and care for the environment are critical elements in the development process'. It gives not one mention to climate change. Even the ICRC, the classic *a priori* international NGO, which, as noted above, is already making public statements about the role of climate change in natural disasters, gives surprisingly little mention

Table 2   Mentions on Websites of Key Words, 8 June 2006

Organisation	URL	'Refugee'	'Health'	'Water'	'Donkey'	'Ice Cream'	'Climate Change'
Human rights							
Amnesty International	www.amnesty.org	366	347	148	0	1	0
Human Rights Watch	http://hrw.org	21,400	52,400	26,800	67	25	16
Physicians for Human Rights	www.phrusa.org	328	26,800	233	11	1	1
Development and disaster relief							
Oxfam US	www.oxfam.org	78	294	319	6	4	1
Oxfam GB	www.oxfam.org.uk	445	34,600	22,000	75	17	729
CARE US	www.care.org	147	903	689	2	1	1
World Vision UK	www.worldvision.org.uk	57	296	301	4	3	14
World Vision US	www.worldvision.org	547	9,500	11,000	63	12	4
International Committee of the Red Cross	www.icrc.org	10,600	45,900	33,000	25	4	73
Save the Children UK	www.savethechildren.org.uk	10,500	17,300	696	42	15	13
CAFOD	www.cafod.org.uk	217	778	761	11	5	178
Indigenous rights							
Survival International	www.survival-international.org	9	13,500	355	4	1	0
Women's issues							
International Women's Health Coalition	www.iwhc.org	49	991	31	0	0	1
Womankind Worldwide	www.womankind.org.uk	11	143	41	1	1	0
Young Women's Christian Association (YWCA)	www.worldywca.info	15	402	29	0	1	0
Refugees							
European Council on Refugees and Exiles	www.ecre.org	9,310	474	78	0	0	3
Refugees International	www.refugeesinternational.org	26,700	17,700	20,000	40	27	4
Health							
Family Health International	www.fhi.org/en/index.htm	109	75,800	426	8	8	0
Labour and unions							
American Federation of Labor-Congress of Industrial Organizations	www.aflcio.org	7	14,800	161	0	1	6
Trades Union Congress (TUC)	www.tuc.org.uk	282	68,600	1,170	13	3	547
Other (for comparison purposes)							
Ben and Jerry's Ice Cream	www.benjerry.com	1	90	233	0	658	13
The Donkey Sanctuary	www.thedonkeysanctuary.org.uk	2	83	70	621	2	0

to climate change on its very large website. The number of mentions is far below that for organisations with only limited engagement. The organisations that gave the greatest mention to climate change were CAFOD, the UK Trades Union Congress and Oxfam GB.

One final observation is worth making: there is a marked difference between US and European organisations. For example, the UK Trades Union Congress and the US AFL-CIO are both voices for their national trades union movements with large websites. Yet the AFL-CIO virtually ignores an issue to which the TUC gives over 500 mentions. Similarly, climate change is clearly not an issue for Oxfam US, despite the attention it receives from its UK sister organisation.

There are always individual reasons for such disparities (for example, Oxfam US is very much smaller than Oxfam GB and works on far fewer issues) but it is also reasonable to assume that the polarised political environment in the US would make organisations wary of tackling climate change. It is hardly surprising, for example, that the AFL-CIO might wish to avoid an issue that has deeply divided unions, many of which campaigned for the US withdrawal from the Kyoto Protocol. Other large major US NGOs have a high level of financial dependence on government funds and have strong reasons not to antagonise the current administration. CARE US receives half of its $561 million budget in this way and gives climate change just one mention on its website. It has also been criticised on similar grounds for its refusal to take any public position on the Iraq war.[36]

Two overall conclusions can be drawn. Firstly, it is clear that major NGO sectors are still not actively engaged with the issue or considering its importance for their core concerns. Secondly, some NGOs appear to be actively distancing themselves from climate change. It is remarkable that large websites concerned with current social and political issues give no mention to a term receiving constant quotation in political speeches, international policy negotiations and media. My tentative explanation is that many organisations define climate change as an issue that they do *not* work on. They therefore consciously exclude it from their materials and the term is actively filtered out of web content.

WHY ARE THESE MAJOR NGOs NOT ENGAGED WITH CLIMATE CHANGE?

To identify the reasons for the low NGO engagement with climate change I conducted formal interviews with five leading figures from the missing NGO sectors above:

Andrew Simms	Policy Director of the New Economics Foundation, former Campaigns Director of Christian Aid, and lead author for the 'Up In Smoke' coalition
Eleanor Monbiot	Director of Humanitarian Learning and Programming, World Vision International
Benedict Southworth	Executive Director of World Development Movement, former Campaigns Director for Amnesty International and Director of the global climate campaign for Greenpeace International
Avner Gidron	Senior Policy Adviser, Amnesty International
John Magrath	Programme researcher for Oxfam GB and contributor to the 'Up in Smoke' series of reports

1. The defence of mission

All of the large NGOs started with limited mandates that established their organisational mission and set the framework for future expansion. For example, Oxfam was founded around famine relief and Amnesty around the release of prisoners of conscience. They are still associated in the public mind with these original defining activities and they continue to promote them as a form of organisational branding. The large NGOs have a strong sense of their mission, and a deep caution about new issues that could weaken their focus. They even have a special phrase for this: 'mission creep'. This threat is a particular concern for human rights organisations such as Amnesty International, which are trying to deal with an issue that, according to its widest definitions, could encompass social, political or economic rights. Climate change, thus, sits outside the historical mission of these organisations, and, to be adopted as a new issue, would have to overcome their reluctance on purely practical grounds as well as an internal culture that equally can influence operational decisions.

2. The perceived ownership by environmental NGOs

Climate change is widely perceived as an 'environmental issue' owned by scientists and environmentalists and to which, at least for many years, NGOs from other sectors felt hampered by their lack of internal expertise. They believed (or chose to believe) that there was little that they could usefully add. However, there are other reasons why the 'environmental' designation has persuaded them to keep away.

Firstly, because the language and messaging of climate change has tended to reflect the interests of scientists and environmentalists, it has failed to highlight the specific human impacts, or use the 'rights' and social justice vocabulary, that energises the wider NGO community. Communication has often been very technical, concerned with the physics of the greenhouse gases and graphs of their accumulation. The impacts have tended to be presented in the form of very abstract predictions of global environmental impact such as the loss of forests, coral, and land vulnerable to a rise in sea-levels.

The development groups have been further challenged and alienated by the solutions proposed by many environmental groups – a rapid phase-out of fossil fuels and constraints on economic growth. These measures are anathema to many working in the development field. Although there have been major moves during the past ten years to find a common ground, largely around the concept of 'sustainable' development, there are still deep antagonisms between the development and environmental communities around the issues of growth and industrialisation. Climate change has the misfortune to sit astride this fault line.

3. The lack of clear role and opportunity for effective intervention

All the large NGOs have survived and flourished because of their capacity to achieve tangible results. Before they can work in any new area they need to establish that there is an identifiable niche and opportunity for their organisation, and that there are worthwhile outcomes that can come from their involvement. This is especially true for any area that is outside their existing range of activities or has a strong advocacy component. All of the NGO officers I interviewed made this point very strongly. Amnesty, for example, 'wants to be strategic and always asks how can we be effective and relevant'. World Vision 'takes on just two or three issues on the basis that it can do them well and achieve tangible results and be effective'.

Climate change is not an issue that these organisations feel offers them an opportunity for active engagement. Eleanor Monbiot for World Vision says:

Climate change is another complex issue with strong and intractable economic interests like trade and tariffs in which organisations have had a very hard and frustrating time in achieving political change and mobilising public concern. It is hard to see what we can do on this – what is the message, what we can achieve?

Even organisations with more involvement in issue-based advocacy are finding it difficult to identify a role for themselves. The international legal framework on climate change and the developing global policy is largely concerned with reducing emissions in the developed world, with a few poorly designed and top-down joint implementation projects in the South. There may be some opportunities for criticism by development groups, but few opportunities for the kind of proactive engagement that can lead to tangible results.

4. The inertia of organisational decision-making structures

As organisations grow they experience an arithmetical increase in the number of stakeholders who need to be consulted and the number of stages required to reach a policy decision. Their capacity to engage with an emerging issue such as climate change has therefore tended to be a reflection of both their size and the complexity of their decision-making structures. Smaller partnership-based organisations, such as Tear Fund or Christian Aid find it easier to respond rapidly to new issues. Large international organisations such as Oxfam require agreement on new policies from across the entire family of national offices. Some development organisations have the scale and turnover of large corporations, with a bureaucracy to match. The American Red Cross, for example, has a budget of $3 billion.[37]

Amnesty International is unusual in having a highly decentralised and democratic decision-making process. Typically, new issues arise through the annual meetings of the national office memberships. If adopted, a proposal is subjected to detailed study before being submitted to the biannual meeting of the international council. Issues are only likely to begin this process if they register with the Amnesty membership which, as noted above, is likely to identify strongly with the established identity of the organisation and is not necessarily qualified to be alert to emerging threats.

Benedict Southworth, who has worked in a senior position in environment, human rights and development organisations, has observed large differences in the process of policy formation between NGOs in different sectors. Environment organisations, he says, tend to develop policy to support the campaigns they wish to run and the outcomes they desire. They are willing to decide on a course of action first and develop the full details of their policy as they go. This strategy is well designed to engage with rapidly developing new issues such as climate change.

Development NGOs are more cautious and formulate a far larger body of internal policy work, much of which never reaches an implementation stage. They are therefore slow to take up issues that are outside their existing expertise and require a full internal analysis before considering involvement. Human rights organisations approach new issues from a legalistic perspective, seeking solutions through a binding legal framework and developing their policy on the basis of either creating or enforcing that framework. This long-term approach makes it hard for them to engage with new and fast-moving issues.

The size and specialisation of large NGOs also militates against cross-sectoral issues such as climate change. Large organisations divide their activities between a wide range of departments: policy, legal, campaigns, media, membership, programmes and so forth. As Andrew Simms comments, 'people tend to sit in their own silos'. He believes that development organisations have not had to deal with an issue that cuts across so many departments since they grappled with gender issues in the 1980s. It is precisely because climate change does not fit neatly within any existing specialism that it has invariably fallen to committed individuals to champion the issue and campaign internally for its acceptance. Simms argues that although new issues are usually introduced to organisations through the field staff, or lower management, climate change has only been accepted when there is also a full understanding at the most senior management level.

The case of Oxfam GB is a good example. Within Oxfam, the internal engagement with climate change is largely attributable to the sustained championing of a few individuals. One of them, John Magrath, could do so because of a mandate given directly by the executive director to scan for upcoming issues. In fact, Oxfam already had a policy position on climate change, reached in 2000. But work on it had stalled in favour of campaigns on unfair trade rules, conflict and small arms. It has therefore taken five years before climate change appeared in any strategic plan and six years before the decision to hire a dedicated staff member for the policy unit.

Clearly, new cross-sectoral issues have a slow and vulnerable gestation requiring the right combination of individuals and opportunity. Oxfam GB is now seriously engaged, but there have undoubtedly been numerous similar processes in other organisations that have foundered because of a loss of a key champion, or the stifling of the initiative of a single staff member.

5. The challenge of competing demands

Managers are warned on business courses never to take their eyes off issues that are important but not urgent. Because these issues can be easily ignored they have the potential to sink their business. Climate change is in precisely this category. Its importance cannot be denied, but we are only now feeling the full impacts of emissions from the 1950s and it still requires an act of imagination to feel the urgency of our current situation.

Organisations concerned with human rights, disaster relief, and Third World poverty occupy a working environment defined by constant, real and tangible urgency. The people interviewed all made a similar point: it is hard to make the case for dedicating resources to a long-term threat when one is working with people who are struggling on a daily basis for survival in a context of severe poverty or violence.

Large NGOs face constant additional demands related to their work and can feel overwhelmed by the urgency of their existing workload: 'we are feeling that we are always under siege' says Avner Gidron from Amnesty. 'We have so many acute pressures to deal with on a day-to-day basis', says Eleanor Monbiot. 'Climate change feels like something on top of everything else.' She lists some of the main pressures faced by senior management in World Vision: there is the demand of donors for quality assurance, the pressure of media for a rapid and visible response, the need to manage other smaller NGOs that may duplicate or undermine relief efforts, or to make work accountable to the people they are assisting, and the constant dilemma between providing short-term relief for individual emergencies and developing long-term solutions that anticipate future demands.

This dilemma between short-term relief and long-term solutions is expressed in an extreme form by climate change. Relief organisations argue that the impacts of weather-related disasters are determined by a combination of both the *hazard* to and the *vulnerability* of the affected population. They may recognise the role of climate change in increasing the *hazard* by creating more extreme weather events but can also identify many more immediate and compelling opportunities to reduce the *vulnerability* side of the equation: poverty, nutrition, health, the level of state preparedness, and the speed of a relief effort.

6. Broader psychology

Finally, it is important to stress that NGOs do not operate in isolation from the wider social and political *Zeitgeist*. Their staff members take their cues from the issues they see in the media, hear from the politicians, and discuss with their friends. Issues that are receiving widespread attention in wider society will have a greater level of awareness within the organisation and are more likely to impact on their membership or donors. Conversely, issues with low public awareness require a far greater effort of internal persuasion before they can be adopted.

For over a decade, the media presented climate change as a matter of unsettled scientific hypothesis. Climate sceptics and politically motivated organisations played to this uncertainty and ran a highly successful campaign to undermine the consensus findings of the IPCC. More subtle sceptics, for example Bjorn Lomborg, accept that climate change is a problem, but argue that the money invested in mitigation would be far better spent on fighting global poverty. NGO officers in progressive organisations are vulnerable to such arguments. They are largely from social science backgrounds and are ill-equipped to interpret the technical scientific debate. There is plentiful anecdotal evidence that senior managers in many organisations have absorbed the sceptical arguments and require detailed and focused briefing before accepting the reality of the threat posed by climate change. Individuals working within NGOs are also subject to wider and more complex psychological responses to climate change. Commentators are increasingly referring to a widespread and self-reinforcing denial of the issue as a means by which people resolve the challenges that it poses to their worldview.[38]

CONCLUSION: MOVING FORWARDS

Most NGOs that have an organisational remit to address global threats to people's livelihoods are not engaged with the greatest global threat: climate change. Although there may be many within the organisations who do not fully appreciate the urgency or scale of the threat, this avoidance does not arise through ignorance or a lack of concern. It is simply too new, large and daunting for organisations that seek clearly defined and achievable goals within their existing area of expertise. Climate change is also widely perceived as a threat for the future. For organisations dealing with urgent and life-threatening situations it is all too readily sidelined as 'important but not urgent'.

Unfortunately, these reasons for non-engagement are exactly those used by governments, businesses and the general public, all of which are actively avoiding the issue or sidelining it as a minor 'environmental' issue. It is for this reason that the involvement of non-environmental NGOs is of such importance because it is only when climate change is recognised as a major threat to economic, social and political stability that it will be taken seriously. Sadly, when it comes to climate change, the 'conscience of humanity' is still largely unconscious.

The momentum of the issue will, inevitably, change this situation. Having established the reality and proof of anthropogenic global warming, the hard science is increasingly concerned with defining the specific impacts. Slowly, the social sciences are incorporating these predictions into their own analyses and providing information of real value to non-environmental organisations. The predictions will increasingly manifest themselves in real, extreme weather events and the issue will stop being important but not urgent and will become both urgent and immediate.

There are also encouraging signs that major players among the non-environmental NGOs are beginning to seriously engage with climate change. This process began in Britain in 2004 with a series of informal meetings between development organisations. This led to the publication in 2005 of the 'Up In Smoke' report,[39] which used the language of social justice and equality to summarise the implications of climate change for global poverty and welfare. Endorsing a coalition report was a simple step that enabled organisations to begin an internal discussion about climate change free from the pressures to adopt a formal policy. The 'Up in Smoke' coalition has inspired similar initiatives in the Netherlands, Germany and Australia.

There is also an emerging and promising tendency for NGOs from different sectors to work together on joint climate change programmes. The British 'Stop Climate Chaos Coalition'[40] brings together the largest environmental and developmental membership NGOs to make joint demands on government. The coalition is consciously modelled on the broad coalition and mass mobilisations achieved by the Jubilee Debt and the Make Poverty History Campaigns.

In the Netherlands, more than 40 nature conservation, environment, development and humanitarian NGOs have joined together to develop a Joint Climate Change Programme.[41] It has secured funding of €16.3 million for 2006–07 from the Dutch Postcode Lottery. This initiative is concerned with building a portfolio of programmatic responses to climate change such as disaster risk reduction, drought management, nature protection and river and coastal zone management, and a package of information and solutions for the general public.[42]

All of these initiatives aim to proselytise and build a higher level of engagement within the wider NGO community. The Dutch initiative aims to 'stimulate a more pro-active role for these organisations internationally'. In other words, we are starting to see a few of the most progressive national offices of the large international NGOs step ahead of their colleagues in other countries and set the pace for internal policy change. It will be a slow and frustrating process, but it is at least an indication that the watchdogs are waking up.

NOTES

1. L. Diamond, 'Rethinking civil society: toward democratic consolidation', *Journal of Democracy*, 5(3): pp. 4–17.
2. James Paul, 'NGOs and global policy-making', *Global Policy Forum*, June 2000: http://www.globalpolicy.org/ngos/analysis/anal00.htm
3. Ibid.
4. International Bank for Reconstruction and Development (World Bank), *Operational Directive 14.70*, cited: http://docs.lib.duke.edu/igo/guides/ngo/define.htm
5. Daniel C. Esty, 'Non-Governmental Organisations at the World Trade Organization: cooperation, competition, or exclusion', *Journal of International Economic Law* 1 (1), pp. 123–48; Steve Charnovitz, 'Two centuries of participation: NGOs and international governance', *Michigan Journal of International Law* 18(2), pp. 281–2.
6. Paul, 'NGOs and global policy-making'.
7. Peter Willetts, ed., '*The Conscience of the World': The Influence of Non-Governmental Organisations in the UN System*, London, Hurst and Washington: Brookings Institution, 1996, p. 38. Updated data available on: http://www.staff.city.ac.uk/p.willetts/NGOS/NGO-GRPH.DOC
8. B. Levinger and J. Mulroy, 'Making a little go a long way: How the World Bank's small grants program promotes civic engagement', Washington, DC: The World Bank, 2003.
9. Paul Wapner, *Environmental Activism and World Civic Politics*, Albany: SUNY Press, 1996.
10. Levinger and Mulroy, 'Making a little go a long way'.
11. These are, in order: International NGOs, Business-oriented International NGOs, Religious International NGOs, Environmental NGOs, Government-Operated NGOs, Quasi-Autonomous NGOs, Donor-Created NGOs, Government-Related NGOs, and Party-Affiliated NGOs.

12. Peter Willetts, 'What is a Non-Governmental Organisation?', Output from the Research Project on Civil Society Networks in Global Governance, UNESCO *Encyclopaedia of Life Support Systems*, 2002: http://www.staff. city.ac.uk/p.willetts/CS-NTWKS/NGO-ART.HTM

13. List of NGOs with observer status under the United Nations Framework Convention on Climate Change, 2006: http://maindb.unfccc.int/public/ ngo.pl?mode=wim&search=A

14. NGOs categorised as 'other' either do not readily fit other categories or are of uncertain categorisation.

15. Categorisation was based on name or information provided on websites in English. Many organisations had names and activities that crossed between environment, business, energy and research categories. These were either allocated on the basis of what appeared to be their primary activity or were included in the category 'other'.

16. Jeremy Leggett, *Carbon War: Global Warming and the End of the Oil Era*, London: Routledge, 2001.

17. Geoffrey Lean, 'UK to go it alone on global warming', *Independent*, 1 April 2001.

18. Michelle Betsill, 'Transnational actors in international environmental politics', in Michelle Betsill, Kathryn Hochstetler and Dimitris Stevis, eds, *Palgrave Advances in International Environmental Politics*, Basingstoke: Palgrave Macmillan, 2005.

19. Ibid.

20. Ibid.

21. Paul, 'NGOs and global policy-making'.

22. Marjorie Mayo, *Global Citizens: Social movements and the challenge of globalisation*, London: Zed Books 2005.

23. Avner Gidron, Senior Policy Adviser, Amnesty International, interview with author, 20 June 2006.

24. Benedict Southworth, Executive Director, World Development Movement, interview with author, 20 June 2006.

25. http://www.ehs.unu.edu/print.php?page=12_October_-_UN_Disaster_ Day

26. *National Geographic*, News, 18 November 2005: http://news.nationalgeo- graphic.com/news/2005/11/1118_051118_disaster_refugee.html

27. Norman Myers, 'Environmental refugees in a globally warmed world', *BioScience*, 43 (11), December 1993, pp. 752–61.

28. *National Geographic*, 2005.

29. Fred Pearce, *When the Rivers Run Dry*, London: Eden Project Books, 2006.

30. 'Water Wars: climate change may spark conflict', *Independent*, 28 February 2006.

31. 'Scientists prepare New York for future climate change', Press Release no. 99–065, National Aeronautics and Space Administration 1999: http:// www.giss.nasa.gov/research/news/

32. Ibid.

33. The search was conducted on 8 June 2006, using the Google 'entire site' search function. The search results include every mention of the chosen term, including multiple references on the same page, and plurals. It also

includes every text file and pdf report and therefore includes much of the published material of an organisation including research documents and annual reports.

34. http://docs.lib.duke.edu/igo/guides/ngo/index.htm
35. See Chapter 2 of this volume.
36. Rano Faroohar, 'Where the money is?', *Newsweek*, 5 September 2005.
37. Ibid.
38. George Marshall, 'Are we in a state of denial about climate change?': http://coinet.org.uk/perspectives/marshall
39. See http://www.neweconomics.org/gen/z_sys_publicationdetail. aspx?pid=196
40. http://www.stopclimatechaos.org
41. http://www.climatecentre.org/downloads/File/articles/Press%20release %20Climate%20Project%20NPL.pdf
42. Ibid.

Part IV

The Challenge Ahead

10
Clearing the Pathways To Transformation

Susan Ballard and David Ballard

As authors elsewhere in this book have identified, climate change is a huge and urgent challenge which is not being met. Current policy processes such as the Kyoto Protocols barely scratch at the surface of the problem and have had little effect so far: global carbon emissions continued to rise between 1997, when the Kyoto treaty was signed, and 2002.[1] Despite cheap and simple technological innovations which could save businesses and consumers energy and money, change is slow and very limited. So why are we failing to respond adequately as individuals, organisations and social institutions? Are we the selfish, morally bankrupt, dysfunctional, witless victims of a powerful geo-oligarchy intent on milking the carbon economy, whatever the long-term cost?

Persuasive though this explanation sometimes is, we tend to think that greater opportunities for progress come from exploring the cock-up rather than the conspiracy view of this crisis, as explored in David Ballard's chapter, 'Mostly Missing the Point: Business Responses to Climate Change', in this volume. That is because, working as strategy consultants in the field of human change and environmental sustainability, we come across individuals who are aware enough of climate change and the threats it poses to want to do something about it, even if they perceive that 'something' as better for the collective rather than in their own interest. What they find out is just how little they can do without an alignment between what they want to do and the facilitative change needed in the wider context beyond their control.

We come across examples of this in many different contexts and at different scales: neighbourhoods keen to stop their rubbish clogging up landfill and giving off methane but whose local authority has been slow to provide kerbside recycling; a construction company wanting to install energy-efficient plant to a new hospital but unable to specify anything which could overcome NHS codes of practice on consistent temperatures; farmers wanting to grow biomass but deterred by the lack of a guaranteed market for their crops. The energy manager of a local business may be tempted by new technology which reduces energy bills and carbon dioxide emissions in the long term but the finance adviser insists that the capital replacement cost is too high and no government grant is available to ease the transition. We know of a business director who got past this hurdle with a creative idea for financing change but was opposed by the local community who did not want a waste-to-energy plant and integrated development in their village.

The devil is in the detail and many good intentions soon go to ground or are limited in scope by constraints over which a change agent has no perceived or actual control. Even elegant and potentially helpful policies such as Contraction and Convergence are in danger of dissolving like bubbles when they hit the ground because no one has thought to remove the sharp obstacles in their way. So what needs to change?

William D. Ruckelshaus, Environmental Protection Agency Administrator under Presidents Nixon and Reagan (not the obvious choice as an advocate of revolution!), suggested that the scale of change needed was comparable to the Agricultural and Industrial Revolutions but with an important difference, 'These revolutions were gradual, spontaneous and largely unconscious. This one will have to be a fully conscious operation, guided by the best foresight that science can provide.'[2]

We too are arguing for a change in the way we think about change. We argue that change is an integrated long-term process which involves what organisational theorists might describe as investment in complementarities. In other words, what the pioneers of complementarities theory in economics, Paul Milgrom and John Roberts,[3] described as 'doing *more* of one thing *increases* the returns to doing *more* of another'. In applying this theory to change for sustainable development we shall be looking at mutually reinforcing conditions for change and a matrix of contextual constraints that require synergistic management.

We shall also argue the need for a change strategy led by a network or ecosystem of champions, as we shall be calling them later, in association with 'proto-champions'; people in a champion role but who are not yet fully committed to doing something specifically on climate change. Certain special qualities characterise climate change champions which we shall be describing in order to highlight the capacity building that is needed for change.

As the first step to clearing a pathway to transformation, we shall outline four mutually reinforcing generic conditions and a learning process which need to be embedded and integrated within a change strategy. Typically, as climate change strategy consultants, we have devised a simple mnemonic, the five As, to help describe what is necessary for change. The first three As: Awareness (understanding at several levels), Agency (the ability to do something meaningful), Association (joining forces with others) are necessary for change at the project level. The fourth A, the process of Action and Reflection (learning through cycles of doing and reviewing), is necessary to keep a project going as change occurs and stop things from running out of steam. The fifth A, Architecture for change (the configuration of people, procedures, processes and resources), ensures that change at the project level is embedded and that questions raised can be addressed by other groups at appropriate organisational levels. This chapter will clarify what we mean by the five As and why we have reached the conclusion that this model is a helpful tool for change agents or champions contributing to the revolutionary scale of change envisaged by Ruckelshaus.

THE FIRST A, AWARENESS, IS INSUFFICIENT WITHOUT THE SECOND, AGENCY

What marketers would describe as brand awareness of climate change, and the mechanisms which cause it (use of energy, driving cars, and so on) is actually high in the UK, with 85 per cent in 2001 thinking that climate change is happening and 71 per cent that humans are causing it. Many fewer, perhaps only 15 per cent, have a sense of the scale and urgency of the challenge. What still needs to be developed beyond this, and few decision makers seem to have it, is an understanding of delays and feedbacks in both climate and social systems, and awareness of intervention points which at certain critical points in time give individuals and organisations the scope to make a very big difference.[4]

By itself, brand awareness of climate change is insufficient to dissolve the many barriers to change. Most people, however aware and well intentioned, simply do not have the energy or the resources to tackle the many factors inhibiting change and may therefore retreat from the issue altogether; a reaction commonly described as fatalism by attitude and opinion surveys. Yet this blanket interpretation of the public as ignorant, selfish or fatalistic is symptomatic of another awareness deficit; a failure to understand the necessary conditions underlying change.

The misunderstanding of change as a one-off event which can be switched on by more information is reflected in recent governmental climate change communication strategies which have opted to focus on awareness-raising, or more recently attitude-changing. It is as if experts, empowered by their role in society, suppose that broadcasting more and more information about climate change will somehow effortlessly erase all the barriers which are currently preventing citizens from changing their lifestyles.

The strategy is reminiscent of jokes about the UK's 'just shout louder' approach to people who do not speak English. It ignores conclusive findings which show that awareness-raising is not only not enough to promote change but can even be counter-productive. This is particularly true of climate change when people feel overwhelmed and disempowered by the huge scale of the issue.

A 1995 study of public perceptions of sustainability in Lancashire, for instance, showed that information about sustainability issues was not enough to engage people. The researchers found that distrust of governmental or local authority commitment to the issues could diminish an individual's interest in taking action and his or her receptiveness to the information. Not surprisingly, many people felt there was no point in acting if their actions were rendered meaningless by a context beyond their control.[5] As a more recent participant in a climate change conversation game put it, 'If I'm going to have to put on a hair shirt, I need to see evidence that it will make a difference.'

THE IMPORTANCE OF THE SECOND A: AGENCY

What people need alongside awareness is a sense of where they can find their agency; in other words, what they can do which seems meaningful to them. We could use ourselves as an example. Having already taken the obvious measures to make our house more energy efficient, we looked to do something more meaningful both in terms of reducing our domestic carbon dioxide emissions and providing a model for friends and neighbours. We wanted to run an electric scooter off electricity generated by a roof-mounted wind turbine. Encouraged by the possibility of a government grant for a microturbine described in several leaflets that came through the letterbox, we applied to our district authority for planning advice. From then on our willingness to engage with government energy policy evaporated. The local planning process was too time-consuming, expensive and financially risky to encourage this material change.

We argue that it is pointless raising awareness of climate change unless people are also enabled to do something meaningful about it. Information about incentives, such as grants, does not increase agency unless other factors impeding change have been removed. In our case, as householders wanting to generate our own electricity, our individual agency was thwarted by the wider planning and political contexts. Although the Office of the Deputy Prime Minister claimed to be reviewing whether household micro wind turbines should require planning permission, the context into which this relatively small step change could be made seems currently to be determined by the anti-wind lobby. Despite the urgency of a need to shift to renewable energy, political fear of an electoral backlash is inhibiting government from following through on its commitments to the Kyoto Protocol and weaning the UK off carbon dependency.

In order to respond to the crisis with the awareness we have, we also seek to extend our agency beyond the individual household level. For instance, writing this chapter, or helping our clients to develop effective climate change action plans, are alternative routes to agency for us. However, our intended response to put a wind turbine on the roof visible from the footpath that runs past our house might have been meaningful not just in reducing our own consumption, but in encouraging others to do the same, had the government attended not just to giving us information but also to removing the local obstacles on the metaphoric path.

THE THIRD A: ASSOCIATION

Research shows that people are much more likely to act on climate change if they band together with other people.[6] We call this 'association'. Besides the obvious reinforcement of will power, like weight watchers, we think that strong association also enhances agency. An individual whose agency has been limited by contextual constraints beyond his or her control, may extend it by influencing an MP or lobbying through a pressure group. However, research also shows that some groups offer more agency than others. Support groups, for instance, if working well, can enhance and develop individual agency. If not, they can degenerate into talking shops and sub-optimal behaviours.

An example of the kind of association which can help to develop individual agency is the community eco club model supported by the charity Global Action Plan. Rather like a book club, the eco club is an opportunity for six to eight households, work colleagues or friends to meet regularly, perhaps once a month, to support and encourage each other to make the pro-environmental changes they choose to make. There are a number of similar initiatives taking place in pockets across the UK and some recent work with the New Economics Foundation (NEF) has enabled us to explore how effective these might be.

One of the ways to awaken a sense of agency through association that the NEF has been developing is by way of a card game which brings groups of people together informally around a table to talk about climate change. The deliberative process of the game helps them to decide where they stand on the issue both as individuals and as a group. It is intended that players are offered both a channel to influence policy and a route to a mutual support group.

The idea grew from the success of previous versions of the game, DEMOCS (Deliberative Meetings of Citizens) which had been used to stimulate informed and non-judgemental public discussions on controversial science issues such as genetically modified organisms and the mumps, measles and rubella vaccine. A version of DEMOCS using climate change as the topic went on trial. At the end of the game players were asked to vote on the kind of policy they wanted to see on climate change. Eventually it is intended to display this information on a website so that players and policy makers can see the voting patterns which may have some influence on policy.

However, a significant number of players were not satisfied with this ending. They wanted to find out more about what they personally could do about climate change. NEF considered a number of options such as issuing a to-do list with the game, setting up a Web-based pledge to action inventory, and so on, but has responded more recently with an informal experiment to convene virtual and real groups of so-called carbon watchers.

Community groups such as this are not new but they seem to be part of a growing movement. Studies of them suggest that success is often due to the weight watchers effect. Participants are more likely to commit to a change and stay committed to it if they have to account for themselves to a group with a shared purpose, as evidenced in this reflection by the convenor of such a group in Ledbury, Herefordshire:

At the initial meeting, I said that I wanted to change over the remaining light bulbs in our house to energy saving ones. It is now four days before our second meeting and for the last week I have felt a growing push to keep to my commitment rather than tell people that I hadn't done it. Somehow meeting with a group of people is a great incentive for action whereas previously it didn't seem to matter whether I did something or not.

Talking about and questioning lifestyle habits can bring about a shift in consciousness which sociologist Anthony Giddens describes as the move from practical to discursive consciousness and has been described in more detail by researcher Kersty Hobson in her study of Global Action Plan's 'Action at Home' programme:[7]

Giddens' concept of practical consciousness, a form of unsaid knowledge that individuals make use of in going about their everyday lives, neatly encapsulates the habits that Action at Home helped to change. What Action at Home does is to bring these habits, hidden away in practical consciousness, into discursive consciousness, where they are considered by the individual, and either altered or contested.

Groups serve to normalise pro-environmental behaviour and, when working well, provide a much bigger resource of creativity, information, skills and power than an individual can access working in isolation. Early feedback from the year-old group in Herefordshire suggests that participants are making pro-environmental behaviour changes and, as importantly, are enjoying doing so.

The NEF's learning journey in the DEMOCS Climate Change project underlines the need for awareness, agency and association to be attended to in parallel rather than in isolation. The card content of the game and the conversations raise players' awareness but it was not enough to offer them agency solely through voting on policy. Players themselves recognised the need to look for agency in their own lives and with others.

Although we come across many examples of awareness-raising alone being ineffective as a catalyst for change, it is just as common to find association alone as a sub-optimal strategy. We invite readers to consider the many examples of climate change associations of the great and the good which have been set up to tackle the issue. In the absence of a strong shared awareness and little real agency it is not surprising that many of these degenerate into rather cosy talking shops which achieve nothing on the pathway to transformation.

However, even when a mutually reinforcing balance is achieved between the first three As: awareness, agency and association, we still find that change initiatives can flounder or become collapsed in scale. They often remain at the project rather than at the programme level unless supported by the remaining two: Action and Reflection, and Architecture.

THE REMAINING TWO As: ACTION/REFLECTION AND ARCHITECTURE

To illustrate the importance of the remaining two As in conjunction with awareness, agency and association, we will draw on an account of one of our consultancy projects in the construction sector.

A UK construction company, which we have called 'Excelsior Holdings' to preserve commercial confidentiality, was required by its parent company to undertake an environmental bench-marking exercise. We were part of a consultancy team called in to help in 2001. Since Excelsior's core business was providing public infrastructure such as schools, hospitals, bridges and roads under the private finance initiative throughout the UK they might have been expected to have engaged with climate change and its impacts long before. In common with the majority of businesses, public bodies and NGOs across the UK, they had not. The level of awareness of climate change across the company was what we described earlier as brand awareness only.

Clearly, there was a huge need to address this awareness deficit across the whole organisation, group, partners, contractors and clients. Typically, we were only contracted with the organisation at one level. Our influence was, therefore, initially constrained.

However, in this particular case, consultation with the client generated a strategic question which was meaningful to the business as a whole: How can we respond profitably and creatively to the challenge of sustainable development? Because the teams framed the question as 'How can we respond ...?', they allowed themselves to use the enquiry to explore what their actual and potential agency might be, alongside learning about the issues in a collaborative association of colleagues and consultants.

In terms of association, a great deal of attention was paid to the dynamics of the group, with effort being put into building mutual trust and confidence and listening skills. This reinforced their ability to reflect together, something that they had not previously been used to doing. The first three As became mutually reinforcing.

Action and Reflection

The project was conducted using a learning process known as Action and Reflection. This process is particularly significant in change initiatives. Practice or behaviour does not change as a result of people being told what to do. For instance, external expert reporting on a problem rarely has an effect, however persuasive the recommendations. What is needed is learning by doing: Action, alongside reviewing both the result of a change in practice and the actions or patterns of thought that led to that outcome: Reflection. We have noticed the absence of this process in countless carbon reduction initiatives which produce little return for the original investment of time and money. Without effective measurement of results or an adequate evaluation process there is little reflexivity or learning. By introducing a structured action/reflection process participants can learn more and change their approach accordingly.[8]

In this case Action phases worked in a number of ways, often with several streams running in parallel. For instance:

- Everybody in the group made small changes to everyday practice; for example, seeing what happened when participants raised sustainability issues in a project meeting. There was no easy opt-out: if someone didn't do the agreed action, then every effort was made to understand what had led to this.
- Focused action in current projects, usually by one member of the group at a time. For instance, one person took a working day to investigate better energy alternatives for a project worth over £600 million; another looked in detail at whether steel or concrete was preferable on a civil engineering project; and a third looked in detail at what had led to significant increases in energy consumption beyond specification on a third project. Each of these investigations gave both content knowledge (for example, on options to reduce energy) and also significantly increased understanding of where 'agency' – a chance to make a major difference – lay on a typical project.
- Clients, sub-contractors and colleagues were asked about their understanding of climate change and its impacts and about what help they needed with various sustainability and business issues it raised for them. Group members found that such

conversations were much easier if they were not undertaken from an expert position but rather from a service position: here are some facts (for example, on climate impacts) provided by reliable third parties; how can we help you to think through what they might mean for your project so that we can help as best we can? In this way, the project process increased association with clients.

As members of the group began to gain trust in each other, in the consultants and in the process of the project, reflection deepened. The value of this became clear when a significant deepening of awareness happened for the group during an informal discussion on the science of climate change. A hasty sketch of data from the Vostok ice-core records had a powerful impact and the group interrupted the presentation because they needed time to assess what it meant for them emotionally, personally and for their business. We believe this deepening of awareness could not have happened without the prerequisite attention to agency and association. Certainly, this group underwent a significant shift in understanding at this point, much more powerful than when less care had been taken with the process.

Overall, the project was a success; the group did identify a realistic and sustainable market position, internal procedures were addressed, and feedback on the bids completed during the project was positive, though it was clear that the company's clients had little grasp of the issues. Opportunities to improve performance at the level of particular projects were identified. Some team members who freely acknowledged having been climate sceptics at the beginning of the project reversed their position to become advocates.

Importantly for our own learning, the project illustrated how vital it is for shallow awareness of climate change to shift to a deeper understanding of what we call 'agency moments'. These are intervention points which open and close quickly at certain critical points in time (for instance in the two or three weeks after a bid has been won and before detailed plans begin to drive out divergent thinking) but which potentially give individuals and organisations the scope to make a very big difference. Those responsible for specifying large infrastructure projects such as building a hospital make decisions which affect how much carbon dioxide is emitted for the next 25 or 50 years. Their decisions determine also whether the infrastructure will be resilient to climate impacts: will the hospital's roof blow off in a severe storm? Will driving rain penetrate the cladding and escalate costs or risk building collapse? It is at these agency moments that if deeper awareness were available, individuals and organisations could exercise greater than usual agency. While they are too often missed, the project showed that they can in principle be opened up.

Architecture

Even though the Excelsior project was rated a success, the scale of change that could potentially have been achieved was still limited in scope. We would suggest that, in common with many such successful projects, this is because an insufficiently robust change architecture (the fifth A) was in place for the learning to spread from project to programme level and beyond.[9]

When we talk about architecture for change we mean a particular configuration of people, procedures, processes and resources which enable change to take root more widely at multiple levels of a social system and across its usual boundaries. In the case of Excelsior, at the individual level, participants clearly increased their capacity to engage with climate change. At project level, a group of people developed who learned how to champion climate change and who would be a resource for other projects in the future. At organisational level the project did change the procedures in place for running projects: changes were made to the project management manual and to the processes to identify and manage risks, for instance.

At the cross- and inter-organisational levels, however, the architecture was weaker. The acceptance of the work at board level had perhaps inevitably depended heavily on the one Director in the project team, but he unexpectedly retired for reasons of ill health towards the end of the project. A new Director took over without the background in the issues and without having taken part in the group's learning journey. Even though the project's conclusions and recommendations were well argued, and so were easy for him to accept and implement, the learning process was inevitably harder to grasp and so the project's edge was quickly lost. While the champion network continued, and did participate in some wider discussions, it did not have counterparts elsewhere in the group and also lacked the leadership that would have been necessary to deal with the many issues in other group companies, so the project petered out before its full potential could be realised. Nor could the champions' group move on to address wider issues in the marketplace by, for instance, participating in initiatives on European competition law, which certainly limited change. While much was done, much more might have been possible.

WHY IS A ROBUST ARCHITECTURE NEEDED?

As a first step to understanding why a change architecture is needed, we present a simple map of the kinds of obstacles blocking the pathway to transformation. The contextual factors which inhibit change initiatives are differentiated on a 2 x 2 matrix developed by the American author Ken Wilber.[10] Obstacles can then be characterised as applying either at the personal level, or at the collective level, and may consist either of subjective issues (for instance, assumptions or group norms which limit action), or objective factors (for instance, the constraints of a job role or of technologies).

1. Individual subjective factors (limiting personal values, worldview, assumptions, etc.)	2. Individual objective factors (limitations of one's role, skills, knowledge, relationship set, etc.)
3. Collective subjective factors (group cultures, shared norms, etc.)	4. Collective objective factors (political, economic, social, technological, legal, environmental)

Barriers to change (after Ken Wilber)

One or another of these obstacles can come into play at any time in the micro-processes which affect decision making in organisations, communities or other groups, and they are often interlinked. For instance, a project in 2004 to introduce a waste-to-energy plant in a Wiltshire village (a technical adaptation response: quadrant 4 in box above) ran into community power dynamics (the integrity of the local proposer of the project was undermined by villagers who distrusted his motives: also quadrant 4). There was significant scepticism about the authenticity of the consultation process (which may have resulted from a shared mindset about how decisions are taken: quadrant 3). The personal skills and role of the facilitator/consultant may have made it difficult to address this mindset (the project facilitator/consultant had not been given enough information about the history of relationships in the village: quadrant 2). There was also evidence of personal assumptions such as 'Why should this village take the risk of new technology and possible devaluation of house prices when others will benefit?' (quadrant 1).

Change efforts continually come up against 'hard' and 'soft' constraints at these different levels. Commonly we see no coordination between efforts in one area of the grid with efforts in another. Just as commonly there is little effort in research communities, with the exception of the Tyndall Centre, to integrate knowledge in one area with knowledge from another. Frequently researchers simply cannot find a mutually comprehensible language in which to communicate, or waste time picking holes in other disciplines' methodologies and ways of validating knowledge.

At policy level, there are at least encouraging signs in the rhetoric of Defra's 2005 sustainable development strategy that policy makers are beginning to see the need for a more orchestrated approach. What is described as a new comprehensive approach to behavioural change by Defra draws on lessons learned from government anti-smoking strategy. For example, before current legislation against smoking in public places could be introduced successfully (collective objective), smoking had to become a minority habit. Therefore, work needed doing in parallel, in the individual subjective domain, by supporting health professionals to run programmes tackling attitudes, habits and addiction. Alongside efforts to change attitudes, public health campaigns (collective subjective), information was needed (individual objective) to help people to make the choice to give up and to find the level of support they needed to sustain this intention. The same issue is recognised by think-tanks, such as the Policy Studies Institute, which argues that fiscal incentives are needed alongside information to persuade householders to adopt more pro-environmental behaviour.

Strategists can develop a robust architecture by using the Wilber matrix to map out the different contextual constraints which will need to be addressed if a change initiative is to be successful. Simple questions, such as 'Who needs to know/do what and when for the change we envisage to occur?' can then be the basis for collective planning and decision making about where to direct resources and organisational processes to catalyse the envisaged transformation. The first three As then become a way to diagnose whether the conditions for change are adequately in balance; the fourth, Action/reflection provides a reminder of the need to set up an adequate and appropriate learning process as part of the fifth, Architecture. This model has proven to be particularly helpful in public sector organisations for department managers who need to devise climate change action plans.

THE ORGANISATION AS ARCHITECT
FOR LARGE-SCALE TRANSFORMATION

Our current work in the public sector has alerted us to the significant role that a linking pin organisation such as a local council might play in developing a strategic change architecture. The potential agency available to a local authority is huge since it is responsible for delivering key services, can influence local communities, has enforcement and convening powers, can scrutinise contractors and partners, has developed practical expertise and has democratic legitimacy. Local government is also a potential bridge between local and regional communities and national government.

Yet in practice many councils are still locked into bureaucratic and hierarchical ways of working designed for the service delivery of yesteryear. They have not developed the adaptive capacity necessary to take on complex cross-cutting policy challenges, the so-called 'wicked issues' first described as such in 1997 by researchers at the University of Birmingham.[11] These do not fall neatly into any single departmental budgeting process or cost code. Climate change, in particular, as a key example of a wicked issue, requires a coordinated matrix of policy from different departments to tackle it effectively.

Frans Berkhout, coordinator of the University of Sussex's Science and Technology Policy Research, Energy and Environment Programme, describes adaptive capacity[12] in this context as the ability of organisations to make changes in technology, policies and practices (another way of defining change architecture) that will help them avoid risks associated with climate change. We have found this capacity lamentably lacking in our strategic work with government at all levels yet it is often evident in individuals. We discovered more about the adaptive capacity of isolated change agents in organisations through some in-depth case study work we undertook in an evaluation of Hampshire County Council's potential climate change champion strategy.

CHAMPIONS CLEAR THE PATH AHEAD

One aspect of architecture often overlooked is the architect. The cathedral remains but the narratives of the individual architect, builders, stonemasons and others, whose collective purpose it was to construct it, are lost. In our case study approach for Hampshire we learned directly from the stories of people whom others identified as champions of climate change. It was in the detail of what we heard that we began to recognise specific characteristics or qualities peculiar to those working on sustainability issues like climate change.

Such people display many of the skills, competencies and behaviours of 'boundary spanners'.[13] They have the interpersonal skills such as fluency in different linguistic registers so that they maintain credibility in different contexts and can frame sustainability issues to meet different agendas. They move easily between different levels of a system, inspiring trust both in a boardroom and in a village hall. They act as conduits for learning, thinking and knowledge between different parts of an organisation or wider system. They can adapt and perform to different management styles: hierarchical or egalitarian. They build relational capital by making connections between people and developing their networks. However, the two most significant characteristics which differentiated sustainability champions from other boundary spanners were their driving passion and a relentless search for greater agency.

These key characteristics are vital, we argue, in the task of clearing the pathways for transformation. Practitioners working on climate change or the wider sustainability agenda invariably come up continually against the contextual constraints typified in the Wilber matrix. They therefore need a driving passion to sustain their efforts to overcome these constraints over long periods of time; in many cases, a lifetime of effort. Their relentless search for greater agency is commonly provoked by their deeper than average awareness of the scale of climate change impacts and the urgency with which we need to respond.

Unlike the tempered radicals described by Debra Meyerson in the book of the same name,[14] who are careful not to rock the organisational boat so hard that they fall overboard, climate change champions will choose to leave the boat if they think they will be able to respond more meaningfully and achieve more elsewhere. Their actions and/or career paths often look risky or radical. What they may be doing is risking their own job or career security in order to remove an obstacle on the pathway to transformation, making it easier for those who follow.

We found examples of a champion who had been prepared to challenge the legitimacy of his organisation's environmental decision making in court, another abandoned a well-paid consultancy career to support business development of environmental management systems, another left a prestigious consultancy to set up a project to exert shareholder pressure on businesses underperforming on carbon emissions. These were relatively high-profile actions.

We also found champions who had managed to outlive organisational upheavals and abandoned career ambitions to remain in a post where they could optimise their influence. It was humbling to hear about the huge and highly motivated efforts they would put in to achieve something that would have been so much easier if more people had helped rather than hindered the process.

Typical examples of this were provided by Dave Pickles OBE, Manager of Newark and Sherwood Energy Agency. In one of the structured conversations that informed our evaluation for Hampshire County Council of the potential for a climate change champions' strategy, Dave told the story of his 28 years as a council officer trying to mainstream sustainable development. This revealed just how much sustained, strategic work was needed by a champion to spearhead a major change initiative. What Dave, and those who have supported his efforts, have achieved is a theoretical 41 per cent reduction of carbon dioxide emissions from Newark and Sherwood's council-owned housing stock between 1990 and 2003, with further theoretical carbon dioxide savings projected in the period to 2020.

Dave was careful to include the word 'theoretical' because the emissions are calculated on the amount of energy needed to heat each property and will never be exact. What can be said with more certainty using April 2003 data is that 98.4 per cent of the council's 7,124 homes are capable of delivering affordable energy to a vulnerable single pensioner. Some tenants, albeit in small apartments, pay as little as £15 a year on heating. Yet to achieve what should be the norm across the UK, Dave has had to invent a new way of accounting, 'holistic cost benefit analysis'; convince the council to accept it as a basis for investing in a comprehensive raft of energy efficiency measures; set up a new database system to record changes to every individual property; devise new ways to measure and audit the energy performance of properties; persuade tenants that spending money on energy efficiency is preferable to modernising their kitchens, as well as surviving a one-time budget cut that removed his department.

Even with this high-profile success behind him (Newark and Sherwood District Council gained beacon status in 2001–03 for tackling fuel poverty), Dave still struggles against obstructions to embed sustainable development more widely. For instance, on one occasion he put a lot of time into developing a brief for ten eco-homes within a development of 150 but it got nowhere because a colleague claimed to have forgotten to do a vital part of the rubber stamping process. On another occasion he failed to get eco-housing built on a former mental hospital site despite overcoming many other constraints because, at the last hurdle, the landowners had to maximise their return on the land.

It is the failures as much as the successes which point to the many complementarities which need to be addressed before significant material change can happen. The majority of climate change champions we have spoken to felt isolated and worn out by constantly having to take on so many different contextual constraints and counter the prevailing culture. From their articulation of their support needs it became more and more obvious that a vital part of architecture for change involves building a network or association of climate change champions. We called it an ecosystem to underline that there are different types of champion working in different capacities horizontally and vertically across an organisation, some with a more visible profile than others, and that all and more are needed. If such a network could work strategically together, to a shared purpose, different champions could be addressing different parts of the matrix rather than each individual having to tackle everything him or herself.

In sharing this idea with managers in Hampshire County Council, we were delighted that we were able to develop in dialogue with them the idea of proto-champions. These are people for whom climate change is not yet an all-consuming passion but who want to do their bit to help in an area that interests them for other reasons and may therefore offer something to an overall strategy without necessarily pledging long-term commitment.

Being able to recognise and then build association with proto-champions enables champions to strengthen their agency. For instance, by catching a senior manager's interest in using the climate change agenda to develop strategic leadership capacity, it might be possible to draw on resources at a much higher level of the organisation than they might normally be able to reach. This strategy also offers a route to intervene in agency moments which a proto-champion would not necessarily have identified as opportunities for agency intervention. For example, in the Excelsior case study the group member who invested time in presenting more creative energy options on a major construction project began as a proto-champion: the project had been framed as relevant to the company's profitability and as being creative and enjoyable in its own right.

Without the climate change consultant's support and prompting he would not have realised how much agency he had to make a meaningful difference by raising the question of energy consumption at this point in a specification.

Although a climate change champion network strategy still invites the criticism that it will give the organisation somewhere to off-load sustainable development responsibility rather than engaging with it as a mainstream issue, we argue that it is a necessary part of the change architecture. Even if sustainable development skills and competencies could be developed across the whole organisation, as they should, there will still be a need for dedicated champions to work collectively and concertedly to lead the scale of change required. This same conclusion is reached by Paul Williams and Alan Thomas in their exploration of an effective system of governance for sustainable development in Wales.[15]

However, it is rare to find a programme of change or a climate change strategy which is not piecemeal. It is just as rare to find a network of champions working together in a way that could be described as systemic. An important dimension of an architecture for change is the development of a network of distributed leadership which needs to be collectively intelligent. In other words, there needs to be enough connectivity between the agents in the system that learning can be shared quickly and easily. This is another aspect of the architecture: the organisation, procedures, processes and learning pathways that will enable this to happen. This may be why Richard Whittington and Andrew Pettigrew describe decentralised, bottom-up approaches as handicapped in delivering change.[16] They describe what we have also found: 'Local experiments and piecemeal initiatives are liable to be abandoned as they fail to find their fit within the rest of the organisation. Only once initiatives are cumulated into complementary packages are they likely to deliver their pay-offs.'

In terms of behavioural responses to climate change this equates to the way many individual local initiatives only achieve small-scale changes or peter out before they can be replicated elsewhere. An effective architecture for change would favour strong central direction to enable each individual project to build on another and contribute to an overall strategy. An ecosystem of champions in this respect would need to include champions at different levels of the organisation as well as across departments.

So where does this leave us? The success of any policy involving behavioural change of the scale needed to address rapid climate change depends on the willingness of a critical mass of nations, organisations and individuals to engage with it. Policies rarely succeed in doing more than creating a broad brushstroke framework for action. Whether or not they achieve their objective depends on how strategically they are interpreted and implemented. In our view, much that is described as strategy is very weak because it does not integrate the five As, learning processes such as Action and reflection are not evident, complementarities thinking is absent and there is not enough collective champion capacity to lead large-scale change. This, as we explained before, is why we favour the cock-up rather than conspiracy view of society's current inertia in the face of looming catastrophe.

In this chapter we have used case study examples from our climate change strategy work with organisations to highlight the micro-processes of change, the everyday obstacles on the pathway to transformation and how climate change champions might most effectively work to remove them. We have been informed by network theory, behavioural change literature, and our own and others' organisational change practices to elucidate the policy to implementation journey. We have made some pragmatic suggestions and offered some frameworks for developing high-quality climate change strategy grounded in a marriage of practice and theory.

Let us now finish with a heroic story. In many cultures, the elephant is a mythic beast. As it walks along the path it encounters many obstacles. Unlike other beasts, it uses its great strength to move these to one side, thereby helping all other beings and exemplifying a moral idea; to delay one's own progress to ease the journey for others.

The story speaks to the issue of responding to the climate change crisis. None of us (or at least no one we know) is perfect in our use of carbon. Even an extremely green person participates in a society that is profligate in its use. It is therefore not a question of those who are perfect, who know, helping those who aren't, who don't, but of participants in a journey, a herd of elephants perhaps, helping each other and the wider world.

NOTES

1. The Worldwatch Institute, *Vital Signs 2003–2004*, London: Earthscan, 2003, p. 41.
2. Donella Meadows, Jorgen Randers and Dennis Meadows, *Limits to Growth: The 30-Year Update*, White River Junction, Vermont: Chelsea Green Publishing Company, 2004, p. 265.

3. Quoted in A.M. Pettigrew, R. Whittington et al., *Innovative Forms of Organizing: International Perspectives*, London: Sage Publications, 2003, p. 128.
4. Data from Department for the Environment, Farming and Rural Affairs, *Survey of Public Attitudes to quality of life and to the Environment*, London: HMSO, 2001. The suggestion that the understanding of climate change leaders is less than perfect is in front of us every day of the week. Why this is can be explored in J.D. Sterman and L. Booth Sweeney, 'Cloudy skies: assessing public understanding of global warming', *Systems Dynamics Review*, 18 (2), 2002.
5. P. MacNaghten, R. Grove-White et al., 'Public perceptions and sustainability in Lancashire', Lancashire County Council, 1995.
6. E. Olli, G. Grendstad et al., 'Correlates of environmental behaviours: bringing back social context', *Environment and Behaviour*, 33 (3), 2001, pp. 181–208.
7. K. Hobson, 'Thinking habits into action: the role of knowledge and process in questioning household consumption practices', *Local Environment*, 8 (1), 2003, pp. 95–112.
8. See D. Schön and M. Rein, *Frame Reflection: towards the resolution of intractable policy controversies*, New York: Basic Books, 1994, for an overview of the field.
9. We thank our colleagues Peter Binns and Mike Jones for suggesting the term 'Architecture for Change' to us.
10. K. Wilber, *Integral Psychology*, Boston, MA: Shambhala, 2000.
11. M. Clark and J. Stewart, 'Handling the wicked issues – a challenge for government', School Discussion Paper, University of Birmingham, 1997.
12. J. Hertin, F. Berkhout, 'How can business adapt to climate change?', *The Edge*, 6, 2001, pp. 4–5.
13. P. Williams, *Public Administration*, 80 (1), spring 2002, pp. 103–24.
14. D. Meyerson, *Tempered Radicals: How everyday leaders inspire change at work*, Boston, MA: Harvard Business School Press, 2003.
15. A. Thomas and P. Williams, *Sustainable Development in Wales: Understanding Effective Governance*, York: Joseph Rowntree Foundation, 2004.
16. Pettigrew, Whittington et al., *Innovative Forms of Organizing*, p. 129.

11
Averting Climate Change: The Need for Enlightened Self-Interest
Jim Scott

FORMS OF PERSUASION

In this chapter, I will argue that persuasion to change people's behaviour in the face of climate chaos is not working, but that dictatorial force should be avoided at all costs. Instead, enlightened self-interest provides the only durable solution to saving the planet from calamitous global warming and climate change. This is an ambitious undertaking. First, an overview of the different forms that persuasion takes will be given, and then some ideas follow on the potential contribution of a more enlightened approach.

The most familiar form of persuasion is perhaps by appealing to the scientific evidence as presented in peer-reviewed journals and conference reports as publicised in parts of the media. However, despite increasingly alarming news pieces confirming the onset of dangerous climate change, there is no real ongoing urgent action that is at all commensurate with the magnitude of the crisis facing us.[1]

Indeed, action can be considered in some respects to have gone into reverse with Tony Blair, when British Prime Minister, upholding a higher priority for economic growth than tackling climate change. In November 2005, Blair stated that no 'external force is (really) going to ... restrict your economic growth' and that 'no country will want to sacrifice its economy in order to meet this challenge'. Just over a year previously he had claimed that the 'UK had demonstrated that economic growth did not have to be at the expense of the environment'. He said: 'between 1990 and 2002 the UK economy [grew] by 36% while greenhouse gas emissions fell by around 15%'. Since much of the latter was due to a freebie from the previous Conservative government in closing down the coal industry, Blair's claim was dubious to say the least, especially given his later admission that 'the government will fail to meet its own target to cut carbon emissions by 20% by 2010'.[2]

DIRECT ACTION

One possible public response to such grievous political failure is direct action. To be effective, this relies upon public coverage in the media. Greenpeace campaigns provide obvious examples: occupying the Brent Spar oil platform, boarding ships involved in whaling and the trade of products of illegal logging, and pulling up genetically modified crops. There are numerous more informal and spontaneous examples, such as the residents of Devizes in Wiltshire defending trees in their town centre and occupations of sites around the UK which are planned for new transport highways and airport expansions.[3]

Examples from other countries include Julia Butterfly's tree-sitting to try to prevent the destruction of one of the last remnants of the great redwood forest in 1997 in California; disruption of Canadian seal culling; the resistence of the Uwa people in Colombia to oil extraction on their land; direct action in Australia to stop uranium mining; and the occupation of land at threat from flooding for dams and hydroelectric power projects, famously supported by the author Arundhati Roy in western India.

Direct action can be highly effective – in the short term. Unfortunately, it can also be employed to promote causes that threaten the environment. Recall the fuel price protests in the UK in 2000. On the other hand, consider, too, the direct action in opposition to the insensitive development of wind-farms in scenic areas.[4]

HIDDEN POWER

While direct action is normally visible, if reported by the media, hidden force is routinely used behind the scenes by powerful financial and commercial interest groups (see also Melanie Jarman's chapter in this volume). This is done in order to counter the persuasive power of scientific evidence, global and national policy making, reports and conferences.

The primary legal responsibility of companies to make profits for their shareholders is often claimed to justify such covert action. As Joel Bakan explains in *The Corporation*, the principle of 'the "best interests of the corporation" [is] now a fixture in the corporate laws of most countries ... The law forbids any other motivation for their [the corporations'] actions, whether to assist workers, improve the environment, or help consumers save money.'[5]

Furthermore, Bakan explains, 'corporate social responsibility is thus illegal – at least when it is genuine ... (for) social responsibility is not appropriate when it could undermine a company's performance'! And he applies this thinking specifically to the oil company BP, in asking: 'Can BP be not just Beyond Petroleum – the clever wordplay used in its ad campaigns – but also Beyond Profit? Can it sacrifice its own interests and those of its shareholders to realize environmental and social goals?'; the standard corporate answer being 'no'.[6]

Granted such licence, it comes as no surprise that: 'today practically all economic activity is carried out under the corporate form', starting with the private sphere, but extending increasingly into the public one – through the process of privatisation, thereby leading to the 'commercialisation of society'.[7] Corporate policies also help to shape cultural norms which may no longer be sustainable. The most obvious of these unsustainable cultural norms is the presumption of the necessity for uninterrupted economic growth. Another damaging norm is the promotion of the consumer society. These corporate-fed notions are taken so much for granted that they are not recognised as chosen values. These norms are expressed in the output of the media, obviously so through the media's corporate ownership and its critical dependence on advertising revenue to survive.

But, more fundamentally, such norms are promoted by the media through its '"societal purpose" to cultivate and defend the economic, social and political agenda of privileged groups that dominate the domestic society and the state', as Edward Herman and Noam Chomsky put it in *Manufacturing Consent*. (See also the chapter in this volume by Theobald and McKiggan.) Herman and Chomsky explain: 'The media serve this purpose in many ways: through selection of topics, distribution of concerns, framing of issues, filtering of information, emphasis and tone, and keeping debate within the bounds of acceptable premises. ... a system so powerful as to be internalised largely without awareness.' As media analyst Ben Bagdikian notes, the institutional bias of the corporate media 'does not merely protect the corporate system. It robs the public of a chance to understand the real world'.[8] As if that were not serious enough, corporations and governments misrepresent facts to suit their purposes, misleading, deceiving and confusing the public with what is now openly, and euphemistically, known as 'spin'.[9]

In the face of such obstacles to genuine sustainability, sufficient to avert climate chaos, I argue that what is needed is enlightened self-interest.

Enlightened self-interest starts with a declaration of the highest order. It could be expressed in many ways, but the one that appears best able to express this viewpoint is: to love and value life itself above all else.

What does this mean? Why take this approach? Why choose this particular declaration? How might it help avert dangerous climate change? And how might it be applied in order to do so? The rest of this chapter is devoted to an attempt to answer these questions.

WHAT DOES ENLIGHTENED SELF-INTEREST MEAN?

The declaration 'to love and value life itself above all else' is not intended to be understood rationally or intellectually alone. It is an openly declared value statement and so derived from the right, intuitive, side of the brain instead of the left, analytical, side. It also originates from a completely different culture from that of the state–corporate politics of persuasion and inducement.

Understanding can be derived from inner experience, as well as through intellect, with both being complementary to each other. Such understanding is not irrational or whimsical. Nor is it an 'off-the-wall' New Age Religion, a smear which anti-greens and climate change contrarians have already employed as a weapon of attack. For example, Deepak Lal, a professor of political economy, writes: 'The green movement is a modern secular religious movement engaged in a world-wide crusade to impose its habits of the heart on the world.'[10]

Although the concept of enlightened self-interest is more fully developed in the Eastern tradition, it has a long tradition in the Western philosophical canon too.[11] There is insufficient space here to trace this history. But, as just one example, consider the words of Alexis de Tocqueville (1805–1859), the French political thinker and historian. He wrote of people's 'enlightened regard for themselves [which] constantly prompts them to assist one another and inclines them willingly to sacrifice a portion of their time and property to the welfare of the state', believing that 'it is the interest of every man to be virtuous ... having found by experience that in the end it is commonly the happiest and the most useful track'.[12] Writing in 1840, de Tocqueville also warned of the dangers of materialism; rightly so, given the subsequent comprehensive attack on the above values by a burgeoning Western culture of consumerism.

Ironically, 'enlightened self-interest' has been invoked by Lord John Browne, former head of BP, when he spins 'social and environmental values ... not [as] ends in themselves but strategic resources to enhance business performance. 'This is not a sudden discovery of moral virtue or a sense of guilt about past errors,' he says of his green agenda. 'It is about long term self-interest – enlightened, I hope, but self-interest none the less.'[13]

In Eastern philosophy, enlightenment is considered the highest goal of spiritual attainment. It is described in the Hindu Yoga Sutra as a state of meditative absorption in which all thoughts, activities and movements of a seeker's awareness have ceased. However, in recent years it has been redefined as no longer incompatible with bodily activity, and with sensory and intellectual functioning. In this more recent view, the enlightened one has no need to close the eyes or to shut off the sensory functions in order to perceive the all-pervading consciousness. One no longer apprehends the world as different from himself or herself.[14] What is more, this understanding can be applied to living in the world and to tackling its problems.

However, the crucial difference between the Western and Eastern concepts of enlightened self-interest lies in the different understandings of 'self'. The Western concept of 'self' refers to separate individuality. In the Eastern view, broadly speaking, the 'self' pervades everything; everyone and everything is the expanded 'self'. This is the meaning of 'self-realisation'.[15] It is in the context of the second, expanded sense that the declaration to love and value life itself above all else is considered here to be 'enlightened self-interest'. Yet it does not preclude a rational recognition that taking a business-as-usual approach to climate change is against the interests of the individual also.

WHY TAKE THIS PARTICULAR APPROACH TO ENLIGHTENED SELF-INTEREST?

If we were to re-trace the human contributions to climate change to their source, we would examine the behaviour of governments, business and private households, and progressively derive the underlying habits, attitudes, priorities and values.

By far the most effort put into persuasion to avert climate change has been into changing *behaviour*. I believe this is part of the reason why that effort has been so unrewarding. For instance, huge efforts were expended on the Kyoto Protocol, but it has been almost immediately undermined by those countries which try to take the minimum action to fulfil their obligations, or which refuse to take part and try to undermine the actions of others. Moreover, companies that have agreed to take part in the UK carbon trading mechanism to support the protocol have prevailed on the government to lower the emissions threshold to the point that it fails to have much effect.[16] And many households have made efforts to save domestic energy and have then lost interest or commitment, and reverted to old habits.

Habits lie behind behaviour, and attitudes lie behind habits. The importance of changing attitudes is now becoming recognised, and is explicit in the UK government's initiative in launching its Climate Challenge Fund in January 2006. However, even at the launch, the Environment Minister, Elliott Morley, offered no solution to the contradictory messages received by the public: endless promotion of cheap air-flights, huge advertising campaigns to entice us to buy the latest car models, and government plans for airport and runway expansion, as well as road-building programmes.

Clearly other priorities of the government override the need to change attitudes to climate change. Similarly, other priorities inform corporate avoidance of reducing carbon emissions through the carbon trading scheme. And, at a domestic level, other priorities may feature higher than saving energy at home or switching to greener sources.

Like many other people, no doubt, I find it awkward to challenge my friends about whether they travel by air to go on holiday. One could argue with people about their priorities, but it is more likely to cause disharmony than change attitudes, habits or behaviour. Our actions derive from what ultimately matters to us most.[17] When it comes to climate change, the seriousness of the issue may cause many people to reflect. But many others have more pressing daily concerns, and they have simply not been able to reflect on the prospects of likely climate chaos – certainly not sufficiently for any significant changes in attitudes, habits or behaviours.

Hence, the importance of focusing on the ultimate values that determine our priorities. The failed 'persuasive approach' is directed towards ameliorative actions, rather than the fundamental goal of loving and valuing life. Even wholesale and global acceptance of the Kyoto Protocol, the Millennium Goals, and the lofty declarations of all World Summits to date would not ensure the continuation of life as we know it on Earth. To focus, instead, on the ultimate goal would yield a full and essential paradigm shift.

This shift would address areas that the ameliorative approach has so far left untouched. These include the destruction of forests, coral reefs and fisheries – the global commons – in the interests of commercial concerns feeding an intensely cultivated culture of consumerism; the presumed 'need' for unlimited air travel; and the presumptions that economic growth and global capitalism are sacrosanct.

But the approach goes deeper and becomes more personal. It is not just a mental paradigm shift but also a deeply felt one that becomes, over time, instinctual. It requires holding up one's personal values to the mirror to ascertain whether they serve or obstruct the overriding one. This may, in turn, affect one's most deeply held beliefs and most entrenched habits before lifestyle changes can become established and durable. It will almost certainly require new learning and new means of support to put that learning into practice.

We will likely rediscover personal qualities that have been left to atrophy in the headlong pursuit of comfort, convenience and possessions: not least service, modesty, integrity, honesty and clarity of intention, perseverance, faith and endurance. If this is too much to ask, life on this planet in its present form will not survive. It is our choice.

WHY CHOOSE THE PARTICULAR DECLARATION OF VALUING LIFE ABOVE ALL ELSE?

In his book *Tomorrow's God*, Neale Donald Walsch writes: 'It is only through PRE-serving ... [that is] serving Life itself before you serve the Little Self ... that Life itself will be preserved in its present form on the earth.'[18] He explains: 'And this is what the New Spirituality is all about.' In other words this is the justification of the entire book. However, do not jump to conclusions about the title, for a whole chapter is devoted to replacing the much fought-over concept of 'God' with 'Life' and arguing that they mean the same thing.

Walsch goes on: 'That this New Spirituality, widely adopted, would change the world, there is no doubt. It could save the world from self-destruction. Because human beings would never do the things they are now doing to the earth, much less the things they are doing to each other, if they thought they were doing all these things to themselves.' This perspective accords with the Eastern view of enlightenment, with respect to regarding the world as not different from oneself. Walsch adds: 'The opportunity now placed before humanity is to preserve life in its present form by pre-serving life in its pre-sent form. That is, in the form in which it was sent to you *before you began changing it. That was its *pre-sent Form.*'[19]

However, I have adopted a simpler wording than Walsch – in the declaration 'to love and value life itself above all else' – so as to avoid debate about just when life may have been 'pre-sent', and in what condition, and whether it is not, in fact, continually changing.

Alternative declarations are difficult to find in order to compare with this one. What one might term 'spiritual environmentalism' is a very new field. Those who are either looking for spiritual solutions to environmental problems or for environmental applications of their spiritual convictions are still relatively rare. One exception is Vandana Shiva PhD, a physicist, environmental activist and feminist. Shiva is the founder of Navdanya, a national movement in India to protect the diversity and integrity of living resources. In her book *Earth Democracy*, she says: 'Earth Democracy is about ecological democracies – the democracy of all life' and that 'living democracy recognizes the intrinsic worth of all species and all people'. She is not attempting an overall declaration of intent, but describing principles which are compatible with valuing and loving life itself above all else.[20]

David Edwards' message in his book *The Compassionate Revolution* is relevant here too. Adopting a Buddhist perspective, he argues 'that despite – or rather because of – the ruthless and violent nature of the system facing us, the only realistic individual, social and political antidote to rampant corporate capitalism is radical awareness rooted in unconditional kindness and compassion'. Further on he adds: 'Surely the world is in such a terrible crisis precisely because it is *not* enough to love ourselves but not others, to love the poor but grind our teeth at the elite, to love women but not men, to grieve for the tortured but hate the torturer, to adore animals but despise people.' Edwards adds: 'Real personal, social and global environmental stability can only be rooted in a commitment to kindness and compassion for All.'[21]

The only disagreement I have with Walsch is that *acceptance and understanding* of 'the New Spirituality' is not enough in itself to effect the changes he seeks. What is missing in Walsch's prescription is addressed in the final two sections of this chapter.

HOW MIGHT LOVING AND VALUING LIFE ITSELF ABOVE ALL ELSE HELP TO AVERT DANGEROUS CLIMATE CHANGE?

Such a radical approach challenges the short-term motivations, expediencies, vested interests, denials and desires for an uninterrupted comfortable life.

In practice, the new approach requires testing every policy proposal and initiative against the principle of loving and valuing life, and rejecting all that fail to uphold this principle. In terms of averting climate change it requires settling for nothing less than immediate global commitment to achieving the necessary greenhouse gas reductions that the best scientific advice provides for stabilising the climate. The means for implementing this commitment naturally follow, of which the Contraction and Convergence framework appears much the most powerful. Ancillary commitments will also follow in agreeing the most equitable method for achieving the required emissions cuts, and in determining which processes, technologies and forms of energy should be adopted to implement these cuts.

More generally, the new approach makes the consideration of underlying values central to the formulation of all polices that might have an impact on climate change. This is already beginning to happen. Defra's launch of its Climate Communications Initiative focused on changing popular attitudes, although the means it proposes still fall under the previous heading of persuasion.

Another new sign is indicated by Jared Diamond's 2005 book, *Collapse: How Societies Choose to Fail or Survive*. Diamond cites examples of societies that 'choose to survive', such as the Netherlands with its highly organised system of reclaimed land in order to sustain normal life below sea-level. Motivation is critical in this context. It requires little imagination to see that the Dutch must have been highly motivated, over the long term, to create and maintain their system of flood control. Strong positive motivation can also be inferred in Diamond's other examples of societies that 'choose to survive'.

What of societies that choose to fail? Do they deny the possibility of a paradigm shift towards enlightened self-interest? Diamond has a chapter entitled 'Why Do Some Societies Make Disastrous Decisions?' with sections following the sequence: Failure to anticipate, Failure to perceive, Rational bad behaviour, Disastrous values. With regard to the climate crisis we cannot claim failure to anticipate or perceive but, as Jonathon Porritt says in a review of Diamond's book, 'Diamond reserves his most insightful analysis for the more "irrational" reasons why we are not yet responding to the scale and urgency of today's converging environmental problems. The often irreconcilable clash between the pursuit of short-term gratification and the defence of future generations' long-term interests features prominently in his collapse case studies.'[22]

One other particular example Diamond gives is highly relevant here. This is the well-known tragedy of the commons. This applies to 'communally owned resources, such as fishermen catching fish in an area of ocean, or herders grazing their sheep on a communal pasture' – to which we can readily add: rainforests, coral reefs and indeed the overheating atmosphere!

Applicable to all these examples is Diamond's diagnosis of ineffective regulation, which is unenforceable at the larger scale – and endemic, as suits the interests of the corporate world. Diamond's most promising solution is also highly relevant to our thesis here:

for the consumers to recognise their common interests and to design, obey, and enforce prudent harvesting quotas themselves. That is likely to happen only if a whole series of conditions is met: the consumers form a homogeneous group; they have learned to trust and communicate with each other; they expect to share a common future and to pass on the resource to their heirs; they are capable of and permitted to organise and police themselves; and the boundaries of the resource and of its pool of customers are well defined.[23]

What better description of enlightened self-interest could we have? Implicitly people will value their shared life together above their differences, if not 'above all else'.

HOW MIGHT LOVING AND VALUING LIFE ITSELF ABOVE ALL ELSE BE PRACTICALLY APPLIED?

First it has to be recognised that short-term gratification in 'liberalised' market economies is collectively suicidal for the human race and likely the death-knell for many other species. However, this message will never be taken seriously, far less acted upon, by the leaders of our 'democratic' institutions because of their dependence on the short-term gratification of their own re-election and continued power. This is intimately connected with the public being misled, confused and led astray.

As well as the environmental crisis, the argument applies to other pressing problems including: AIDS, redressing obscene disparities of wealth, the causes of 'terrorism' and the prospect of starvation for millions across the world. Note, too, that the consumerist ideology in the West requires the resources of three planet earths to maintain the affluent lifestyle of Europe and six in the USA.[24] This is simply not sustainable.

Governments and electorates are thus caught up in a codependent vicious circle of short-term gratification. To escape this vicious circle, we need a movement which will first draw attention to the awful consequences of present policies, while alerting the public to the pernicious ways in which it is being misinformed, confused and led astray. Such a movement must also point to alternative values and beliefs about individual and collective survival, and promote the requisite attitudes, motivation, will, habits and lifestyles to ensure survival.

One possibility is a 'coalition of the willing' who have already 'got the message', forming a core group of those 'living the talk', snowballing out to include an increasing number of people who may only take action when the group grows to a critical size. This 'Movement for Survival' has been proposed by Save our World, a grassroots organisation based in the UK. The aim is to develop a determined critical mass of public insistence that world governments take commensurate action in order to avert calamitous climate change within the necessary timescale of ten years or less. However, the movement must address not only the onset of climate change but all the other threats to the preservation of life in its present form since they all spring from the same dysfunctional but dominant worldwide value system.

Such a movement would transcend loyalties to particular technical solutions and policies – over which advocating organisations frequently fall out – and accommodate a variety of short-term or long-term coalitions and campaigns which can coalesce, dissolve and reform with increasing ease with the use of the Internet.[25]

This is not the first 'Movement for Survival' to be proposed. In 1970, a similarly named movement was proposed as a way of realising the 'Blueprint for Survival' manifesto that launched *The Ecologist* magazine. This led to the creation of the Ecology Party, at a time when the founders 'believed that if politicians were alerted to what was happening to the planet, they would do something about it'.[26] Such a view is no longer credible. A different Movement for Survival was launched in 1997 by the Ogoni people of Nigeria to protect themselves from pollution and exploitation related to oil and gas extraction.

The values of reciprocity and cooperation are an inherent part of the make-up of *Homo sapiens*. Despite our aberrant and dysfunctional values and ideological systems, these better values often appear spontaneously at times of community crisis and among oppressed people.

As Neale Walsch states:

If your survival is directly threatened, you will do what you have to do. You will even change your most sacred and long-held beliefs about yourselves, about God, about Life, about everything, if you have to. You will always choose survival, make no mistake about that. You are encoded to do so ... Life is functional, adaptable, and sustainable. Always. ... You would abandon those beliefs that are killing you, that are impairing your ability to survive, right now, but the negative effect of most of your most damaging beliefs is so insidious, is so slow in showing itself, that you do not recognise them as being damaging.[27]

Walsch adds: 'If large numbers of people get together, create a team, and choose to experience conscious evolution, humanity could reach critical mass within a very short period. Decades, not centuries. Perhaps not even decades, but years.'[28]

Human life is at a crossroads. The situation can be viewed negatively as a dire threat with inevitable consequences. However, a growing number of people see it instead as an opportunity for transformation at all levels; an intensely exciting process which is already under way, and the necessary next step in evolution. After all, it is not just humanity that is at risk but the fate of the planet that we share with so many other lifeforms.

NOTES

1. The most notable reports include: *Guardian*, 28 July 2003: 'Global warming is now a weapon of mass destruction' by Sir John Houghton, formerly co-chair of the Intergovernmental Panel on Climate Change (IPCC); *Guardian*, 7 August 2003: 'World to warm by 8C says think tank' – the Institute of Public Policy Research (IPPR); *Independent*, 24 January 2005: 'Countdown to global catastrophe: report warns point of no return may be reached in 10 years'; *Guardian*, 11 August 2005: 'Warming hits "tipping point"'; *Guardian*, 6 October 2005: 'Climate change and pollution are killing millions'; *Guardian*, 25 November 2005: 'Sea level rise doubles in 150 years'; *Guardian*, 1 December 2005: 'Alarm over dramatic weakening of Gulf Stream'. As to governmental responses: *Guardian*, 9 January 2004: 'Top scientist attacks US over global warming' reporting on the UK chief scientist's claim that climate change is a more serious threat to the world than terrorism; *Guardian*, 2 May 2005: 'Unearthly silence: Climate change poses a greater threat than terrorism, yet has barely registered as an election issue'; *Guardian*, 16 May 2005: [UK] 'Climate change policy in tatters'; *Guardian*, 15 November 2005: 'Campaigners attack [UK government] plans to "buy way out" of CO_2 goal'; *Independent*

on *Sunday*, 4 December 2005: 'What planet are you on, Mr Bush? (and do you care, Mr Blair?)' – in which President Bush is quoted as having 'been assiduously trying to sabotage the [Kyoto] protocol and has ruled out even talking about setting targets for reducing the pollution that causes global warming ... And Margaret Beckett, the Secretary of State for the Environment [in the UK] said that anyone who believed that the [Montreal Conference of the Parties] meeting was going to agree to new pollution reduction targets was "living in cloud-cuckoo land"'; *Guardian*, 22 December 2005: 'US emission of global warming gases nearly doubled over 14 years'.

2. 'Blair signals shift over climate change', *Guardian*, 2 November 2005, and 'Blair calls for UK lead on climate change' *Guardian*, 15 September 2004.

3. See J. Barry and E. Frankland, eds, *International Encyclopedia of Environmental Politics* London: Routledge, 2001, p. 353.

4. For example, 'Storm of protest over planned windfarm', *Guardian*, 5 July 2004.

5. Joel Bakan, *The Corporation*, London: Constable & Robinson Ltd, 2004, p. 37.

6. Ibid., pp. 45 and 41.

7. Ibid., pp. 113 and 119.

8. Edward S. Herman and Noam Chomsky, *Manufacturing Consent – the Political Economy of the Mass Media*, London: Vintage, Random House, 1994, pp. 298, 302 and 303.

9. Epitomised in Sharon Beder, *Global Spin: The Corporate Assault on Environmentalism*, Totnes: Green Books, 1997.

10. *Guardian*, 18 February 2004, Ecoquotes in Society Section, from Deepak Lal, Professor Emeritus of Political Economy, University College London.

11. Discussed in the Introduction by Renfrew Brooks to *Meditation Revolution, a History and Theology of the Siddha Yoga Lineage*, New York: Agama Press, 1997, pp. xxi.

12. Alexis de Tocqueville, *Democracy in America*, translation by Henry Reeve, Ware: Wordsworth Classics, 1998, p. 230.

13. Bakan, *The Corporation*, p. 44.

14. Ibid., pp. 213 and 212, where these concepts are explained much more fully than space allows here.

15. For example in the Sri Guru Gita text, vv 4, 126 and 163, in the latter part of Sri Skanda Purana, *The Nectar of Chanting*, New York: SYDA Foundation, 1983.

16. 'Kyoto sacrificed to competitiveness', *Guardian*, 28 October 2004.

17. See 'Boiling Point' for November 2001 at http://www.save-our-world. net/archive/nov2001.html

18. Neale Donald Walsch, *Tomorrow's God*, London: Hodder and Stoughton, 2004, pp. 48 and 50 interpolated together; and, later, pp. 69 and 72.

19. Ibid., p. 63.

20. Vandana Shiva, *Earth Democracy – Justice, Sustainability and Peace*, London: Zed Books Ltd, 2006, pp. 62 and 9 respectively.

21. David Edwards, *The Compassionate Revolution – Radical Politics and Buddhism*, Totnes: Green Books, 1998, pp. 18, 23 and 202.

22. Review by Jonathon Porritt in *Guardian Review*, 15 January 2005, under the title of 'Man vs nature'.
23. Jared Diamond, *Collapse: How Societies Choose to Fail or Survive*, London: Allen Lane, 2005, p. 428.
24. Pooran Desai and Sue Riddlestone, 'Bioregional solutions for living on one planet', *Schumacher Society Briefing* (8), 2002, generally but specifically pp. 15 and 28.
25. This 'New Movement for Survival' is currently proposed on the Save our World websites: http://www.save-our-world.net (global) and http://www.save-our-world.org.uk and support for it is invited there.
26. Details have been obtained from websites: http://www.theecologist.org/archive and http://www.wdm.org.uk/campaign/history
27. Walsch, *Tomorrow's God*, p. 109.
28. Ibid., p. 215.

Afterword:
Where Do We Go From Here?

Mayer Hillman[1]

Few readers of this book can now doubt the gravity of the effects of climate change. Most days bring alarming new evidence, whether about the capacity of oceans, forests and soils reaching their limits in acting as major reservoirs for emissions from our burning fossil fuels and thereby accelerating the rise in carbon dioxide concentrations, about the release of colossal quantities of methane from the world's tundra regions and peat swamps or about the growth in air, road and rail travel and the investments being made to accommodate it. The obstacles to overcome or get round are so great that it is clear we are living on borrowed time. A drastic curtailment of our use of fossil fuels can now only slow down the changes in climate, not reverse them.

Even a major reversal of current policy offers the world a bleak future. Sea-level and temperature rises and changes in weather patterns around the world are inevitable. This century will see tens, if not hundreds of millions of ecological refugees fleeing inundated or drought-stricken regions of the world at a time when international demographers predict a large global population increase. Where will these refugees go, against the backdrop of a shrinking habitable land mass caused by the effects of climate change? This intractable problem will have to be faced imminently.

The chapters of this book consider why the looming catastrophe has not resulted in the degree of behavioural change that the world *must* make to limit the impacts of the evolving catastrophe. It may be that the preservation instinct of looking the other way when faced with unpalatable truths stands in the way of rational contemplation because of the immensity of the task ahead.

Many of the chapters provide valuable insights into the causes of our collective predicament, the remedial efforts being made substantially to reduce carbon dioxide emissions and the insufficiency of the forces that, directly or indirectly, have brought us to this lamentable position. In the last decade, there has been little change in the UK's level of emissions. This fact becomes all the more significant because even the short-lived reduction in previous trends of increasing annual emissions is due principally to extraneous factors, such as the 'dash for gas' and the export of energy-intensive manufacturing to other countries. The contribution that can be attributed to direct policy on emissions reduction is relatively small.

Some of the chapters have highlighted the questionable methods employed to further the objectives of vested interests' attempts to achieve minimal government interference in their activities through more prescriptive legislation and higher levels of tax. Almost every sector of society appears to be complicit. The business and academic communities, the media and NGOs, have been weighed in the balance by several authors and often found wanting. To a large extent, the source of the problem is their terms of reference and narrow account-ability. These limit their ability to prioritise actions in the light of the overriding implications of climate change, even when they recognise the desirability of doing so. And the outcome can be to sow seeds of doubt that hinder or delay the adoption of the necessary policies.

Areas of industry which support energy-intensive lifestyles attempt to shield themselves from accusations of hypocrisy by demonstrating their green credentials in their internal ongoing policies on saving fuel. However, it must be clear to them from their understanding the nature of the consequences of rising carbon dioxide concentrations in the atmosphere that maintaining energy-profligate lifestyles at their current levels is making the planet less habitable.

Other chapters have explained why nearly every institution, from governments downwards, has not acted with sufficient resolve, and have warned of population migration on a far greater scale than the world has ever seen and the frightening immobilising techniques now available to governments to prevent it. The global political process has been analysed to reveal its in-built failure until now to agree and implement policies that depend on international agreement and engage the world community in recognising its collective responsi-bility on this issue.

ECONOMIC GROWTH

It is easy to understand why both politicians and the general public find it difficult to face up to the scale of change that must take place if catastrophe is to be averted. The former British Prime Minister, Tony Blair, and the American President, George W. Bush, have been explicit in their rejection of any proposition which would risk economic slow-down and cause unemployment in order to counter what is described as a 'long-term environmental problem'. The phenomenal growth in air travel, the promotion of second homes overseas, the encouragement given to higher levels of public investment in the transport infrastructure, all suggest that people can relax and that, even if there is a problem, it need not affect the here and now.

It is clear, however, that even though the consequences cannot be accurately predicted, strategies based on continuous economic growth *must* be replaced by ones based on the objective of a massive reduction in fossil fuel use. Although growth can be de-coupled from this source, it is totally unrealistic to plan on the basis that this process can prove adequate to the task. Moreover, it is not simply a question of restraining growth, as is often argued when addressing, say, the future of air travel. Given its energy-intensity and the fact that, within the foreseeable future, aircraft will be fuelled only by kerosene, with the resulting release of greenhouse gas emissions into the delicately balanced atmosphere, this form of travel must decline sharply. Its present level is an obvious and avoidable contributor to the excess emissions that the planet can tolerate if the climate is not to be seriously destabilised and if other more basic needs for fossil fuels in the home and in commerce and industry are to be available. And even that condition is based on the immoral position that future generations have no claim whatsoever on the world's remaining finite reserves.

Many crucial areas of public policy are predicated on the assumption that economic growth, as conventionally interpreted and pursued, can be maintained in perpetuity. It is suggested that hugely problematic outcomes will stem from having to abandon it, and from having to cope with a massive decline in the demand for the goods and services which cater for the energy-profligate ways of life damaging our planet so catastrophically. Once people understand that they must take account of the effects of their decisions on the global environment, there will be a huge growth of interest in activities and products with low energy impacts.

The implications for enterprise and businesses anticipating these massive changes are phenomenal. Realistically, only those activities which add a modest level of greenhouse gas emissions to the atmosphere can have a future. In richer countries, current levels of funding education, the health service, the transport infrastructure, and the contribution that pension funds make to act as a buffer against poverty in old age presuppose a continuously burgeoning economy as the source of their financial support. A considerable dilemma is posed, on the other hand, as devastating consequences will inevitably follow from the maintenance of business as usual policies.[2]

LOOKING FOR EXCUSES

With such prospects on the horizon, it is not surprising that the great majority of people turn a blind eye to the evidence. Escape routes have been sought to justify an understandable preference for present policies, perhaps marginally modified to reflect environmental concerns. However, they are rapidly being closed off, obliging those who have sought to side-step the implications of business as usual to face the facts.

A catalogue of excuses for adequate action can easily be set out, ranging from denial that human activity is the source of the excess of greenhouse gases in the atmosphere and that therefore no case has been made for having to choose between averting climate change and promoting growth and development. Mirroring this is the questioning of whether there is any realistic prospect of preventing economic growth from accelerating the world towards ecological Armageddon. To deflect accusations of excessive consumption patterns, critics ask 'Why take a course of action that can be shown to be insufficient? Why make a personal gesture when others – such as the Americans – are not sharing the burden? Why pick on climate change when the world is crying out for solutions to more urgent problems such as poverty, AIDS and water shortages? Why be so concerned when surely global warming will mean fewer people will die of hypothermia, and the south coast of England will have French Riviera weather?'

In the UK, it is often asserted that the public will not be prepared to go along with severe limitations on their preferred lifestyles and that progress cannot be made unless there is an all-party consensus on the direction to be taken; that it is unrealistic to expect government to introduce draconian measures on climate change in the absence of public support; that something will turn up to reveal that government need not have intervened after all; that there is not the remotest chance of affordable alternatives replacing fossil fuels if economic growth is abandoned as a societal goal; that individual efforts pale into insignificance when set against the totality of what must be done; and that there is no point in proceeding until the public is convinced.

It is argued, for instance, in the Stern Review, published in October 2006,[3] that huge reductions in fossil fuel use can be achieved by ensuring that they are used more efficiently, and that this can be achieved by the removal of barriers standing in the way of a wider adoption of proven measures to that end. However, this overlooks the fact that, to take cars as an example, evidence of the last few decades shows that, without a strict cap on emissions, more people will buy the more efficient vehicles and drive further because the unit cost of travel has thereby been lowered.

As a reason for not doing enough, growing weight is being placed on carbon offsetting in its various forms, including emissions trading, and the pursuit of so-called 'carbon-neutral' practices. Its attractions for the proponents of the expansion of air travel, for instance, are obvious. However, its morality is arguable. It entails paying for people in developing countries to limit their emissions by adopting energy-saving measures because it is cheaper for them than for people in affluent parts of the world to do so. This approach needs serious attention, as it allows rich people both to maintain their energy-intensive lifestyles *and* superficially to assuage their consciences.

THE ROLE OF TECHNOLOGY

Perhaps the most common excuse for inaction is the proposition that technology can provide the means of enabling growth to continue without the need for substantial behavioural changes. All that is required is more investment for innovation and the deployment of low carbon technologies and encouragement of the take-up of opportunities for minimising fossil fuel use. It cannot be denied that the scope for doing so is considerable. Indeed, it could well be safe to rely on if only a small reduction in emissions were required. But any objective examination casts considerable doubt that it would prove sufficient to prevent serious climate change, particularly when set against a limited time scale. Subscription to the view that technology can ride to the rescue is whistling in the wind! It is inconceivable that it could deliver the required reduction of *90* per cent, not 60 per cent, of emissions, which is needed urgently, certainly not later than 2030, rather than 2050 (see below).

For example, take some of the front runners of carbon-reducing options. It is now claimed that electricity generation through nuclear fission is far less fraught with risk than it used to be. But most of the current sites proposed for new reactors in the UK, for instance, will be vulnerable to flooding and coastal erosion as a result of climate change this century. Moreover, in spite of the considerable sums spent on research and development, no solution has yet been found for the safe disposal of radioactive waste, nor is there an answer to the morality of obliging future generations to take responsibility for these toxic byproducts.

Energy renewables could contribute far more to energy supply, particularly as economies of scale would be able to be made. Their future depends very much on government policy. However, critical analysis of their prospects points to the conclusion that they are likely to bring about only a small fraction of the huge reductions that must be achieved. Of course, the easiest way of increasing the *proportion* of our energy requirements from renewables – and at no cost – would be to reduce energy consumption! In an ideal world, with better storage systems and much lower levels of demand through improved efficiency of production and changed lifestyles, renewables could supply the majority of our needs.

Major sequestration projects have been proposed in the form of growing trees to absorb carbon dioxide. However, in the case of afforestation, totally unrealistic areas of land would have to be planted each year and the trees would have to be constantly replaced when they died. In addition, the carbon balances of forests, particularly under a changing climate, are uncertain. Thus the number of trees to look after would rise annually in order to continue to store in them all the carbon dioxide from the use of fossil fuels in previous years. In the case of carbon capture, for instance, at coal-fired power stations, even setting aside the high costs entailed in the process, safe storage underground would have to be totally reliable over the long term – a very difficult condition to meet.

Hydrogen power and associated technologies have, without doubt, considerable prospects. However, if they are to be carbon-free, their future application depends on a surplus of electricity generated from renewable sources. Major technological advances and infrastructure changes would also be required for them to replace a significant amount of fossil fuel use. As this is unlikely for several decades, any benefit to be gained from transfer to it must be ruled out as a component addressing the current problem.

This is not to suggest that technology cannot help reduce the impact of energy use. But it cannot play a crucial role in mitigating climate change in a business as usual world where forces for energy-dependent growth continue to dominate. The idea that every little bit helps is a dangerous one. Even the combined and most optimistic projections of technological developments will not begin to deliver the reductions required. Only in the context of a strict cap on carbon dioxide emissions can the technological options play a meaningful role in averting climate catastrophe.

BARRIERS TO PROGRESS

Complementing the instinctive attractions of finding excuses for inaction or insufficient action is the mantra of problems representing barriers that must be removed before the obvious policy directions can be followed. These problems vary in complexity and resolution. They include the perhaps understandable reaction of 'not wanting to know', because of the implications for moving into the unknown. Their exemplar is the view of world leaders that a future without growth cannot be contemplated even in the light of evidence of its damaging effects.

It is often stated that, in a democracy, decisions cannot be taken unless the public acquiesces and that it would be unreasonable to expect people to agree to stringent measures if it was not totally persuaded that they were essential. These difficulties are aggravated by the observation that the sceptics' arguments have to be effectively refuted before the public can be expected to support the necessary changes, especially when they perceive that these run counter to their own preferences, no more obviously than in the field of air travel.

The difficulties of giving sufficient attention to the long-term are compounded by the fact that decisions on public investment are driven by short-term considerations and the fact that the most attractive options for government are those which maximise its chances of re-election. In view of this further short-term perspective, the desirability of introducing only minimal measures are obvious. At the same time, ambitious long-term targets can be set to demonstrate 'vision' as that suggests that the needs of future generations have been considered, as well as letting itself off the hook by not being able to be held to account if the targets are not met.

The UK government's target for dealing with climate change at the national level is for a 60 per cent reduction in carbon emissions by 2050. Yet climate scientists tell us that with this degree of reduction, carbon dioxide concentration in the atmosphere will be in the region of 550 parts per million by volume (ppmv). But these same scientists have calculated that *400* ppmv represents the tipping point beyond which the whole process of climate change becomes irreversible. One often hears the statement that we only have 10–15 years left before the tipping point is reached. This lulls people into a false sense of security at a time when responses to climate change need immediate attention.

The British government's approach is to aim to persuade people to see the need for the changes it wishes to see adopted. From its perspective, this is far preferable to obliging people to adapt which then runs the risk of generating rejection by those opposed to state interference in their lives and the consequent damaging political fallout. The attractions of promoting behavioural change through the medium of regulation to lower demand are obvious. But the hazards of attempting this are greater. To be effective, it requires, as the Stern Review attempted, attaching a monetary value to the impacts of carbon dioxide emissions that will adequately cover the damage, and implies that this value can take account of all the costs entailed over at least the next 100 years. It cannot. Stern puts the current value at $85 on a tonne of carbon dioxide. This cannot be realistic. This value does not cover some unquantifiable future costs such as the mass migration and resettlement of ecological refugees. Moreover, and critically, at this price, the continuing rise in temperatures and sea-levels and accelerated climate change will not be stopped.

Government can also be accused of side-stepping its responsibility for implementing the necessary action by arguing that it is everybody's responsibility, implying that if individuals do not respond sufficiently, government is absolved. This type of 'buck-passing' would only be acceptable if government takes the first step by obliging everyone to share responsibility. That sharing will not happen voluntarily.

Some may be persuaded that the necessary change can be achieved when they realise that enlightened self-interest is the way forward. However, such a view rests on a questionable belief that a critical mass of people can be created speedily enough to cover nearly everyone's actions and thereby avoid the risk of 'free-riders' who in evading their responsibilities erode the resolve of the majority. This key point is illustrated by considering the response of government to members of the public in the late 1930s had they asked – what steps can individuals take in the fight to prevent the spread of fascism?

The construction of conventional economics when applied to this area of policy is that demand is best regulated through price and, therefore, if greenhouse gas emissions are to be reduced, price rises should be applied to limit demand. This may hold true where demand has to be lowered somewhat, but it cannot be seen to apply where greenhouse gases have to be speedily reduced to a considerable degree. Associated with this widely accepted approach to curbing demand is the introduction of green taxes adjusted to prevent media accusations of stealth taxes being introduced by government. This would entail a revenue-neutral process rewarding green practices and penalising brown ones. Whilst the climate change levy to which some industries have been subject has the prospect of promoting substantial energy conservation, its application in the form of higher taxes and prices on the consumer would necessarily be severely socially regressive, impacting disproportionately on poorer people, especially in developing countries who would have to spend far more on their basic fuel needs even though they are the least responsible for the damaging effects of climate change.

The extent of the prospective failure of the economists' approach is illustrated by one of the conclusions of the Stern Review, which is based on the assumption that the cost burden on the world's economy of adequate action is relatively low – about one per cent of global GDP. The implications of this are that against a background of current patterns of energy use, costs will have to rise – but that these are manageable. This is highly questionable.

Moreover, there is an assumption that change is possible only with considerable investment of capital, overlooking the fact that any target on emissions reduction may well lead to policies requiring much lower investment, for instance, on the transport infrastructure. The Review also makes the bold and unsubstantiated claim that 'The world does not need to choose between averting climate change and promoting growth and development.'

Another problem arises when individuals, industry or government cite the progressive steps being taken to limit the effects of climate change by, for instance, turning off the standby on their television, using public transport rather than the car when possible or recycling the waste products from their activities. It is a simple option to set targets for improvement which are easily realisable or so distant in time as to raise no opposition. However, in the totality of the steps that must be taken, these actions are grossly inadequate. They produce complacency stemming from the view that progress, however slow or modest, is good as long as it reflects some improvement on what went before. It is totally unrealistic to expect that sufficient numbers of people will take sufficient steps in sufficient time, on a voluntary basis, to prevent global catastrophe.

In all likelihood, the most difficult problem stems from our instinctive rejection of any proposition that requires giving up what we have taken as an inalienable right. Restriction on freedom to do as our circumstances allow, without regard for the wider social and environmental impacts, and a future containing fewer choices than have been enjoyed until now, with the prospect of a lowered quality of life, would be difficult for many to accept. There is, too, an instinctive reaction which leads people to evaluate new proposals in order to find flaws justifying their rejection. All too often this results in support for a business as usual approach even though it would be likely to bring in its wake far greater difficulties than the new proposals.

Only government can take the necessary measures to slow down the effects of climate change. Individual action is meaningless unless it is within a national or internationally agreed framework. Such a framework is now seen widely to be essential both by the UK government in its call for a 'Climate Covenant' and in industrialists' call on government in 2004 to provide such a framework for its forward planning.

SO WHAT MUST WE DO?

It is widely accepted that there would be little point in individuals or indeed any one country going it alone. Sufficient change could not be achieved by such an approach. It is unrealistic to believe that the necessary massive reduction in the energy-profligacy of the current lifestyles of many of the world's people, such as when flying, can come about on a voluntary basis. A global framework based on a collective view of long-term goals is essential. Such a framework was formulated more than ten years ago by the Global Commons Institute: Contraction and Convergence (C&C) is based on principles of limits and equal rights, with each country making a fair contribution to the survival of the planet.[4]

C&C was described fully in Chapter 1 and its fundamental logic explained. Its application reveals in an alarming way the need for urgent action: greenhouse gas concentrations are increasing faster than they have been even in the recent past and now show signs of rising at an uncontrollable rate. It argues in support of a long overdue 'consensus-backed rationale for action' to slow this down.

The chapter also outlined its author's history in guiding his C&C proposal through the political minefield of obfuscation and procrastination. It is the only framework within which success in mitigating the effects of climate change and reversing them can be assured. In the judgement of its proponents, including most of the authors of this book, there is no realistic alternative. Once agreed, its success in reducing emissions is assured because the rates of contraction and convergence are set to that end.

Its national application is in the form of carbon rationing or allowances[5] or Domestic Tradable Quotas (DTQs).[6] Scientists have calculated that the capacity of the planet to absorb greenhouse gases without serious destabilisation of the climate is finite, so who could reasonably support the proposition that the contraction should converge towards an *unequal* distribution? If that capacity is therefore divided by the world's population, each person's equitable annual allocation of emissions must now not exceed about one tonne. At present, the UK's average carbon dioxide emissions are about 10 tonnes – two-and-a-half times the current world average.

Clearly, it would be impracticable for the people of richer countries or for the global economy to cope with an immediate reduction to the one tonne ration – despite the fact that it must be achieved without delay. A year-on-year reduction will be necessary. But, by giving advance warning of each future annual allowance, the necessary changes can be planned, at least, and costed in the most efficient and preferred way. By including all personal transport and household energy use in individual allowances, a significant proportion of total emissions will be covered. Units of the allowance will be surrendered when gas and electricity bills are paid, petrol is purchased and air tickets bought. The contribution made by the business and public sectors which produce our goods and services will be included at a later date, within a wider allowance and trading system, and further application of the current climate change levy.

Carbon allowances will act as a parallel currency to real money as well as creating an ecologically virtuous circle. Since a key feature of the proposal is buying and selling, a 'conserver gains' principle will complement the conventional 'polluter pays' principle. Those who lead less energy-intensive lives, and invest in energy efficiency and renewable energy, are unlikely to use all their allowance. They will then not only spend less on fuel but also have the added incentive of increasing their incomes by selling their surplus units. But the cost of buying these units will rise steadily in line with the reduction of the allowance as it will be determined by the availability of the surplus set against the demand for it. The process will act as a fast driver by encouraging individuals to adopt green practices far more effectively than they would through regulation, pricing, exhortation or appeals to conscience.

Not only does C&C offer the only prospect of ensuring that the worst effects of climate change are avoided, it also brings in its wake a range of other hugely beneficial outcomes as a result of personal, national and international economies being driven by *economy*. In this way, policy on social justice will be enormously advanced. Moreover, as the ration is reduced, demand for fossil fuel dependent products and activities will fall away, easing considerably the problems associated with energy scarcity and security of supply.

So who has the prime responsibility for the adoption of Contraction and Convergence and the essential and urgent transformation that it will deliver? Of course, it can only result from resolute action on the part of governments – and this well before 2010.

CONCLUSIONS

In the introduction to this book, the editors ask, in effect, 'How will the public wake up to the new realities and acquiesce to what must be done?' The book provides irrefutable evidence for recognising Contraction and Convergence as the only practical framework for international negotiations on limiting damage to the world's climate, and on providing a strategy by which responsibility for the requisite action is shared equitably by the world's population.

Without doubt, it is essential to achieve both public backing and political leadership in climate negotiations so that every country is committed to the shared vision of the way ahead. That consensus will ensure continuity in application of the policy beyond each government's administration. The political, institutional and professional support around the world that C&C has gained over the last ten years offers strong grounds for asserting that governments will indeed come together very soon to commit themselves to this essential, practical and moral strategic framework. Without it, we will be bequeathing a dying planet to the next generation. Further procrastination is out of the question.

NOTES

1. M. Hillman, 'Why climate change must top the agenda', in M. Hillman, ed., 'Special section: climate change', *Town and Country Planning*, October 1998; M. Hillman with T. Fawcett, *How We Can Save the Planet*, Penguin Books, 2004.
2. A. Gore, *An Inconvenient Truth: The Planetary Emergency of Global Warming and What We Can Do About It*, Bloomsbury Publishing PLC, August 2006.
3. N. Stern, *Review: The Economics of Climate Change*, Cambridge University Press, 2007, or http://www.sternreview.org.uk, October 2006.
4. A. Meyer, *Contraction and Convergence: the Global Solution to Climate Change*, Green Books, 2000.
5. M. Carley, I. Christie and M. Hillman, 'Towards the next environment white paper', *Policy Studies*, vol. 12, no. 1, 1991 (on the proposal for carbon rationing); M. Hillman, 'Carbon budget watchers', in M. Hillman, ed., *Town and Country Planning*, October 1998.
6. R. Starkey and A. Anderson, 'Domestic Tradable Quotas: a policy instrument for reducing greenhouse gas emissions from energy use', Technical Report 39, Tyndall Centre for Climate Change Research, 2005.

Appendix 1
A Layperson's Glossary of the Global Politics of Climate Change

Tim Helweg-Larsen and Jo Abbess

ADAPTATION: The term used for those **Climate Change** responses that deal with the consequences of **Climate Change** rather than preventing it (**Mitigation** against it).

AFRICA GROUP: A major player in **Climate Negotiations**. Africa has been experiencing disastrous **Climate Change** for over 30 years in the form of famines and droughts.

AGENDA 21 (LOCAL AGENDA 21): Built on the articles of the **Rio Declaration**, it provides funding for local groups to pursue the **Sustainability** agenda for the twenty-first century. It is supported widely and internationally at all levels of government.

ANNEX 1 COUNTRIES (ANNEX 1 PARTIES, ANNEX 1 NATIONS, ANNEX 1): Those defined by the UNFCCC as heavily reliant on **Fossil Fuel** energy. These nation states are obliged to make major changes in net **Greenhouse Gas Emissions** trends. Typically these are wealthy nations with large current and historic **Emissions**.

ANTHROPOGENIC CLIMATE CHANGE: Human-made **Climate Change**. The component of **Climate Change** resulting from human activity rather than natural processes.

ANTHROPOGENIC GREENHOUSE GAS EMISSIONS: Those **Greenhouse Gas Emissions**, principally **Carbon Dioxide** (CO_2) from human activities, that exceed the balanced **Carbon Cycle**. This is predominantly from the burning of **Fossil Fuels** that have been mined or pumped from the ground.

APPROPRIATE TECHNOLOGY (PRINCIPLE OF APPROPRIATE TECHNOLOGY): Technology appropriate to the situation in which it is being deployed, and sensitive to wider environmental considerations. Appropriate Technologies have provided simple and often low-technology solutions to environmental problems around the world. Low levels of technology imply low **Carbon Dioxide Emissions**.

BINGO: Business and Industry Non-Governmental Organisation. A constituency recognised by the UNFCCC.

BIOMASS: Living plants and animals on the surface of the Earth and in the Oceans. Reproduction of plants and animals soaks up **Carbon Dioxide** (CO_2) from the atmosphere. Burning Biomass releases **Carbon Dioxide** back into the atmosphere. Decomposing Biomass releases **Methane** (CH_4) into the atmosphere under many conditions.

BIOSPHERE: The band of living plants and animals that circles the surface of the earth. Includes soils, rocks and those parts of the lakes, seas and oceans that contain marine life; and also the lower layers of the atmosphere, where birds and insects and microscopic life-forms are found.

BIOSYSTEM: A clearly delineated part of the **Biosphere**, normally having its own distinct flora and fauna, and possibly its own unique micro-climate.

BRAZILIAN PROPOSAL: Proposed reductions towards an overall **Emissions** ceiling for all **Annex I Parties**. **Emissions** reductions would be shared among individual **Annex I Parties** proportional to their relative share of responsibility for **Climate Change**. The scientific and methodological aspects of the proposal were considered questionably complex.

CAP & TRADE: A scheme by which an absolute upper limit or quota on annual **Carbon Dioxide Emissions** is agreed upon. Within this **Carbon Budget**, **Carbon Emissions** are then distributed in the form of permissions to burn **Fossil Fuels** (**Carbon Permits**) which can be traded.

CARBON BUDGET: A fixed amount of net **Carbon Dioxide Emissions** to the atmosphere, usually measured per year. Processes such as **Biomass** growth reduce the net **Carbon Dioxide Emissions** to the atmosphere, as **Biomass** is a **Carbon Sink**.

CARBON CREDIT: A Carbon Credit can be exchanged for a **Carbon Permit**; in other words, a licence to make net **Carbon Emissions** into the atmosphere.

CARBON CYCLE: The biological and atmospheric processes that circulate carbon chemical compounds between the earth, ocean and atmosphere.

CARBON DIOXIDE (CO_2): Emissions of CO_2 from burning **Fossil Fuels** constitutes humanity's largest contribution to net **Greenhouse Gas Emissions** and therefore **Climate Change**.

CARBON DIOXIDE INFORMATION ANALYSIS CENTER (CDIAC): Responds to data and information concerning the **Greenhouse Effect** and global **Climate Change**. Produces research reports, news and articles.

CARBON EMISSIONS (CARBON DIOXIDE EMISSIONS): The release of **Carbon Dioxide** (CO_2) through natural and industrial processes. Since the start of the industrial revolution, the combustion of **Fossil Fuels** has been the largest contribution to net **Carbon Emissions** and consequently **Global Warming**.

CARBON MARKETS: Several Carbon Markets not formed under the **Kyoto Protocol** are already in existence. These are likely to grow in importance and numbers in the coming years. These include the New South Wales Greenhouse Gas Abatement Scheme, the Regional Greenhouse Gas Initiative (RGGI) in the United States, the Chicago Climate Exchange, the State of California's recent initiative to reduce emissions: Assembly Bill 32 (AB 32 which will be known as The California Global Warming Solutions Act of 2006), the commitment of 131 US mayors to adopt Kyoto targets for their cities, and the State of Oregon's emissions abatement programme.

CARBON OFFSETTING: The concept asserts that **Carbon Emissions** by one person can be neutralised or offset by reductions in **Carbon Emissions** by another. Carbon Offsetting has developed as an industry in which customers voluntarily pay a fee to cover their own **Carbon Emissions**. This income is used to fund **Biomass** growth projects and **Renewable Energy** investments. In the absence of a **Global Carbon Cap** however, Carbon Offsetting cannot of itself guarantee to reduce net global **Carbon Emissions**.

CARBON PERMIT: A licence to pollute by producing net **Carbon Dioxide Emissions**.

CARBON QUOTA (CARBON ALLOWANCE, CARBON RATION, CARBON ALLOCATION): Sharing out a **Carbon Budget** between polluters. An example would be a personal annual **Carbon Ration** which would give a personal budget for the use of **Fossil Fuels** via electricity and natural gas utility bills throughout the year.

CARBON RATIONING: Implies a **Cap & Trade** scheme in which **Carbon Permits** are distributed to individuals and/or industry within a fixed **Carbon Budget**.

CARBON SEQUESTRATION: Any natural **Biomass** or mechanical means for holding **Carbon Dioxide** back from entering the atmosphere. Examples include: growing trees, or pumping Carbon Dioxide into depleted oil wells.

CARBON SINK: A net soak of Carbon; for example, the solution of **Carbon Dioxide** into the oceans, or the inspiration of **Carbon Dioxide** by large forests via the process of photosynthesis.

CARBON SOURCE: a net source of Carbon; for example, combustion of **Biomass** as in large-scale wildfire, or the production of cement.

CARBON TAXATION: Tax placed on **Carbon Dioxide Emissions**. Carbon Taxes are a means of internalising the global cost of pollution. Carbon Taxes do not provide an effective means of applying an absolute limit to regional or global **Carbon Emissions**. They cannot therefore set a **Global Carbon Cap**. There is some discussion around the world to replace income taxation with Carbon Taxes, as **Carbon Dioxide Emissions** are closely correlated with wealth.

CARBON TRADING: The purchase and sale of any of the following: **Carbon Dioxide Emissions**, avoided **Carbon Emissions**, **Carbon Sequestration** and **Carbon Permits** or **Carbon Quotas**. **Carbon Markets** include the **European Union Emissions Trading Scheme (EU ETS)**.

CHINA: Has per capita (per person) **Carbon Emissions** close to the world average of 3.89 metric tonnes of **Carbon Dioxide** per person (2002 IEA) (just over 1 metric tonne of Carbon). With a Chinese population in excess of 1.28 billion (2002 IEA), it is the second only to the USA in total **Carbon Emissions**. The USA emits approximately 23 per cent of global Carbon Emissions (2003

CDIAC) and China roughly 16 per cent (2003 CDIAC). China is pursuing aggressive industrial and economic growth as well as making significant strides in developing and deploying **Renewable Energy** technologies.

CLEAN DEVELOPMENT MECHANISM (CDM): A component of the **Kyoto Protocol**. It allows **Annex I Countries** to substitute reductions of their own **Carbon Emissions** with investments and projects leading to avoided Carbon Emissions in **Non-Annex I Countries**.

CLIMATE CHANGE: The cumulative effects of **Global Warming** on the Climate's natural patterns. These changing patterns include: unprecedented cyclone systems, sudden storms and more violent hurricanes (typhoons), changes in rainfall patterns (including monsoons) and wind patterns (trade winds and jet streams). Many of these are seriously impacting habitat and **Biosystem** viability.

CLIMATE CHANGE LEVY: A tax on large consumers of **Fossil Fuels** set at a fixed percentage of their **Carbon Emissions**. Came into effect in the United Kingdom in 2001.

CLIMATE NEGOTIATIONS: International conferences organised under the auspices of the United Nations with the aim of addressing **Climate Change**.

CLIMATE TREATY: A treaty made between nations, following international **Climate Negotiations**.

CONFERENCE OF THE PARTIES (COP) TO THE CONVENTION (ON CLIMATE CHANGE): Were held annually by the UNFCCC between 1995 (COP-1) through to 2005 (COP-11) with rotating host nation and chair.

CONSERVATION (PRINCIPLE OF CONSERVATION)· The recognition that we should not waste the resources of the **Biosphere** through unnecessary consumption and the consequent pollution.

CONTRACTION AND CONVERGENCE (C&C): A proposal from the **Global Commons Institute** and derived from the UNFCCC's **Precautionary Principle** and **Principle of Equity**. C&C is a planning tool for resolving the global **Climate Change** problem. A Global **Carbon Budget** is agreed upon, defining the amount of Carbon permitted to be burnt annually. Annual permits to burn Carbon are distributed between nations, and are progressively reduced over time to ensure stabilisation of **Greenhouse Gas** concentrations in the atmosphere (Contraction). The distribution initially reflects current **Carbon Emissions** patterns, but converges over time to equal per capita allocations. The Convergence date is negotiated between **Parties**.

DEVELOPED COUNTRIES (DEVELOPED NATIONS): Typically countries with high per capita **Carbon Emissions** and incomes. Generally **Annex I Nations**.

DEVELOPING COUNTRIES (DEVELOPING NATIONS): Typically countries with low per capita **Carbon Emissions** and incomes. Generally **Non-Annex I Nations**.

DOMESTIC TRADABLE QUOTAS (DTQs): A proposal for a national **Carbon Dioxide** emissions trading scheme for rationing, and rapidly reducing, the use of **Fossil Fuels**, by sharing out access to fuel among every individual and organisation in the economy. DTQs are nowadays known as **Tradable Energy Quotas (TEQs)**.

EARTH CHARTER: Informed the **Rio Declaration**. After an unsuccessful release in 1992 it was officially re-launched in 2000, as the result of an extensive consultation of grassroots environmental and development groups.

EMISSIONS: Normally **Greenhouse Gas Emissions**. This term is used to describe the net transfer of **Carbon Dioxide** and other **Greenhouse Gases** into the atmosphere. The principal cause of Emissions is the burning of **Fossil Fuels**. **Carbon Dioxide** is a good and qualifying proxy for determining the level of all **Greenhouse Gas Emissions**.

ENGO: Environmental Non-Governmental Organisation. A constituency recognised by the **UNFCCC**.

EQUITY (PRINCIPLE OF EQUITY): This principle supports the belief that all people are born equal. In the context of **Climate Change**, people have equal rights to the use of the atmosphere, and equal responsibilities for its protection.

EUROPEAN UNION EMISSIONS TRADING SCHEME (EU ETS): Under **Kyoto** rules, the EU elected to be treated as a single block or bubble, and created the EU Emissions Trading Scheme (EU ETS) as a **Carbon Market**. The ETS's currency is an EUA (EU Allowance) a **Carbon Allocation** to large Energy Producers and Users, allocated under National Allocation Plans (NAP). The scheme went into operation on 1 January 2005, although a forward market had existed since 2003.

FIRST WORLD CLIMATE CONFERENCE: Geneva 1979, sponsored by the **World Meteorological Organization (WMO)**. Led to the establishment of the World Climate Programme (WCP) to research **Climate Change**.

FOSSIL FUELS: Principally coal, oil and natural gas found in geological deposits. These carbon-based fuels were formed from plant or animal remains that were subjected to heat and pressure in the earth's crust over many millions of years.

G77: The Group of 77 **Developing Nations**, sometimes G77 plus **China**, working to pursue common negotiating positions. Where consensus is not held, member nations are not restricted from negotiating individually or as other smaller groups. These include: **Africa Group**, the Alliance of Small Island States (AOSIS) and the group of Least Developed Countries.

GLOBAL CARBON CAP: In order to stabilise the concentrations of **Greenhouse Gases** in the earth's atmosphere, and to avoid dangerous **Climate Change**, an upper limit on **Carbon Emissions** must be enforced, and progressively reduced over time. This Global Carbon Cap can only be attained by setting a Global **Carbon Budget**.

GLOBAL COMMONS INSTITUTE: An independent UK group concerned with the protection of the global commons. GCI was founded in 1990 after the Second World Climate Conference. Its director is co-founder Aubrey Meyer. GCI originated the proposal of **Contraction and Convergence**.

GLOBAL DIMMING: The global cooling effect of large quantities of particulates (soot and such-like) in the upper atmosphere, associated with the burning of **Fossil Fuels**. These particles reflect incoming solar radiation causing a dimming or cooling effect. This has partially compensated for **Global Warming**, but this effect is being lost as air pollution is being controlled in urban areas for health reasons, and to protect against acid rain.

GLOBAL WARMING: A term used to describe the increase in the average global land surface temperature due to a build-up in the **Greenhouse Gases** in the atmosphere.

GREENHOUSE EFFECT: The mechanism by which the Earth maintains a warm and stable temperature (like a thermal blanket). **Greenhouse Gases** in the atmosphere act like the glass panes of a greenhouse, allowing short-wave light radiation to enter, and preventing long-wave heat radiation from exiting. Excessive **Emissions** have resulted in an enhanced Greenhouse Effect.

GREENHOUSE GASES (GHGs, GHG EMISSIONS, GREENHOUSE GAS EMISSIONS): The **Kyoto Protocol** legislates over the emissions of the principal Greenhouse Gases (GHGs): **Carbon Dioxide** (CO_2), **Methane** (CH_4), Dinitrogen Oxide (Nitrous Oxide N_2O), Hydrofluorocarbons (HFCs), Per-fluorocarbons (PFCs) and Sulphur Hexafluoride (SF_6). Water is also a powerful Greenhouse Gas, but its presence in the atmosphere is a consequence of higher global temperatures from **Global Warming**, rather than as a direct result of human activities.

INDIA: With a population of just over 1 billion and growing, India has per capita **Carbon Emissions** of around 1.2 metric tonnes Carbon Dioxide (0.32 metric tonnes Carbon: Little Green Data Book, World Bank, 2006). India has been vocal in pursuing **Equity** in international **Climate Negotiations**.

INDIGENOUS PEOPLES ORGANISATION (IPO): A constituency recognised by the UNFCCC.

INDUSTRIALISING COUNTRIES: China, India and Brazil are undergoing rapid changes in their economies, often referred to as industrialisation. This industry includes the manufacture of export goods to **Developed Nations**, raising the question of which nation should account for the associated **Carbon Emissions**.

INTERGOVERNMENTAL PANEL ON CLIMATE CHANGE (IPCC): was created by UNEP and WMO in 1988 to assess the scientific knowledge on **Global Warming**. It concluded in 1990 that there was broad international consensus that **Climate Change** was human-induced, leading the way to the application of the **Precautionary Principle** through the UNFCCC.

INTERNATIONAL ENERGY AGENCY (IEA): An intergovernmental body committed to advancing security of energy supply, economic growth and environmental **Sustainability** through energy policy cooperation.

INTERNATIONAL NEGOTIATING COMMITTEE (INC): became the central forum for the international effort to develop the **UNFCCC**. It was negotiated between February 1991 and May 1992.

IRREVERSIBILITY: There are many **Climate Change** processes that have been assessed as being irreversible – such as the melting of the Greenland Ice Cap, the burning of the Amazon Rainforest, or the release of massive stores of Methane (CH_4) from melting Siberian tundra.

JOHANNESBURG SUMMIT 2002 (RIO + 10): The second World Summit on **Sustainable Development**.

JOINT IMPLEMENTATION (JI) MECHANISM: One of the provisions of the **Kyoto Protocol**. It allows the creation of **Carbon Credits** through developing **Carbon Emissions** reduction projects in **Annex I Countries**.

JUSSCANNZ: A regional group coalition of non-EU developed countries, which was active during the **Kyoto Protocol** negotiations. JUSSCANNZ stands for Japan, the US, Switzerland, Canada, Australia, Norway and New Zealand.

KYOTO PROTOCOL: An amendment to the **UNFCCC** assigning mandatory targets for the reduction of **Greenhouse Gas Emissions** to the **Annex I Countries (Developed Nations)**. Kyoto requires countries to reduce their collective **Greenhouse Gas Emissions** 5.2 per cent below their 1990 baseline over the period 2008–12. The United Kingdom has a commitment to reduce the 1990 figures by 12.5 per cent in the 'basket' of **Greenhouse Gases**.

LGMA: Local Government and Municipal Authorities. A constituency recognised by the **UNFCCC**.

LINEAR AND NON-LINEAR CHANGE: Linear changes are steady trends, such as sea-level rise due to the gradual warming of the oceans (water expands in a linear way), which is caused by general **Global Warming**. Non-Linear changes are accelerating effects, experienced in the Climate system when there are sufficient **Positive Feedbacks** in the systems.

MEETING OF THE PARTIES (MOP) TO THE (KYOTO) PROTOCOL: Began after ratification of the **Kyoto Protocol** in 2005 (MOP-1).

METHANE: The chemical compound methane, chemical symbol CH_4, is a hydrocarbon between 8 and 20 times more potent a **Greenhouse Gas** than **Carbon Dioxide**.

MITIGATION: The term used when describing measures that work to avoid **Climate Change**. Mitigating activities will include reduction in the use of **Fossil Fuels**.

NEGATIVE FEEDBACK: A mechanism that dampens a trend – for example, increased concentrations of atmospheric **Carbon Dioxide** increase the rate of **Biomass** growth in a forest and therefore the rate of capture of Carbon Dioxide.

NGOs: Non-Governmental Organisations, including privately run charities.

NON-ANNEX 1 COUNTRIES (NON-ANNEX 1 NATIONS): Those countries which are not identified by the UNFCCC under **Annex 1**. Typically poorer nations with low per capita **Greenhouse Gas Emissions**.

NUCLEAR FISSION: The decomposition of matter by the use of neutron bombardment from radioactive (unstable) elements of large molecular weight, causing the emission of heat. This is the process used in all nuclear power stations to generate electricity.

NUCLEAR FUSION: The combination of low molecular weight elements to produce larger molecular elements, releasing energy in the process. This is the process that all stars, including the sun, use to emit energy. It is theoretically possible to reproduce this on earth, but has not been demonstrated sustainably and hence is not yet commercially viable.

ORGANISATION OF PETROLEUM EXPORTING COUNTRIES (OPEC): Has historically controlled the price of oil. Negotiates mostly through member states and **G77**. One member, Saudi Arabia, is pursuing the argument that any **Climate Treaty** should not restrict their 'right' to sell oil.

PARADIGM SHIFT: A complete shift in our mental approach to an issue – such as seeing Carbon as a pollutant rather than simply an energy source.

PARTIES (PARTIES TO THE CONVENTION): United Nations terminology for a country recognised by the United Nations that has signed the UNFCCC.

PEAK OIL: A reference to the shape of the global oil production curve. Oil is a finite resource. Production has historically risen exponentially, but it is now reaching an all-time peak which will be followed by an inevitable decline.

'POLLUTER PAYS' PRINCIPLE: Born of the recognition that ecological damages are unsustainable and cannot therefore be externalised in the accounting of corporate activities. An externalised cost is borne by systems outside of the corporation. An example would be a town that suffers damage to its water supply arising from the side-effects of nearby commercial agriculture using petrochemical fertilisers. By internalising the clean-up costs of pollution, the polluter pays.

POSITIVE FEEDBACK: A mechanism that exacerbates or accelerates a trend – for example **Global Warming** causes forest fires which increase **Carbon Dioxide Emissions** causing increased **Climate Change**. The expression 'Positive Feedback' is not a value judgement on whether something is good or bad.

PRECAUTIONARY PRINCIPLE (PRECAUTION): Asserts that if human activities hold the risk, however small, of unlimited damages, those activities should be stopped as a precautionary measure. In the early years of the **Climate Negotiations**, consensus was still fragile as to the certainty of human-induced **Global Warming**. The risk, however, had been identified, and its implications demanded that the Precautionary Principle be adopted.

RATIFICATION: The Kyoto Protocol required 55 **Parties to the Convention** to individually ratify the Protocol in order to come into force. These 55 Parties had to represent in excess of 55 per cent of global **Carbon Dioxide Emissions** of all the Parties in **Annex 1 Countries**, as measured in 1990.

RENEWABLE ENERGY: Those energy sources whose availability will not diminish over meaningful human time scales. These include wind, wave, **Biomass** and solar energy, all derived from the sun directly or indirectly. Other sources include tidal energy which is derived from the gravitational pull of the moon, and geothermal energy derived from heat generated in the earth's core.

RINGO: Research and Independent Non-Governmental Organisation. A constituency recognised by the UNFCCC.

RIO DECLARATION (THE): A statement of 27 Articles, encapsulating the fundamental principles of **Sustainable Development**. It has had a major impact in promoting, amongst others, the Principles of: **Equity, Precaution, Polluter Pays, Subsidiarity, Conservation** and **Appropriate Technology**.

RIO SUMMIT, 1992: The **United Nations Conference on Environment and Development** (UNCED), also referred to as the 'Earth Summit'. The main outcomes were: the **Rio Declaration, Agenda 21** and the United Nations Framework Conventions on Biodiversity, Desertification and **Climate Change** (UNFCCC).

RUNAWAY CLIMATE CHANGE: If too many **Positive Feedback** mechanisms kick in, they would reinforce each other. This could result in a greater force for **Global Warming** than **Anthropogenic Greenhouse Gas Emissions**. At this point **Climate Change** would have reached a runaway state and the cessation of burning **Fossil Fuels** will be insufficient to stop continued Climate Change.

RUSSIA: The third largest source of **Carbon Dioxide Emissions** of the **Annex I Countries** after the USA and China (2003 CDIAC). Unlike most Annex I Countries, Russia saw its Carbon Dioxide Emissions drop from 1990 levels due to economic collapse, but they have now picked up again.

SUBSIDIARITY (PRINCIPLE OF SUBSIDIARITY, OR LOCALISATION): This principle asserts that decisions should be taken at the lowest appropriate level of social organisation. The basis for this is that decisions made on this level will most accurately reflect the local situation. They will therefore be more democratic and more efficient.

SUSTAINABILITY: The ability of a system to maintain itself indefinitely. This includes ecological processes, ecological systems, human social systems and energy production.

SUSTAINABLE DEVELOPMENT: By definition must be a process of enrichment, and thus be able to perpetuate itself. Physical growth, or growth in numbers or wealth of a system does not guarantee that it can persist indefinitely, and so is not a measure of Sustainable Development.

TARGETS: The **Kyoto Protocol** identifies target annual **Greenhouse Gas Emissions** reductions, which are defined as percentage reductions from 1990 levels.

TECHNICAL FIX (TECHNOLOGICAL FIX, TECHNOFIX): A technological response to a problem, as opposed to a policy response to a problem.

TRADABLE ENERGY QUOTAS (TEQs): Previously known as **Domestic Tradable Quotas**, or DTQs. A system proposed for allocation and trade of **Carbon Permits** or **Carbon Rations** amongst the domestic United Kingdom population.

UNFCCC GROUPINGS: Similar in style to the Economic Groupings in other international negotiations, and include: Regional Groups, **Developing Countries (G77)**, Alliance of Small Island States (AOSIS), European Union, Least Developed States, the Umbrella Group (formed out of **JUSSCANNZ**) and the Environmental Integrity Group.

UNITED KINGDOM (UK): The main British actors on Climate Change include, significantly, the RCEP (the Royal Commission on Environmental Pollution), the EAC (the Environmental Audit Committee), the Hadley Centre (a department of the UK Meteorological Office and a major contributor to the work of the **IPCC**). They also include the Stop Climate Chaos coalition (aid, development and environment NGOs).

UNITED NATIONS ENVIRONMENT PROGRAMME (UNEP): Has a mission to provide leadership and encourage partnership in caring for the environment by inspiring, informing and enabling nations and peoples to improve their quality of life without compromising that of future generations.

UNITED NATIONS FRAMEWORK CONVENTION ON CLIMATE CHANGE (UNFCCC): Signed by most UN members when it came into force in 1994. The UNFCCC contains 26 Articles, is funded by UN member states and provides a forum within which international policy is formed with the goal of reaching **Climate Treaty** consensus.

UNITED STATES OF AMERICA (USA): A signatory to the UNFCCC that notably has not ratified the **Kyoto Protocol**. Has recently recognised **Climate Change** as a human-made threat to the world. Is pursuing solutions through technology and economic growth. The USA is responsible for some 23 per cent of the world's **Carbon Emissions**.

WORKING GROUP 1 (WG1): IPCC Group, addressing the scientific aspects of the Climate system and **Climate Change** (including predictions).

WORKING GROUP 2 (WG2): IPCC Group, concerned with the sensitivities of the socio-economic and natural systems to **Climate Change**, and with both negative and positive impacts of Climate Change, including **Adaptation** measures.

WORKING GROUP 3 (WG3): IPCC Group, addressing strategies for the **Mitigation** of Climate Change, for example, limiting **Emissions**.

WORLD BANK: One of the largest international development agencies. Currently one of the major actors in the **CDM Carbon Market.**

WORLD HEALTH ORGANISATION (WHO): Has identified Climate Change as a fundamental long-term threat to human health.

WORLD METEOROLOGICAL ORGANISATION (WMO): A Specialised Agency of the UN. It is the UN system's authoritative voice on the state and behaviour of the earth's atmosphere, its interaction with the oceans, the Climate it produces and the resulting distribution of water resources.

Appendix 2
Climate-related Groups and Other Relevant Websites

The following list is not intended to be comprehensive, but rather to give some flavour of available online resources.

Camp for Climate Action (Climate Camp)
http://www.climatecamp.org.uk
Climate Camp aims to bring people together to explore grassroots solutions to climate change through workshops, skill-sharing, education, debate and entertainment and to take non-violent direct action against the root causes of climate change.

The Climate Crisis Coalition
http://www.climatecrisiscoalition.org
The Climate Crisis Coalition seeks to broaden the circle of individuals, organisations and constituencies in North America and beyond for engagement on the issue of global warming, to link it with other issues, and to provide a structure to forge a common agenda and united front.

Climate Outreach and Information Network (COIN)
http://www.coinet.org.uk
Through education and innovative approaches to learning COIN aims to achieve permanent reductions in household greenhouse gas emissions; reducing them to levels which can be sustained, and which result in no further degradation of ecological systems and human livelihood.

The Corner House
http://www.thecornerhouse.org.uk
Since its founding in 1997, The Corner House has aimed to support democratic and community movements for environmental and social justice. The Corner House carries out analyses, research and advocacy with the aim of linking issues, of stimulating informed discussion and strategic thought on critical environmental and social concerns, and of encouraging broad alliances to tackle them.

Crisis Forum (Forum for the Study of Crisis in the Twenty-First Century)
http://www.crisis-forum.org.uk/index.html
Founded in 2002 by Mark Levene and David Cromwell, two Southampton-based academics, the Forum's aims are to bring together committed people from diverse college-based academic disciplines, as well as independent researchers, to analyse the nature of our twenty-first-century crisis in a

genuinely holistic way; to put that knowledge to positive use so that ordinary people can apply global knowledge to local contexts; and to develop this initiative as an independent research-based 'centre' through projects, publications and study programmes.

Friends of Wisdom
http://www.knowledgetowisdom.org/index.htm
The website of Friends of Wisdom sets out the case for transforming academic inquiry so that it takes up the task of seeking and promoting wisdom. Friends of Wisdom is an association of people sympathetic to the idea that academic enquiry should help humanity acquire more wisdom by rational means.

Global Commons Institute
http://www.gci.org.uk
GCI is an independent group founded in 1990 and based in London. Its focus is the protection of the global commons of the global climate system. Since 1996, GCI has encouraged awareness of ' Contraction and Convergence' (C&C). C&C is GCI's suggested international framework for sharing the arrest of global greenhouse gas emissions. This site details C&C and its growing support around the world.

Intergovernmental Panel on Climate Change
http://www.ipcc.ch
The Intergovernmental Panel on Climate Change (IPCC) was established by the United Nations in 1988 to assess scientific, technical and socio-economic information relevant for the understanding of climate change, its potential impacts and options for adaptation and mitigation.

Media Lens
http://www.medialens.org
A UK-based media watchdog founded in 2001 by David Edwards and David Cromwell. The site offers authoritative criticism of mainstream media bias and censorship, primarily via frequent free 'media alerts', and an active message board and forum with archived articles and debates.

Rescue!History
http://rescue-history-from-climate-change.org/indexClassic.php
Rescue!History seeks to develop research, curricula and other educational programmes of past and present societies that will contribute to disseminating knowledge about the human origins, impacts and consequences of anthropogenic climate change, while also enabling and empowering the broader public to make the epochal changes which are going to be needed in the face of it.

Rising Tide
http://www.risingtide.org.uk
Rising Tide is a grassroots network of independent groups and individuals committed to taking action and building a movement against climate change. The network has no formal membership structure – anyone who supports the

political statement on the website can become a part of the network. Rising Tide in the UK is part of the international Rising Tide Network.

Save Our World
http://www.save-our-world.org.uk
Save our World is a UK-based charity which acts to help protect and sustain the natural world through increasing awareness and caring for human beings and all other species, as well as inspiring and empowering people to change attitudes, habits and lifestyles – personally, locally, nationally and globally.

Stop Climate Chaos
http://www.stopclimatechaos.org
Stop Climate Chaos is a coalition of environment and development groups, faith groups, humanitarian organisations, women's groups, and trade unions whose aim is to build a massive coalition that will create an irresistible public mandate for political action to stop human-induced climate change.

Tyndall Centre for Climate Change Research
http://www.tyndall.ac.uk
The Tyndall Centre brings together scientists, economists, engineers and social scientists, who together are working to develop sustainable responses to climate change through transdisciplinary research and dialogue on both a national and international level – not just within the research community, but also with business leaders, policy advisers, the media and the public in general.

Worldwatch Institute
http://www.worldwatch.org
The Worldwatch Institute is a non-profit independent organisation that has been offering its unique blend of interdisciplinary research, global focus, and accessible writing via its publication *WorldWatch* since 1975. It is a leading source of information on the interactions among key environmental, social and economic trends.

Notes on Contributors

Jo Abbess is a climate and energy policy activist. She is currently working on a project to generate and support climate change action groups in several London boroughs. Her next project will be a London-based School of Global Change.

David Ballard is a Visiting Fellow at the Centre for Action Research in Professional Practice in the School of Management at the University of Bath. With Susan Ballard, David is co-founding editor of Oxford University's online learning community/magazine http://www.changingclimate.org.

Susan Ballard is a social learning and communication consultant in the field of environmental sustainability and a practising journalist who works regularly in the field of science communication for the UK's Research Councils.

David Cromwell is a researcher at the National Oceanography Centre, Southampton. He is author of *Private Planet* (Jon Carpenter Publishing, 2001), co-founder and co-editor of Media Lens (http://www.medialens.org), and of the Crisis Forum (http://www.crisis-forum.org.uk). He is co-author, with David Edwards, of *Guardians of Power* (Pluto Press, 2006).

Tim Helweg-Larsen is a lecturer at the Centre for Alternative Technology at Machynlleth, Wales. He has also worked with the Global Commons Institute on climate change policy.

Mayer Hillman is Senior Fellow Emeritus of the *Policy Studies Institute*, and head of its Environment and Quality of Life Research Programme. He is the author, or co-author, of more than 40 books on these topics, most recently (with Tina Fawcett), *How We Can Save the Planet* (Penguin Books, 2004).

James Humphreys is a writer, broadcaster and consultant in the field of media, politics and decision making. He is the author of *Negotiating in the European Union* (Century, 1997).

Melanie Jarman writes a column on climate change related issues for *Red Pepper* magazine, edits the supporters' magazine for Campaign Against the Arms Trade and is an adviser to Corporate Watch UK. Her latest book *Climate Change* is in the Oxfam Small Guides to Big Issues (Pluto Press, 2007).

Mark Levene is Reader in Comparative History at the University of Southampton and co-founder of the Crisis Forum. Volumes 1 and 2 of his multi-volume *Genocide in the Age of the Nation-State* (Tauris) were published in 2005.

George Marshall is co-director of the Climate Outreach and Information Network (COIN). He was a founder and coordinator of Rising Tide, a national network of grassroots climate change campaign groups.

Marianne McKiggan is the webweaver for the Crisis Forum website and an activist.

Aubrey Meyer co-founded the Global Commons Institute (GCI) in London in 1990. He is the author of *Contraction and Convergence* (Green Books, 2000) and has recently accepted an Honorary Fellowship of the Royal Institute of British Architects.

Jim Scott trained as an architect and is the founder of Save our World, an environmental NGO.

John Theobald was associate professor in modern languages at Southampton Solent University. He wrote and co-edited several books, *including The Media and the Making of History* (Ashgate, 2004) and *Radical Mass Media Criticism* (Black Rose Books, 2005). He launched and co-edited the media-critical Web journal *Fifth-Estate-Online*. He died in 2006.

Jonathan Ward is a research assistant in the human radiation effects group at the University of Bristol.

Dave Webb is both Professor of Engineering at Leeds Metropolitan University and a co-founder of its Praxis Centre for the 'Study of Information and Technology for Peace, Conflict Resolution and Human Rights'. He co-edited *Cyberwar, Netwar and the Revolution in Military Affairs* (Palgrave Macmillan, 2006).

Steve Wright is a visiting professor at Leeds Metropolitan University and an associate director of the Praxis Centre, where he specialises in tracking the transfer of military security and police technologies. He is also a trustee of the Mines Advisory Group.

Index

Compiled by Sue Carlton